Microfinance and Financial Inclusion

Published by
ACADEMIC FOUNDATION
in association with
Institute of Public Enterprise

Microfinance and Financial Inclusion

S. Teki and R.K. Mishra

ACADEMIC FOUNDATION
NEW DELHI

www.academicfoundation.com

First published in 2012
by

ACADEMIC FOUNDATION
4772-73 / 23 Bharat Ram Road, (23 Ansari Road),
Darya Ganj, New Delhi - 110 002 (India).
Phones : 23245001 / 02 / 03 / 04.
Fax : +91-11-23245005.
E-mail : books@academicfoundation.com
www.academicfoundation.com

in association with

Institute of Public Enterprise, Hyderabad

Microfinance and Financial Inclusion
by S. Teki and R.K. Mishra

ISBN 13: 9788171889488
ISBN 10: 8171889484

Typeset by Italics India, New Delhi.
Printed and bound in India.

Contents

Part I

Conceptual Framework and Perspectives

Part II

Specialised Financial Institutions (SC/ST/BC/FDC) and Financial Inclusion

List of Tables and Figures

TABLES

FIGURES

About the Authors

S. Teki is currently Professor and Head of the Department of Management Studies, at Adikavi Nannaya University, Rajahmundry, Andhra Pradesh, India. He has 17 years of premier academic industry experience. He is a versatile trainer and has conducted many training programmes for various government departments officers including IFS, IAS, IDAS, IA&AS, ICAS, IRAS, IRS, IES, IPoS, IP&TAS, officers and various state civil services Group A officers, and also executives of NGOs, and SHGs office bearers. He is a prolific writer and vivid development thinker. His academic background includes management and commerce disciplines. He is a hardcore researcher in microfinance and development, and has completed many research projects funded by international reputed organisations like UNESCO. He has published more than 30 papers in national and international journals. He has presented number of papers at international and national conferences. He has travelled throughout the world and visited more than 20 countries in Europe, Asia, Australia, Africa and South America to disseminate his research works for the benefit of the common. He is a renowned consultant and has completed a number of consultancy assignments including World Bank funded projects and Government of India sponsored consultancy assignment. He formerly worked as faculty member at National Institute of Financial Management, Faridabad; Indian Institute of Forest Management, Bhopal and North Maharashtra University, Jalgaon.

R.K. Mishra is Senior Professor and Director, Institute of Public Enterprise, Hyderabad, India. PhD from the University of Rajasthan and a visiting fellow at London Business School, he studied for International Teachers programme at SDA Bocconi, Milan. Dr. Mishra taught at the University of Bradford, and was a visiting Professor at Maison

Des Sciences De L' Homme, Paris and Faculty of Economics, University of Ljubljana, Slovenia. He is a member of the UN Task Force on International Standards of Excellence in Public Administration and Education. He is a special invitee on OECD Working Group on Privatisation and Corporate Governance of SOEs and Asian Network of Corporate Governance. He is Non-Executive Director on some public and private enterprise boards in India. He has a considerable experience of teaching and guiding research for doctoral degree in management, economics, public administration and commerce. His areas of interest include corporate governance, international management, international finance, public-private partnership, restructuring and environmental administration.

Preface

This is a unique book that combines financial inclusion, microfinance and special financial institutions striving for providing access to financial services to the poor. Inclusive growth and financial inclusion are currently global and national concerns. The present Eleventh Five Year Plan (2007-2012) of India focusses on financial inclusion, as it is for an indispensible sustainable economic development of India. Financial inclusion is instrumental to the inclusive growth process and sustainable development of the country. There has been an increasing awareness and realisation that financial services to the poor and disadvantaged hold the key to their mainstreaming with the development of the country. Inadequacies in rural access to formal financial system and the seemingly extortionary terms of informal finance for the poor warrant a strong need and ample space for innovative approaches to serve the financial needs of India's rural poor. Over the last decade and half, toils have been made by government financial institutions, and NGOs, often in partnership, to develop new financial delivery approaches. Financial inclusion stands for provision of important financial services like credit, savings, insurance and remittances for an affordable cost to the disadvantaged, marginal and low-income groups across sections of the society. The primary goal of financial inclusion is to broaden the scope of activities of the informal financial system that could tag the poor people with low incomes into formal financial system in a gradual manner with focus on freeing the poor people from poverty. The book has indeed come of age, and would become significant source of work on microfinance and financial inclusion in India. This book is aptly timed and relevant to the academic world, policymakers, government, business organisations, not for profit organisations and development thinkers.

Part I

Conceptual Framework and Perspectives

1 Introduction and Overview

Poverty in India is one of the persisting problems since long time. Governments have been striving hard to alleviate poverty out forever. A variety of socioeconomic and welfare strategic programmes like Integrated Rural Development Programme (IRDP), District Rural Development Agency (DRDA), self-employment schemes etc., have been activated to address the problem. All these strategic programmes could attain the desired results up to some extent. The Government's quest for alternative endeavours is a continuous process. Thus, it has been realised that unequal growth and financial exclusion are major causes for this syndrome. This in turn paved a way to the concept of microfinance and financial inclusion that has been emerging in India since late 1980s. This evolution has been proving to be result-oriented and effective. This is changing the classical phenomenon that says, 'poor people in India born in debt, survive in debt and die in debt'.

Poverty is a multifaceted phenomenon, described as a situation where people are deprived of income generating activities, adequate food, clothing, housing, health care, sanitary facilities, access to formal credit, opportunity for education, poor infrastructure and high incidence of corruption adds to the woes of an already deprived group. Causes of poverty vary from nation to nation. Currently about one and half billion people live on less than \$1.5 a day, a majority being from third world. India alone (1999-2000) accounts for 260.3 million poor people. As per the *Human Development Report 2004* by the United Nations Development Programme (UNDP), India's 34.7 per cent population income is in below poverty line (\$1.5 a day). As per national assessment, 28.6 per cent population is living below poverty line. Poor agricultural systems in developing agriculture-based economies worsen poverty by increase in the cost of living. Inefficient provisioning coupled with leakages in (social) expenditures led to deteriorating quality of service that resulted in slow human development indicators during liberalisation era in South Asia (UNDP, 2001). Poverty was not (Grameen Bank) a personal problem due to laziness or lack of intelligence, but a structural one: lack of capital. Poor people during rainy season (lean season) strive hard to find income generating opportunities. Unable to secure any opportunity and no access to formal credit, forces them to resort to either moneylenders who often lend money at exorbitantly high interest or alternately depend on traders/landlords for obtaining subsistence and for absorbing shocks like illness. This also often forces the poor to enter into distress sale of harvest or labour leading to a vicious poverty trap (Figure 1.1). What is needed then from developmental agencies, be it public administration, multilateral agencies or local institutions, is access to microfinance (financial inclusion) rather than subsidies to assist the poor to come out of the poverty cycle.

Figure 1.1

Informal Financial System Leading to Poverty

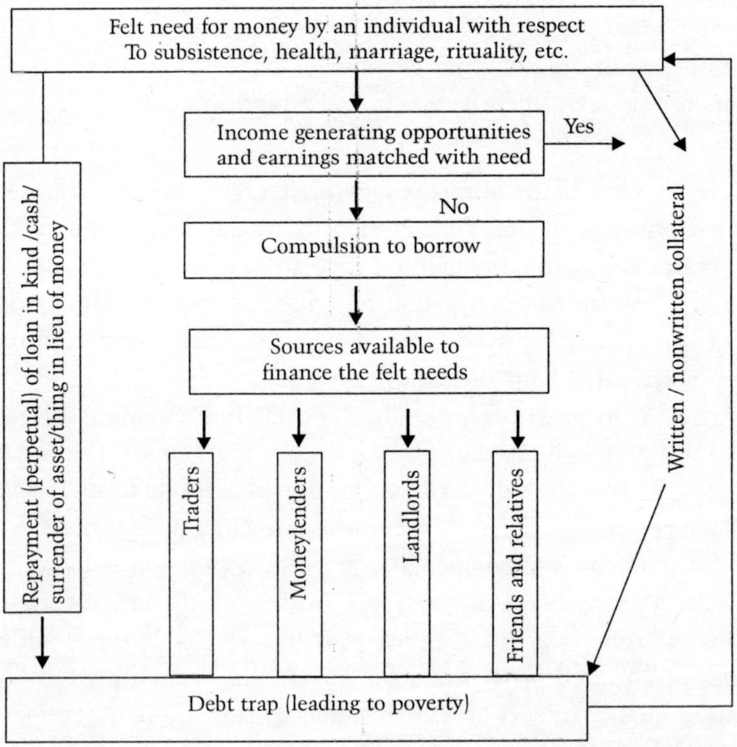

As shown in Figure 1.1, when the poor borrows from friends and relatives, the interest rate is generally reasonable and may not be exploitative. Borrowing from other three sources *viz*., moneylender, trader and landlord, push the poor into a debt trap that lands him in utter poverty. Perpetual repayment of loan is largely applicable where poor people borrow money from moneylenders, traders and landlords. It may or may not be applicable where friends and relatives are the source. And also to other sources when the borrower improves repaying capacity and repays loan effectively. After the microfinance intervention in the rural areas, the scenario is slowly metamorphosing.

Though financial exclusion is not the only cause for poverty, this book is largely confined to role of financial inclusion in reducing and eliminating poverty. The other causes like cultural liberty etc., as reported in UNDP's recent report attributable to poverty are not denied. The scope of poverty is wide and immense, this book seeks to review microfinance and financial inclusion in poverty reduction.

Poverty is a multifaceted phenomenon, described as state of deprivation of people from a variety of basic needs. It can otherwise be defined as a structural problem partly due to illiteracy, lack of access to finance, access to capacity building, health care, ineffective and inefficient public administration, leakages in social expenditure, etc. Microfinancial services are needed by the poor for loan for subsistence, loan for shock absorption, working capital loans, consumer credit, loan for asset building, savings, pensions, insurance, and money transfer services. The impact of participation of the rural poor in developmental and poverty alleviation programmes can only be visualised in terms of improved accessibility to social infrastructure in the form of employment, health, agricultural productivity and education. The importance of specially building a robust financial infrastructure is apparent when about 290 million of these people survive on less than Rs. 20 a day and more than half of them do not have any access to either banking or formal funding infrastructure.

Rural population constitute 72.22 per cent of the total population in India and is dependent on agriculture and allied activities for their livelihood (Census, 2001). Due to the unsuccessful implementation and adoption of farmer-oriented agricultural policy, the growth rate of employment in agriculture sector is continuously declining. This also contributes to declining of GDP from agriculture contribution. The development through rural economy will be a real socioeconomic growth of the country. Lack of access to funding infrastructure creates opportunity for local moneylenders to thrive by charging exorbitant lending rates to their clientele. A majority of them are rural poor and sometimes their inability to repay leads to either selling of their assets or taking of extreme steps like committing suicides! The restricted access to capital and the high cost of servicing create a major social problem; in the absence of inadequate rural enterprises *vis-à-vis* job opportunities, the young generation has been migrating from rural to urban areas for a better living. Not only does this create an opportunity for exploitation of these young men and women, it also leads to an incredible pressure on the urban infrastructure in the cities and metros. There is a real need for establishing sustainable rural enterprises to strengthen financial infrastructure at the grassroots.

A 2006 National Sample Survey Organisation (NSSO) study found that 40 per cent of Indian farmers want a different job. Roughly 80,000 farmers—with landholdings and landless alike—are thought to be moving to cities every year. Studies show that by 2020, 70 per cent of Tamil Nadu's farmers, 65 per cent of those in Punjab and nearly 55 per cent of Uttar Pradesh's farmers will move to urban centres. Meanwhile the agriculture's share in India's GDP has steadily declined from 46 per cent in 1960 to 20 per cent today, even though 70 per cent of population is still engaged in the sector. Sociologist Shiv Viswanathan says it is no wonder that the farmer has been written off. He says, 'Kisaan has become an object in the experiment of Biotechnology, and that too without any sense of modernity. If only agriculture in India is more modern, the farmer wouldn't look so out of place and out of breath.' (*Times of India*, 9th August 2009). Recently the Government of India exhibited an unprecedented generosity by handing out a whopping Rs. 60,000 crore of largesse as a farmers' debt-relief scheme. One can only imagine the level of impact had this been provided for as part of creating an enabling financial infrastructure in the hinterland rather than a largesse as a post-remedial measure. The question arises, how many times, the government can do it? The implantation of National Rural Employment Guarantee Scheme (NREGS), Pradhan Mantri Gram Sadak Yojana (PMGSY), Swarnjayanti Gram Swarozgar Yojana (SGSY) and various other government sponsored schemes are yet to yield any expected result for uplifting the bottom line of the socioeconomic pyramid. The rural credit schemes were fully politicised. Participation of poorer members of cooperatives in decision-making was less. The rich members used loans and other financial facilities. Most of the cooperatives were formed with selfish motives of big landlords. Long-term credit institutions were more necessarily needed to finance for long period so as to enable the farmers to bring about lasting improvement. There was lack of mobilising for local savings. Regional distributions of agriculture credit were inequitable. There is a huge network of institutions of development in India to alleviate poverty and generate employment but its poor implementation has not solved the purpose of alleviation of poverty. Findings on anti-poverty programmes by some researchers are quite shocking as the rural development programmes were centrally invented (lacking participation of local level institutions), politically motivated, having leakage and misappropriation and heavy administrative expenses (Ansari, 1980; Jain, 1984; Chaturvedi and Mitra, 1987; Ray, 1992). As a result, very poor quality assets were provided to the beneficiaries for productive purposes. Similar is the story of rural banking sector (see Basu, 1979; Chippa, 1987; The Netherlands Ministry of Development Cooperation, 1992; Rayudu, 1992). Studies on the effectiveness of cooperatives in agriculture sector show that it is not only the process of production and distribution which leads to success or failure of cooperatives in different regions of India, but also more importantly, the social system has a bearing on the same (Attwood, 1984; Baviskar and Attwood, 1984; Attwood and Baviskar, 1987). There are also other problems of development related to education, health, environment, housing, sanitation and atrocities on women and people of backward castes and minorities. Failure of institutional initiatives in providing microcredit to the poor people in starting their enterprises and meeting household requirements gave way to non-institutional sources of credit. In other words, financial and organisational health of the rural financial institutions (RFIs) is very poor due to the reasons of political interference, bureaucratic functioning, high degree of regulatory control, poor industrial relations and lack of customer-driven functioning. Moreover, banks see rural lending as social obligation than as business proposition. One can only wonder on the impact it would have, had a fraction of this fund been spent as a pre-policy funding measure to intensify the growth of self-generating funding like microfinancing at the grassroots.

There are multiple instances where pre-policy measures have proved to be a better alternative than the post-policy remedial measure like the present debt-relief scheme. Instead of any direct funding, the government should provide a suitable incentive-oriented scheme to foster the growth of microfinancing *vis-à-vis* microenterprises at our grassroots.

It has been seen that in rural landscape, the poor lack all the facilities starting from employment to education. They hardly get three square meals per day. The poor lead a very precarious social as well as economic life. The poverty forces them to depend upon the moneylenders (usually landlords in the village), to feed their family and self. The entire family works with the landlord for a meagre amount, which only can feed them at night time, and half in the morning. They usually depend upon the landlord for the day time food, which is also very less and fulfill only half of their need. For every occasion of their life, from health to marriage, they have to ask the moneylenders or landlords for help. The small and marginal farmers also depend upon the moneylenders to cultivate their land and to get seeds for sowing and, feeding their family with a promise to give extra 25 per cent in addition to the lending paddy from the whole produce during the harvesting season. They also end up paying an exorbitant 60 per cent of interest on the money lent or the paddy at a throw away price. Moreover, the Government help hardly reaches to them and everything is taken away by high and mighty in terms of their contact and influence. Personally, I feel the present rural funding which has been traditionally dominated by local moneylenders needs to be replaced by more accessible, clientele-friendly, self-sustaining funding systems and in this, the self-help groups (SHGs), non-governmental organisations (NGOs) and microfinance institutions (MFIs) can be a great help.

Microfinancing system, in the recent past, has developed into a business model that, other than providing credits and fund monitoring, advises in all other aspects of business. The borrowers required to be well versed with services of microfinance to promote growth in the country. There are also legal or cultural biases against fair sex, barring them from taking advantage of such services even when available. Illiteracy and lack of financial experience are stumbling blocks to the growth of microfinancial services. For increasing growth of investment opportunities, efforts are being made to eradicate above-mentioned problems through SHGs and

NGOs. These organisations can be major players for removing bottlenecks in propagating microfinancing for total development. Gradually the SHGs are proving to be a better source to finance the poor people' microfinance needs and thus paving an exit path for the moneylenders The SHGs (consisting 10-20 poor people) usually create a common fund by contributing their small savings on a regular basis. Most of the groups themselves, or with help of NGOs, evolve flexible systems of working and managing their pooled resources in a democratic way, with participation of every member in decision-making. Request for loans are considered by the group in their periodic meetings and competing claims on limited resources are settled by consensus. Loaning is done mainly on trust with a bare minimum documentation and without any physical security. The amounts loaned are small, frequent and for short duration. The loans cover a variety of purposes, some of which are non-traditional and rather unconventional. The formation of cluster and federation are worked out by the help of an NGO to see growth at a bigger level.

It is perhaps the time to recall the nation's demand for 'Purna Swaraj' or 'Total Independence'. And this dream can only be fulfilled by developing social infrastructure and economic independence at grassroots in totality i.e., planning from micro-level to macro-level to place the nation on the world map with other developed nations. Orissa is vulnerable to repeated natural calamities like droughts, floods and cyclones. The recurring natural calamities further exacerbate distress of the people, particularly small and marginal farmers and landless labourers. The Orissa's agrarian architecture is predominated by small and marginal farmers whose capacity to invest is limited. Rural funding landscape traditionally dominated by local moneylenders needs total replacement by more accessible, clientele-friendly, self-sustaining funding systems, which is yet to be fulfilled by banking networks of the country as well as the states, as the banking system is a friend of high and mighty in their own ways. Also, the poor agricultural productivity has resulted in virtually stagnant agricultural growth and employment generation. This has been further aggravated by poor infrastructural facilities and essential socioeconomic amenities like connective roads, schools and hospitals. Forest resources are an important source of sustenance to a majority of rural poor but the forest protection is not adequate. Also a long-term sustenance avenue is eroding for them, which requires immediate attention to protect the forest and provide livelihood. The credit deposit ratio of the state is one of the lowest in the country. The plan expenditure of Orissa for development is not encouraging. The major problems to development of below poverty line population (BPL) in Orissa are lack of credit at the time of need. Microfinance through group activity can be a major boost for micro-level planning for the needy and poor. And these results can be evaluated and translated from micro-level to macro-level and future growth of the state as a whole. The outlines for micro-level and macro-level planning are given below:

- At micro-level—Need to meet the immediate credit requirement as money for consumption and capital for livelihood activity. Precisely, due to lack of credit in time, the poor fall in the debt trap i.e., lack of banking facilities in rural area as well as difficulty in getting loans from banks to get the day to day operation working by poor people.
- At macro-level—Need to develop socioeconomic infrastructure for generating employment opportunities and improving the socioeconomic indicators.

There are 30 districts in Orissa having unique cultural amalgamation and tradition. The above mentioned are the core developmental issues of Orissa and efforts are made by Government to form women self-help groups (WSHGs) through Mission Shakti. Further efforts to complement microfinance and earning of livelihood may put the state in the right track of development in true sense. Microfinance has become a process of poverty reduction and strengthening livelihood of the rural poor.

This work on microfinance can be used as a baseline for further planning and a tool to achieve the social infrastructure and economic upliftment of poor, and also provides an opportunity (conducive atmosphere) for individual growth, group cohesiveness to understand each other's problem i.e., rural empowerment in true sense—decision-making in the group as well as at individual level to perform outside job. Microfinance can directly and indirectly be used as a vehicle for employment generation for youth belonging to group member's family by establishing individual enterprises (grocery shop, cattle rearing unit, agriculture production and horticulture units) and outsiders as well. This is a better source of finance for the poor people, as no collateral is required like any other banking units and paves an exit path for the moneylenders. Assessment of microfinance as a useful tool is not only an economic development approach for benefitting below poverty line people by providing basic financial services i.e., loans, savings, and other basic financial services to the poor to run businesses, build assets, stabilise consumption, and shield against risks but also a tool to help above poverty line people to achieve their goals and objectives of maximising wealth.

Microfinance implementation in true spirit can be a useful tool for achieving a vibrant growth in country's village economy as well as country's sociocultural awakening along with true rural empowerment and growth of country as a whole. Micro-level planning for self-sustenance and earning of livelihood with the help of microfinance through SHGs for making people self-reliant and enterprising to become a developed country by eliminating the structural problems of poverty needs greater attention. Looking at the recent success of the microfinancing system especially in the developing countries, it could be a viable funding model for growth of sustainable rural enterprises in India. Microfinancing policy has several merits along with several inherent challenges like small transactions may entail high administrative costs and lending terms may be inappropriate for a particular group of clientele who are conversant with traditional practices of borrowing as well as inadequate knowledge of cash flow and investment opportunities.

Microfinance is a new reality in the world of development discourse and financial intermediation. Broadly speaking, microfinance means providing financial services to the poor, long excluded by mainstream banking and finance market. Neoliberals support it as it does not disturb the status quo. The concept of social capital is the key theoretical element in social intermediation, derived from the anthropological and sociological literature. The historical account of the emergence and growth of microfinance sector at the global level need a post-mortem to understand the basics of socioeconomic status of different countries. According to the *World Development Report* (World Bank, 2000), 1.8 billion people live in extreme poverty, subsisting on less than US $1 a day and almost half of the world population (2.8 billion) live on less than US $2 a day. South Asia is the home to half of the world's poor. In African countries, women account for more than 60 per cent of the agriculture labour force and contribute up to 80 per cent of the total food production, yet receive less than 10 per cent of the credit provided to small farmers. The underdeveloped and developing countries of the world have tried to develop their own models for improving socioeconomic status of the needy and low income groups. Pischke (1991) observed that microfinance is primarily social as the Latin root of the term credit (*crèdere*) is to believe or entrust. Commercial banks see it as a new profitable area of credit with a high repayment rate in a world of mounting non-performing assets (NPAs) and sub-prime hazards. Many governments welcome it as a less burdensome manner of fighting poverty. The most important economic rationale in bringing financial services to the door steps of the poor households is the economy in the transaction costs. In India, various estimates put the requirements of microcredit at Rs. 150 billion to Rs. 500 billion per year. As against these estimates, bank advances to weaker sections aggregated about Rs. 100 billion per year and SHGs are estimated to provide about Rs. 1 billion per year. About 36 per cent of the rural households are outside the fold of institutional credit. The Indian financial system comprises an elaborate network of banks, financial institutions, non-banking financial companies (NBFCs) and a wide range of financial instruments. For formal banks, it will be costly to mobilise the small savings of the poor families lying widely scattered. Equally prohibitive is the cost to the conventional banks in financing a large number of these families who require credit frequently and in small volume and that too not backed by collateral securities. The cooperative banks failed to play their due role in the achievement of avowed objectives of economic development because of duality of control, high incidence of loan delinquencies, mounting NPAs and heavy accumulated losses caused by poor income, high cost of management, injudicious funds management, poor deposit mobilisation and excessive reliance on funds from higher financing institutions. Despite a considerable widening and deepening of the Indian regulated financial institution (RFI) system, the extension of banking and other financial facilities to a larger cross-section of society and increase in all indicators of social and economic infrastructure through rural banking system continued to be inefficient.

To understand the concept of microfinance, it would be worthwhile to first understand the term microcredit as both are closely related to each other. Poor people need microcredit for various purposes. It may be to meet the major household expenses, emergency needs or even basic livelihood support. There are two main systems of microcredit (Chauhan, 1990). One is formal financial institutions, banks and cooperatives, which provide microcredit to the poor people under different schemes for livelihood support or helping them to start microenterprises. The other is informal system comprising traditional moneylenders, pawnbrokers and trade-specific lenders. Both the systems have their own positive and negative aspects. The positive aspects of formal financial system are that under this system, microcredit is available at low rate of interest with easy and periodical repayments and moratorium period. The most important aspect of this type of credit is that it is available for income generating activities. But at the same time microcredit from formal financial system is not easily available. The system requires collateral or security. It has complex legal and operational procedures, involving lot of paper work. Since the process of credit disbursement is time-consuming, many a times credit is not available on time. Finally, there is a stigma attached to the poor people, therefore, the bankers do not think them creditworthy and feel that the recovery rate is unsatisfactory. But this may not necessarily be true. The positive aspects of informal system of microcredit are that the credit disbursement is easy and relatively quick. No collateral is required and there is least paper work. Credit can be given for any activity, especially for consumption and emergency purposes. Credit is generally given for non-productive purposes as well. But at the same time there is very high interest rate in informal microcredit system (Fisher *et al.*, 1997; Light, 1998; Mahajan, 2001; Martin *et al.*, 2002). Exploitation is also attached with this system. Moneylender takes repayment at one time only. Based on these two systems of microcredit, we can define 'microcredit as the provision wherein debtor takes money either from formal or informal sources of credit on unilaterally decided terms by the creditor'. If we combine together positive aspects of both the systems like low rate of interest, easy and periodical repayments with moratorium period, credit for income generating activities, easy process of disbursement, no collateral or security and less paper work etc., we come closer to understanding the concept of microfinance.

Microfinance has emerged and grown rapidly at global level. Microfinance as a major financial service emerged in the 1970s, notably after

Muhammad Yunus now of Nobel Prize fame, started the Grameen Bank in Bangladesh (Yunus, 2003). The Bank began to offer financial services to the poor once excluded from formal banking primarily because they lacked collateral. Today microfinance has emerged as an industry in which even big multinational and national banks are interested because they are sure of repayment and it fetches profit. For such institutions fighting poverty is a facade.

Microfinance and Socioeconomic Status

Microfinance: The term microfinance has been in use for the last one and a half decade or so. A number of definitions and interpretations have been discussed in various publications worldwide on microfinance. The financial (Pethiya and Teki, 2003a) assistance rendered by various agencies to the village/countryside poor people towards self-employment, enhancing income levels through better utilisation of available resources, and income generating activities. Microfinance can be defined as a loan fund especially meant for microenterprises (including agriculture, forestry, agroforestry, horticulture, animal husbandry, handicrafts, processing of NTFPs for value addition, fisheries, bamboo and jute crafting, mushroom cultivation, etc.) to provide required start-up capital for local needy people in an organised manner (Pethiya and Teki, 2003a). Provision (Task Force Report) of thrift, credit and other financial services and products of very small amounts mainly to the poor in rural, semi-urban or urban areas for enabling them to raise their income level and improve living standards. Microfinance (like Consultative Group to Assist the Poor, CGAP) is the supply of loans, savings, and other basic financial services to the poor.

The emergence of microfinance as a viable and strategic option to alleviate poverty and empower the poor has given visible results. The easy access of credit used to attract the poor people to the door of moneylenders (also include indigeneous bankers, landlords, village level traders etc.) who were available round the clock (24 X 7) quite like current days' sophisticated technology-supported ATMs. This was the biggest strength of the moneylenders who used it to exploit the needy poor. This is one of the grassroot causes for poverty in India. But the timely intervention of microfinance is also functioning as rescuer of poor people from the vicious debt trap of moneylenders, besides promoting saving habits and income generating activities, group cohesiveness, and social security amongst the poor masses.

The experience of microfinance (Patel, 2002) shows that the poor are bankable and that poverty alleviation is possible without subsidies. The sharp visible impact (UNDP, 2001) of the community banking programme (CBP) is seen in its outreach to the poorest of the poor in backward and remote locations and curbing the moneylender's activities of upfront usurious interest rate. Substantial resource mobilisation and more than 98 per cent repayment pattern with negligible NPAs are other quantitative indicators helping to further upscale the programme. Qualitative indicators like cadre of poor women as leaders, strength of collectives as social support structure creating an identity of women in the home as well as in the village, confidence, physical mobility, access to public space and increased control on financial resources are to be observed and believed. As a group (UNDP, 2001) the members have been able to change rules of credit markets and engage with government departments involved in social service delivery.

India has about 400 million poor people, more than any other country in the world (The Virtual Library on Microcredit). These poor live on the brink of subsistence. Thus, microfinance is one option to help and improve the income of poor people. Traditionally, microfinance is seen as providing credit through small loans to poor people to help them to engage in productive activities or expand their own small business enterprises. In fact microfinance is more than credit and now includes a much broader range of financial products which can be accessed and used by both poor and very poor people. Typical users of microfinance institutions are people with low income who cannot access formal finance. They are generally self-employed and engage in small business enterprises such as farming, petty trade, shop keeping, street vendors and food production. To cope with their disadvantage, the poor often take small loans, during crisis periods, from moneylenders who charge exploitative rates of interest. If poor people are given access to low interest loans during times of crisis, they can avoid falling into such debt trap. Microfinance is the extension of small loans to entrepreneurs too poor to qualify for traditional bank loans. It has proven an effective and popular measure in the ongoing struggle against poverty, enabling those without access to lending institutions to borrow at bank rates, and start small business. But with the current explosion of interest on microfinance issues, several developmental objectives have come to be associated with it, besides those of only 'micro' and 'credit'. Of particular importance is that of savings—as an end in it, and as a guarantee for loans.

Microfinance programmes extend small loans to very poor people for self-employment projects that generate income, allowing them to care for themselves and their families. Definitions differ, of course, from country to country. Some of the defining criteria used include: size—loans are micro, or very small in size, target users—microenterpreneur and low-income households, utilisation—the use of funds for income generation, and enterprise development, but also for community use (health/education) etc., terms and conditions—most terms and conditions for microcredit loans are flexible and easy to understand, and suited to the local conditions of the community.

A working definition proposes to define microfinance as: 'Provision of thrift, credit and other financial services and products of very small amounts to the poor in rural, semi urban or urban areas for enabling them to raise their income levels and improve living standards'. It does not only cover consumption and production loans, but also include other credit needs such as housing and shelter improvement, financial services like savings and insurance under it. It may be left to the MFIs to identify the poor. However, the selection criterion so adopted will have to be in conformity with the poverty line adopted by the GoI. Microfinance is very often accompanied by non-financial and other business services like capacity building, forward and backward linkages, etc., provided either by the same or by some other institutions, mainly for enhancing the productivity of credit.

Microfinance is an economic development approach intended to benefit by supply of loans, savings, and other basic financial services to the poor i.e., people living in poverty. It is also true that microfinance can be a useful model for the needy and low income group people to run businesses, build assets, stabilise consumption, and shield against risks. This can also be a suitable model to reduce the poverty of our country not only mentally but also structurally, if all the facets are suitably taken care by the users as well as other stakeholders. The institutional initiatives taken in extending microcredit in India after independence can be understood in conjunction with the process of rural development and the role played by several developmental institutions for poverty alleviation and employment generation programmes. This process can be categorised under community development programme, RFI programmes and development of cooperatives programmes. Apart from these, public distribution system (PDS) and agricultural/land reforms are also supposed to be major initiatives for providing the benefit to the poor section of the society and attacking poverty. Microfinance may be stated as 'an approach to develop the socioeconomic status of needy and low income group people by providing a capacity to absorb shock and build assets as well as social empowerment'.

Mainstream Microfinance Institutions

In India major sources of microfinance are: (a) organised sector (banks, government agencies etc.); and (b) unorganised sector (moneylender, traders, relatives, friends etc.). The former is regulated by government bodies like Reserve Bank of India (RBI), banking regulation acts etc., and the later has no formal regulatory bodies. Microfinance falls under the primary sector and they are supposed to meet specific pre-decided targets. The major contributors for microfinance supply in India are shown in Table 1.1.

Table 1.1

Sources of Credit for Rural Households, 1991

Credit Agency	*% of Rural Households*
Government etc.	6.1
Cooperative societies	21.6
Commercial banks and RRBs	33.7
Insurance	0.3
Provident Fund	0.7
Other institutional sources	1.6
All institutional agencies	64.0
Landlord	4.0
Agricultural moneylenders	7.0
Professional moneylenders	10.5
Relatives and Friends	5.5
Others	9.0
All non-institutional agencies	36.0
All agencies	100.0

Source: *http://www.basixindia.com*

The SHG-Bank Linkage Phenomenon

The SHG-bank linkage phenomenon saw a hesitant beginning in 1993-1996. Three basic models of linking emerged.

Model-I: Bank-SHG Members (Bank as SHPI)

In this model, the bank itself acts as a self-help group promoting institution (SHPI). The bank takes the initiative to form the groups, nurture them, open their savings accounts and provide them credit.

Model-II: Bank-Facilitator Agency-SHG Members

The second group is formed by NGOs (in most of the cases) or by government agencies. The groups are nurtured and trained by these agencies. Government or other community-based organisations to take the lead in forming the SHGs, and then provide savings and credit facilities by the banks. Even after the linkage with banks, these facilitating agencies continue interacting with the groups. Most linkage experiences begin with this model with NGOs playing a major role. This model has also been popular and more acceptable to banks, as some of the difficult functions of social dynamics are externalised.

Model-III: Bank-NGO-MFI-SHG Members

Due to various reasons, banks in some areas are not in a position to even finance SHGs promoted and nurtured by other agencies. In such cases, the NGOs promoted and nurtured the groups and also act as financial intermediaries. First, they promote the groups, nurture and train them and then approach banks for bulk loans for on-lending to the SHGs. The banks lend to these intermediaries for onward financing to the groups or their members.

Three C's of Credit

- *Character:* means how a person has handled past debt obligations. From credit history and personal background, honesty and reliability of the borrower to pay credit debts is determined.
- *Capacity:* means how much debt a borrower can comfortably handle. Income streams are analysed and any legal obligations looked into, which could interfere in repayment.

- *Capital:* means current available assets of the borrower, such as real estate, savings or investment that could be used to repay debt if income should be unavailable.

Microfinance may play a vital role for improving social and economic infrastructure by providing microfinancial services needed by the poor for loan for subsistence, loan for shock absorption, working capital loans, consumer credit, loan for asset building, savings, pensions, insurance, and money transfer services. Figure 1.2 explains the potential impacts of microfinance at a household and community level. Survey of literature on the role of microfinance through SHG for development of socioeconomic indicators is limited.

Harper (1998) reported on 72 SHGs—covering over 1,000 SHG members in Orissa, Uttar Pradesh, Maharashtra and Karnataka—and concluded that there is improvement in members' diet, assets and education. The evidence suggested that nearly all members benefitted to some extent although the benefits to poorer members were less or delayed compared to the better-off. Borrowing for income generation activities increased from 50 per cent to 70 per cent. It was estimated that 112 households or 47.8 per cent of the poor had crossed the poverty line. Another significant finding was that a standard of living index of sample households comprising socioeconomic parameters rose for both economic and social parameters. The study findings also reveal that social impact was found to be stronger in the case of groups promoted by NGOs than in groups promoted by banks. Other positive impacts experienced by SHG members related to increase in self-worth, communication skills, and desire to protest social evils, improved response to problem situations and a decrease in domestic violence. A consistent increased access to various amenities such as water, health and sanitation, schools and markets is also indicated. Thus, only 31 per cent of the families of poorer members increased their assets, 44 per cent improved their food consumption and 15 per cent improved their education. On the question of the access to benefits and power of poorer members of groups, the findings from data collected from six Mysore Resettlement and Development Agency (MYRADA) groups, however, suggest that the poorest were not marginalised in terms of access to loans, though their loans were mainly for consumption purposes (Fernandez, 2000). In its 70 case studies, the National Bank for Agriculture and Rural Development's (NABARD) impact evaluation of SHGs covered by the bank-linkage programme indicate the changes in socioeconomic conditions of 560 members of 223 SHGs in 11 states before and after (spanning a three-year period) their association with the SHG (Puhazhendi and Satyasai, 2000). On impact of the SHGs in terms of economic status of the households, the study found an average value of assets per household (including livestock and consumer durables) rose by 72.3 per cent to Rs. 11,793 during the three-year period. Average net income per household from income generating activities where loan amounts were deployed, increased from Rs. 20,177 prior to group formation to Rs. 26,889. Employment increased by 17 per cent and average saving per member was about Rs. 1,000 in 1998-99.

Another study of 70 SHGs promoted in Tamil Nadu through four leading NGOs: Association for Sarva Seva Farms (ASSEFA), MYRADA, Development of Humane Action (DHAN) Foundation and League for Education and Development (LEAD), Trichy was undertaken by NABARD during 1996-97 (Puhazhendi, 2000). The performance of groups was assessed using a scoring system covering indicators such as homogeneity of groups, regularity in holding meetings, attendance at meetings, increase in rate of savings, share of production loan to total loan, training, NGO involvement and effective leadership. As much as 61 per cent of groups were found to be performing well, 29 per cent average and 10 per cent poorly. In the Tamil Nadu study, economic impact was assessed through net increase in family income, which was found to have more than doubled for the sample groups during the period of participation in the SHG. Social impacts identified related to literacy levels, housing facilities and food security. Empowerment of women was observed in the form of participation of financial decisions in the family, checking liquor addiction of male family members and sending children to school. The groups were also found to be influential in the community with some women becoming members of *panchayats*. SHGs are cohesive and are characterised by a strong sense of ownership, voluntary participation, diversified management, leadership skills and provision of ongoing support services for meeting emergent credit needs of its members as decided by the group. With the extraordinary success of SHGs in several states including Orissa, Karnataka, Tamil Nadu, Kerala, Andhra Pradesh and Uttar Pradesh in

Figure 1.2

Potential Impact of Microfinance at a Household and Community Level

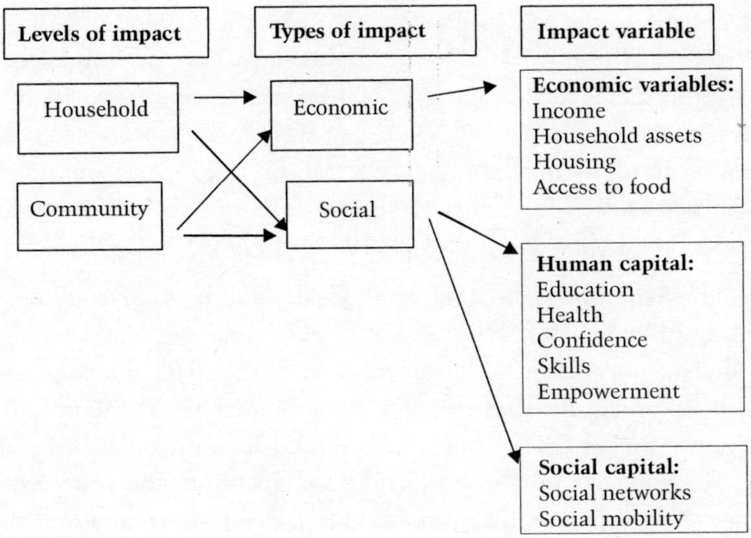

Source: After Wrenn, 2005.

setting in motion the socioeconomic transformation of the rural poor, SHGs emphasising functional literacy, group building and solidarity, conflict resolution and consensus approach now need to be formed all over the country in a big way and increasingly linked to the banks to be meaningful and effective in the present day context. Such linkages like the Shakespearean quality of mercy is 'twice-blessed': it benefits both the banks and SHGs. While banks benefit by: (a) dispensing with pre-sanction appraisal, monitoring and post-disbursement supervision, (b) assured recoveries, (c) reduced transaction cost by eliminating large number of small borrowers at frequent intervals, and (d) mobilisation of small savings; SHGs: (a) have access to mainstream institutions for augmenting their resource base, and (b) shift from non-productive to productive activities with consequential increase in income of its members (Puhazhendi, 1995; Girija and Satish, 1999).

Findings of a study on SHG-Bank Linkage Programme conducted by NABARD (2002) among 115 SHG members of 60 groups in states namely Orissa, Chhattisgarh and Jharkhand also reveal the positive impact of SHGs. According to this study, there was an increase of Rs. 12,319 in the family income of the SHG members after the intervention of SHGs while 45 per cent of the households were observed to have accumulated assets after joining the SHG. As far as social impact is concerned there was a significant improvement in the status of women in aspects such as joint decision-making at household level, talking freely with outsiders and officials, demanding for rights, resisting domestic violence, exposure to outside world etc., (NABARD, 1994; 1999a; 1999b; 1999c; 2002).

Studies conducted by Andhra Pradesh Mahila Abhivruddhi Society (APMAS) (2005) for 400 SHGs observed that employment opportunities for the poor had not significantly increased after the SHG intervention. The study also pointed out that realisation of improvement in family income was better for upper caste people than that of backward and scheduled caste people. A significant proportion of the respondents in the study expressed that they were not quite free from local moneylenders yet, and that they did not spend as much on food as they needed to spend. Levels of confidence, self-reliance, ability to make decisions, leadership quality etc., had all increased. Education levels and ability to negotiate with other bodies had also improved (Ibid.). Microfinance is an intervention based on social intermediation in which poor people can mobilise their savings, link it with credit and finally become self-employed. It results in building social capital. In the present chapter an attempt has been made to understand the growth of microfinance at global level in general and in India in particular and how microfinance sector can contribute significantly for building social capital. From the review of literature on microfinance, it has been revealed that there is a high demand of microfinance all over the world. Moreover, microfinance is not limited to rural society or developing countries only; it is equally applicable to urban society and developed countries as well. In India, the need for microfinance is higher as the demand for credit to start microenterprises by the poor people could not be met by the institutional initiatives of rural finance up to large scale. Due to the failure of percolation theory of social development, poor people are highly dependent on non-institutional sources of credit. Growth of microfinance in India has been in response to the failure of institutional initiatives of rural credit and exploitation attached with informal system of credit. Learning from the success of Grameen Bank in Bangladesh, many NGOs in India came forward to promote microfinance. At present about 1,000 NGOs are implementing microfinance projects in India. Some of them are leading MFIs building and playing the role of social intermediation. These MFIs have adopted different strategies for improving people's livelihood through microfinance delivery (APMAS, 1995; 2005; *http://www.sasnet.lu.se/EASASpapers/20NareshSingh. pdf)*.

Majority of the poor population depends on informal financial system for their credit needs. The financial management experts feel that this sector should be treated like an industry sector. It means that any microfinance project should be financially viable to cover the cost of credit management, cost of default and cost of devaluation from its spread (difference between the cost of borrowing and cost of lending). On the other hand development management practitioners view microfinance as a social sector. According to them microfinance can be one of the best poverty alleviation social programme but not a business-like entity where ultimate motive is to sell its product in a competitive environment and earn a profit. In nutshell, any microfinance project should have three basic components namely, financial, economic and social. It should be financially viable, should help the poor people to build their productive capacity for self-employment and overall it should improve the quality of life of the poor people. Attempt has been made to understand the growth of microfinance in India.

The Task Force on Supportive Policy and Regulatory Framework for Microfinance is constituted by NABARD (1999c). The microfinance is defined as 'the provision of thrift, saving, credit and financial services and products of very small amounts to the poor in rural, semi-urban and urban areas for enabling them to raise their income levels and improve their standard of living'. The emphasis of support under microfinance is on the poor in 'pre-microenterprise' stage for building up their capabilities to handle larger resources. This perception is quite significant, keeping in view the limitations of any approach of microenterprise development to help the poorest of the poor for self-employment (Awasthi, 1994; 1996). The Task Force has not specified limit for the 'small' amount of financial services envisaged. Services of microfinance are being provided by various MFIs. Task Force has classified these MFIs under three important categories such as:

- *Not-for-profit MFIs:* These include societies registered under Societies Registration Act, 1860 or similar State Acts, public trusts registered under the Indian Trust Act, 1882 and non-profit companies registered under Section 25 of the Companies Act, 1956.
- *Mutual benefit MFIs:* Such as state credit cooperatives, national credit cooperatives and mutually aided cooperative societies (MACS).
- *For-profit MFIs:* Bodies like NBFCs registered under the Companies Act, 1956 and banks which provide microfinance along with their other usual banking services could be termed as microfinance service providers of this type.

Different Models of Microfinance

Rural credit markets are characterised by high cost of legal enforcement, imperfect information, high collateral security, underdevelopment in complimentary institutions and covariant risks. Consequently, a number of alternative strategies have to be devised to attract greater inward investment and unleash latent indigeneous potential in the form of entrepreneurship and helping existing businesses to realise their expansion plans. This requires the active involvement and full support of rural banking in the country. Thus, the concept of rural banking has itself become an issue of debate and discussion. The main strands of this debate bring into question the known paradigms of rural banking, direction of development for fostering dispersed industrial growth and the attempt to replicate western models of development without considering the socioeconomic conditions peculiar to India. Institutional development could be enhanced by strengthening of institutions, promotion of sustainable and equitable agriculture, effective credit support, improving the outreach of the banking system, modification of the regulatory framework and the promotion of competition and privatisation (Capoor, 2001; Hulme and Paul, 1996; Jain, 1984; Karmakar, 1999; Korten, 1981; Papopla, 1991; Patel, 1994).

Cooperatives are basically concerned with provision of credit and other inputs to the members to support production, particularly the agricultural production and provision of post-harvest support to farmers. The cooperative credit sector consists of state cooperative banks (SCBs), district central cooperative banks (DCCBs), primary agricultural credit societies (PACSs)/large size adivasi multipurpose societies (LAMPSs) for meeting production credit needs, state land development banks (SLDBs) and primary land development banks (PLDBs) for meeting investment credit needs. Cooperatives provide the critical forward and backward linkages to their members, enhancing the technical feasibility and in turn the viability of the activities. Despite these impressive features, the performance of the cooperative banks has been unsatisfactory because of the complex interplay of organisational, financial and managerial inadequacies of the cooperative credit system. However, there have been significant changes in the share of various agencies in providing institutional credit to agriculture and allied activities with the shares of commercial banks and RRBs rising from 40 per cent in 1987-88 to 50 per cent and from 1 per cent to 10 per cent, respectively during 2002-03 and the share of cooperatives declining from 58 per cent to about 40 per cent during this period.

An elaborate network of the formal sector, as it has evolved in the post-independent India, relates to multi-agency institutional credit structure comprising 91 commercial banks, 196 RRBs and 1,149 co-operative banks. The basic framework of the credit dispensation attempted to increase the quantum of credit for improving production and productivity without being oblivious to the credit requirements of the vulnerable sections of the society and backward areas (Reddy, 2000). Thus there are today 1,34,000 rural credit outlets, i.e., one branch outlet for every 4,700 population. However, 39 per cent of rural indebted households continue to be served by informal credit sector comprising moneylenders, indigeneous bankers, friends, relatives, traders, etc. NGOs, SHGs/ federations and credit unions also play an increasingly important role in credit dispensation.

Three different approaches could be identified in the evolution of microfinance in the world: (i) the Latin American model i.e., cooperative model, (ii) the Grameen Bank model, and (iii) the SHG-based model. Latin

American model is a commercial model. Emphasis on social and community development of poor women is totally missing in such a model. The Grameen model, on the other hand, is basically centred on women and poverty. The SHG-based model is the Indian variant of microfinance popularised and institutionalised by NABARD, largely through the commercial banking system (Oomen, 2008).

The Kudumbashree Mission (KDS) of Kerala, launched in May 1998 but effectively implemented from early 2000, does not seem to follow any of these models though its economic base is patterned on the SHG-based microfinance system. Its organisational set up could be traced to the three-tier community development system (CDS) that evolved in the Alappuzha municipality in the early 1990s. In order to highlight how the KDS of Kerala differs from the general run of the mill microfinance and has evolved into a unique community-based organisation (CBO), designed to 'eradicate poverty' through a process of women empowerment. For identifying poverty and the official poverty line in India, the nine-point poverty index is followed by KDS to identify the poor from the non-poor. As far as the KDS is concerned, poor are those who match with four or more of the nine criteria given below:

(a) *kutcha* house;
(b) no access to safe drinking water;
(c) no access to sanitary latrine;
(d) illiterate adult in the family;
(e) family having not more than one earning member;
(f) family getting barely two meals a day or less;
(g) presence of children below five years in the family;
(h) alcoholic or drug addict in the family; and
(i) scheduled caste or scheduled tribe family.

A meaningful poverty assessment should be based on sound conceptual foundations and must serve at least four purposes:

(a) Identify the poor from the non-poor.
(b) Find out how deep is poverty through an appropriate scale that facilitates comparison over time and space.

(c) Make a meaningful aggregation about the magnitude of poverty in a jurisdiction, be it a country, a state or even a *panchayat* or whatever be the level of aggregation required.

(d) Throw policy insights for reducing poverty. The official poverty line (PL) as well as the above nine-point index of KDS cannot be said to be based on sound conceptual foundations and do not satisfy all the purposes mentioned. While the official income poverty line anchored on a minimum calorie norm of 2,400 calories per capita per day in rural areas and 2,100 calories per capita per day in urban areas has been subjected to considerable scholarly debate (and it still continues!), the KDS's nine-point criteria have not attracted any such debate or review.

Oomen (2008) tried to measure empowerment from five major angles:

(a) organisational empowerment;
(b) economic empowerment;
(c) knowledge empowerment;
(d) leadership empowerment; and
(e) social capital.

The various models for microfinance and development of poor are as outlined below with discussions.

1. *Grameen bank model:* This model basically provides finance by careful targetting of the poor entrepreneurial women already doing small jobs (Yunus, 2003). This is a field-intensive work by staff to motivate and supervise the borrower groups. The key feature of the model is group-based and graduated financing that substitute collateral as tools to mitigate default and delinquency risk. Groups normally consist of five members who guarantee each other's loans and meets weekly. This model is very successful in eradicating poverty.

   Salient features: five member group, centre/village *sangam* consists of maximum of 8-10 groups and weekly meetings.

2. *Cooperative model:* It can be of two main types like village bank model and credit unions (Stiglitz, 1994).

(i) *Village bank model:* This model involves an implementing agency that establishes individual village banks with about 30 to 50 members and provides 'external' capital for onward financing to individual members. Individual loans are repaid at weekly intervals over four months, at which time the village bank returns the principal with interest/profits to the implementing agency. A bank repaying in full is eligible for subsequent loans, with loan sizes linked to the performance of village bank members in accumulating savings. Peer pressure operates to maintain full repayment, thus assuring further injections of capital, and also encourages savings. Savings accumulated in a village bank is also used for financing. This model has been very successfully implemented in a *Shari'ah*-compliant manner in Jabal al-Hoss, Syria.

(ii) *Credit union:* This model is based on the concept of mutuality. It is in the nature of non-profit financial cooperative owned and controlled by its members. Credit union mobilises savings, provides loans for productive and provident purposes and have memberships which are generally based on some common bond. Credit union generally relates to an apex body that promotes primary credit unions and provides training while monitoring their financial performance. Credit union is quite popular in Asia, notably in Sri Lanka.

Salient features: Individuals are members and size is 100-400. Monthly meetings and member-owned governing board.

3. *Self-help groups-Federation Model:* This model is indigeneous in nature and it promotes development through SHGs (Singh and Gain, 1995). Each SHG is formed with about 10-15 members who are relatively homogeneous in terms of income. An SHG essentially pools together its members' savings and uses it for lending. SHGs also seek external funding to supplement internal resources. The terms and conditions of loans differ among SHGs, depending on the democratic decisions of members. Typical SHGs are promoted and supported by NGOs, but the objective (as with village banks) is for them to become self-sustaining institutions. Some NGOs act as financial intermediaries for SHGs, while others act solely as 'social'

intermediaries seeking to facilitate linkages of SHGs with either licensed financial institutions or other funding agencies.

Salient features: Support services to voluntary organisations (VOs), secure linkage with government departments, auditing of the groups, social security & risk management, support services to the SHGs, arrange line of credit to the SHGs, social action and link with PRIs, access services at village level, thrift and credit activities, participatory monitoring of the groups and group level poverty reduction plans.

a. *SHG promotion strategy:* SHG promotion approach is based on the premise that the NGO promotes SHGs and provides them services as financial advisor as well as capacity builder. SHGs is involved in terms of savings mobilisation, linking them with banks and providing technical support in starting viable micro-enterprises by the members of SHGs members. In this approach NGO basically is a mediating contact between SHGs and banks. NGO also examines creditworthiness of the SHGs so that bank can lend money to the SHGs. In all this, NGO gets some financial support in terms of grant from apex financial institutions (AFIs) like NABARD and Rashtriya Mahila Kosh (RMK). The examples of such NGOs who are following SHG promotion approach are: MYRADA in Karnataka, SHARE in Andhra Pradesh, Rural Development Organisation (RDO) in Manipur, People's Right and Environment Movement (PREM) in Orissa and Andhra Pradesh, Youth Charitable Organisation (YCO) in Andhra Pradesh, Acil Navsarjan Rural Development Foundation (ANARDE) in Gujarat, Professional Assistance for Development Action (PRADAN) in Delhi, Rural Development Society for Vocational Training (RUDSOVAT) in Rajasthan and Adithi in Bihar.

b. *Microfinance institution strategy:* The approach of promoting MFIs is based on the premise that AFIs like Small Industries Development Bank of India (SIDBI), RMK and other donor agencies provide bulk lending, soft loans and some grant to such NGOs which can act as MFIs by on-lending the money to the poor people/SHGs/federations/smaller NGOs (RMK, 1998;

SIDBI, 1999; Singh and Gain, 1995). These MFIs stimulate the credit demand of the poor people. They also provide technical support for the beneficiaries to ensure proper utilisation of loans and repayment. At the same time they meet their cost of funds, credit management and cost of default through the spread of interest and generate surplus for the viable operation of microfinance. The examples of such MFIs are Sewa Bank & Friends of Women's World Banking (FWWB) in Gujarat, BASIX in Andhra Pradesh and Rashtriya Gramin Vikas Nidhi (RGVN) in northeastern states, Orissa and Bihar (APMAS, 2005; Puhazhendi and Satyasai, 2000; Singh and Gain, 1995).

c. *Microenterprise development strategy:* Entrepreneurship is one of the most important inputs in the economic development of a country and of the regions within the country. Economic growth and industrialisation are the byproducts of entrepreneurship. It is a breeding ground for the development of small-scale enterprises. The Entrepreneurship Development Programme (EDP) is designed to help a person in strengthening his/her entrepreneurial motive and in acquiring skills and capabilities necessary for playing his/her entrepreneurial role effectively. It inculcates entrepreneurial traits into a person and develops his/her personal, financial, technical, managerial and marketing skills. There are number of programmes which are aimed at providing informational or managerial inputs required by a new entrepreneur. However, a programme not touching upon entrepreneurial motivation and behaviour cannot be called an EDP (Desai, 1991; Desai and Namboodiri, 1994a, 1994b, 1996). EDP covers mainly three variables: (i) target group, (ii) location, and (iii) enterprise development or entrepreneurial activities. All of these variables are strongly interlinked with each other. To make EDP successful and effective, the role of the NGOs has significant importance in terms of identification of place or location, pre-promotional activities, selection of potential entrepreneurs, entrepreneurial training, monitoring and follow-up mechanism. NGOs are playing important role as catalyst in helping the rural unemployed persons to acquire training through Micro-Enterprise Development Programmes

(MEDPs) so that they can become self-employed by starting their enterprises in rural non-farm sector (RNFS). Moreover, they can also become job providers instead of job seekers. Thus, institutionalisation of MEDPs through NGOs can be an alternative approach to rural development in India. The success of any MEDP in terms of starting the enterprises by the trainees trained under it depends mainly upon the availability of loan. Microfinance sector can provide help to solve this problem. Microfinance for microenterprise development is a proper approach in India. Some of the NGOs in India have adopted the approach of microenterprise development through microfinance. The examples are Co-operative Development Foundation (CDF) in Andhra Pradesh, Lupin Human Welfare Research Foundation (LHWRF) in Rajasthan, Uttar Pradesh Land Development Corporation (UPLDC) in Uttar Pradesh and Group Enterprise Development Project of Entrepreneurship Development Institute of India (EDI) in Nagaland.

The Role of SHGs for Improving Socioeconomic Status

SHG movement is currently going on in different parts of the world. The effectiveness and efficacy of SHGs in reaching out to the poor has been successfully demonstrated in various contexts, new questions are being asked about the impact of the SHGs on the lives of the poor. SHGs with their thrift and credit model, who can really pull out a poor family out of poverty, are being assessed time and again to know the true status. There is enough evidence to show that SHGs are good at providing finance to meet urgent and priority consumption needs, but lot more is required to solve important life cycle needs. In a holistic perspective, microfinance is a process of social intermediation and building social capital. Process of social intermediation is an investment that is made for development of both human resources and institutional capital to make marginalised groups self-reliant in preparing them to engage in formal financial intermediation. It is also a financial intermediation with a capacity building component, aimed at those sectors of society that lack access to credit and savings facilities. It can be understood by transformation of beneficiaries into clients or customers and creation of local institutions that bridge the gap between the formal financial institutions and marginalised groups (Elaine and Barton, 1998; Pethiya and Teki, 2000a; 2000b; 2003).

In the recent times, SHGs are growing but at slow rate, as per the provisional information made available by NABARD in its annual report of 2007-08, the number of new groups credit-linked with banks declined to 0.552 million during the year, compared to 0.68 million groups in the previous year. The cumulative number of groups that have borrowed from a bank at least once has increased to 3.48 million by the end of March 2008 from 2.92 million, at the same time last year (Table 1.2).

Major form of microfinance in India, is based on women's SHGs, which are small groups of 10-20 members. These groups collect savings from their members and provide loans in turn. However, unlike most accumulating savings and credit associations (ASCAs) found in several countries, these groups also obtain loans from banks and on-lend them to their members. Over 700,000 groups had obtained over Rs. 20 billion (US $425 million) in loans from banks benefitting more than 10 million people by the year 2003. Delinquencies on these loans are reported to be less than 5 per cent. Savings in these groups is estimated to be at least Rs.8 billion (US $170 million) (Nair, 2001). SHG federations that provide a wide range of services and help SHGs become institutionally and financially sustainable because they provide the economies of scale that reduce transaction costs and make the provision of these services viable. 'Livelihoods financing' has been advocated to convey that the poor require higher capital investment if they really have to come out of poverty. An individual SHG does not meet the full credit requirement on its own and needs to access higher finances through different sources. The role of SHGs in tackling crucial social problems that become a barrier in achieving economic progress for the poor, for instance, social discrimination, gender discrimination, etc., have also been questioned. It is observed that the voice of an individual SHG is too feeble to challenge these social practices that are deep-rooted in historical traditions. But their sustainability is constrained by several factors—both internal, related to the federations themselves, and external, related to the other stakeholders (Nair, 2005).

The social development approach of microfinance is based on the premise that people should earn money by investing in viable micro-enterprises. They should earn profit from their enterprises. Major share of the profit should be reinvested in enterprises for their growth. The other share of the profit should be spent on social development that is, health, education, housing, sanitation etc. By earning profit from the viable micro-enterprises, people will increase their paying ability for services delivered to them under different social development projects run by NGO and states/ Central government. For the NGOs and government it can be a process of gradual withdrawal and, for people, decreased dependency on the NGOs and Government. Such projects have microfinance as a major component coupled with social service delivery (Gain and Satish, 1996; Girija, 1998).

NABARD initiated the process of microfinance in India through linkage programme of SHGs under Automatic Refinance Scheme (ARS). SIDBI is second important player in microfinance, providing bulk lending to MFIs. RMK is the third player providing loans to NGOs for on-lending to the women SHGs. These are the three major AFIs in India. Each has a different approach in microfinance sector. While NABARD's emphasis is entirely on SHGs linkage programme by mobilising their own savings, also SIDBI is focussing on building and creating larger MFIs and RMK is lending money to smaller NGOs as well. Taking into consideration the growth and potential of microfinance sector in India, other organisations and international agencies have also made their entry in the microfinance sector by providing loans and grants to NGOs for different income generating projects as well as for incorporating microfinance component in the service delivery projects of social development (UNDP, 2001). The important names among them are Housing and Urban Development Corporation Ltd. (HUDCO), National Backward Classes Finance Development Corporation (NBCFDC), National Minorities Finance Development Corporation (NMFDC), National Handicrafts Development Corporation (NHDC), UNDP, British Department of Foreign and International Development (DFID) and Consultative Group to Assist the Poor (CGAP) etc. Though in its young age, microfinance sector has a diversified growth and multiplicity of impact. It is seen as an important phenomenon in the process of development, especially in context of globalisation and liberalisation wherein subsidy and grant-based

Table 1.2

Growth Trends in SHG-Bank Linkage Programme

	2002	*2003*	*2004*	*2005*	*2006*	*2007*	*2008*
No. of new SHGs provided with bank loans (cumulative)	4,61,478	7,17,360	1,079,091	1,618,456	22,38,565	29,24,973	3,477,965
Of which in southern region (cumulative)	–	–	–	9,38,941	12,14,431	15,22,144	16,74,811
Per cent in southern region (%)	–	–	–	58	54	52	48.1
No. of new SHGs financed during the year	1,97,653	2,55,882	3,61,731	5,39,365	6,20,109	6,86,408	5,52,992
Of which in southern region	–	–	–	–	2,75,490	3,07,713	1,52,667
Per cent in southern region	–	–	–	–	44	45	27.6
Rate of growth of loans to new SHGs (%)	32	29	41	49	15	11	(-)16 decline
No. of SHGs receiving repeat loans	41,413	1,02,391	1,71,669	2,58,092	3,44,502	4,57,410	1,86,883 Provisional and incomplete
Rate of growth of repeat loans	91	147	68	50	33	33	NA
Proportion of repeat loans in total loans	17	29	40	32	36	40	NA
Bank loan disbursed cumulative (in crore)	1,026	2,049	3,904	6,896	11,398	18,0402	2,268
Bank loan disbursed during year (in crore)	545	1,023	1,855	2,994	4,499	6,643	4,228
Of which, disbursed to new groups (in crore)	453	691	1,158	1,727	2,330	3,044	2,542
Of which, disbursed as repeat loans (in crore)	92	332	698	1,268	2,169	3,599	1,686 Provisional and incomplete
Proportion of repeat loans in total disbursed (%)	17	33	38	42	48	54	NA
Average loan sizes—new	22,919	27,005	32,013	32,019	37,574	44,343	45,960
Repeat loan sizes	22,215	32,425	40,660	49,130	62,960	78,682	90,195*

Note: * Based on the information available on number and amount of repeat loans, which is provisional and incomplete.
NA = not available.
Source: Srinivas (2008).

programmes/schemes is losing their importance. Microfinance sector is seen as the best option based on saving mobilisation of the poor people and credit linkages. In India, many AFIs have come forward to lend money to the MFIs. MFIs of different nature (NGO registered under Societies Registration Act, trusts under Public Trust Act, cooperatives under Cooperative Societies Act, NBFCs under Company Act and local area banks (LABs) under Banking Act etc.) have also come up with different strategies of promoting people's livelihood. The poor people, on whose shoulders the success of sector is depending, are also participating in the growth of this sector. Government is also interested and is closely monitoring the sector from the policy and regulatory point of view. The sector has also opened scope for research, training and consultancy.

Nurturing and strengthening of the SHGs and creating solid foundations for the movement to promote strong SHG federations for real socioeconomic development in the country as a whole by capacity building and creating awareness. The grassroot level initiatives on the part of several voluntary organisations/NGOs became necessary to overcome the reticence of the banks. The banking institutions could help by utilising the existing voluntary organisations in a selective manner on the basis of an assessment of the capability of each such organisation. In several parts of the world, NGOs have demonstrated that promotion of SHGs of resource-poor persons with some basic traditional skills for undertaking different kind of income generating activities could foster proper grassroot level initiatives for motivating the banks to extend credit support to such groups at the appropriate juncture. The Indian experience demonstrates that some of the key elements of successful SHGs relate to:

- Formation around 'felt needs' of group members.
- Membership generally based on concept of 'some common economic interest'.
- Evolution of structure and byelaws in line with development and maturity of groups.
- Emergence of a disciplined group evolving and imposing byelaws and contributing to collective deliberation and action.
- Creation of an awareness and confidence building in the target group.

Microfinance: A Tool for Improving Socioeconomic Status

Microfinance can change the lives of the poor. There may not be a quantum jump in the income but it is possible still to ensure a reasonable rise in the income of the poor. This experiment clearly shows how a programme that is mainly intended for improving the economic conditions, and which effectively improves other parameters of a better quality of life. The socioeconomic conditions of the rural poor is being improved and has resulted in higher flow of credit to support a much broader production base. These groups have to graduate into promoting microenterprises. Though microenterprises are not a panacea for the complex problems of chronic unemployment and poverty, yet their promotion is a viable and effective strategy for achieving significant gains in income and assets for poor and marginalised people. The SHG improves the socio-economy by giving survival, subsistence and sustainable support to the economically deprived sections of the society. The three S's are defined below:

- At the first level, households use microfinance to meet 'survival' requirements where small savings and loans serve as a buffer in the event of an emergency or to smoothen consumption or even service previous debt to give itself more liquidity during lean times.
- At the second level, 'subsistence' needs are met through microfinance, where a household begins to utilise microfinance to diversify its basket of income generating activities, or to meet working capital requirements in traditional activities.
- At the third level, as households reach a stage where they can assume a higher degree of risk, microfinance would be used to invest in setting up an enterprise or facilitating entry into employment in one way or the other so that the household becomes 'sustainable'.

The progress of the SHG movement in India so far has been promising (Rangarajan, 2005). It has reached out to nearly 20 million households over the last decade. It has shown that the poor can organise themselves and do things to promote their well-being. It has also had a tremendous social impact. A survey on 70,000 women of 4,500 SHGs in Kurnool district. Andhra Pradesh has revealed the following:-

- More than 79 per cent of Development of Women and Children in Rural Areas (DWCRA) women had undergone family planning operations.
- More than 60 per cent of the children availed of *anganwadi* facilities.
- Cent per cent of the children had been immunised in the pulse polio programme.
- Ten per cent of the women were able to approach banks on their own for accessing institutional credit.

An attempt has been made to ascertain the socioeconomic status of women involved in different SHGs. See Table 1.3 for better understanding.

Benefits of SHGs to Donors and Government

SHGs are helping donors and government in accomplishing their broad goals of poverty eradication and empowerment of women and deprived sections of the society. SHGs are effectively implementing a number of programmes of donors, official agencies, and civil society organisations; for example, the vast network of SHG federations in Andhra Pradesh is implementing a pension distribution programme, managing mid-day meals at schools, and are working on awareness building for health, legal issues as well as social empowerment. The SHG federations are seen by governments as an alternative channel for service delivery of government programmes. SHGs individually should provide very little 'plus' services, but SHG federations not only reduce the regional inequalities but also promotes equitability for greater development. The government and donors should take a proactive role in strengthening the SHG movement in the country. The important roles are:

Focus: Governments should play a facilitating role, should not be target-oriented and restrain from enlarging the agenda of SHGs. Government and donors should provide funds to credible NGOs for capacity building of all the stakeholders.

Facilitate federations: Organising of SHGs into federations is to be treated as a public investment in terms of funds, which is required to be made available for research, experimentation and advocacy. SHG

Table 1.3

Showing Socioeconomic Status of Group Members in Different States

Total SHGs Covered	*Total Members Covered*	*Status of Socioeconomic Parameters*	*Result*	*States Covered*	*Reference*
72	1,000	Improvement in diet	+	Orissa, Uttar Pradesh, Maharashtra, Karnataka	Harper, 1998
		Improvement in assets,	+		
		Education	+		
70	-	Improvement in saving	+	Tamil Nadu	Puhazhendi, 2000
		Improvement in income	+		
		Improvement in assets	+		
		Improvement in food security			
		Employment	+		
		Education	+		
		Reduction in liquor consumption of male members	+		
		Women empowerment	+		
223	560	Improvement in income	+	Orissa, Uttar Pradesh, Maharashtra, Karnataka, Rajasthan, Bihar, Tamil Nadu, Andhra Pradesh	Puhazhendi and Satyasai, 2000
		Improvement in assets	+		
		Employment	+		
400	-	Improvement in income	+	Andhra Pradesh	APMAS, 2005
		Empowerment	+		
		Education	+		

Note: + = increase in status.

federations could be appropriately incorporated to optimise the benefits of both informal and formal institutions.

Build capacity: It is required for decentralised capacity building and support services for the SHG movement to thrive. The federation must cultivate 5-10 SHGs. Federations' staff should be trained to be trainers, auditors, motivators, and para-professionals to support the agenda of the SHGs.

Innovate: Continuous innovation is required to promote growth and ensure sustainability. With the advent of technology, SHGs could take on several intermediary or agent roles that benefit their members. There is a great potential if the movement is supported with a vision and strategy. SHG is a unique model with many challenges and many more

Table 1.4

SHG-Bank Linkage Programme in India

S. No.	*Particulars*	*Cumulative as on 31st March 2007*
1.	Number of SHGs linked	29,24,973
2.	% of women groups	90%
3.	No. of participating banks	498
	i) Commercial banks	50
	ii) Regional rural banks	96
	iii) Cooperative banks	352
4.	Number of states/UTs	31
5.	Number of district covered	587
6.	Bank loan (Rs. in billion)	180.41
7.	Refinance (Rs. in billion)	54.59
8.	Number of poor households assisted (in million)	40.95
9.	Average loan/SHG – new (Rs.)	44,342
	– repeat (Rs.)	78,693
10.	Average loan/family – new (Rs.)	4,167
	– repeat (Rs.)	5,612
11.	Model-wise Linkage (cumulative)	
	i) SHGs formed and financed by banks	17%
	ii) SHGs formed by other agencies but directly financed by banks	75%
	iii) SHGs financed by banks using financial intermediaries	08%

Source: *www.nabard.com*

opportunities i.e., giving aid to poor women and providing opportunity to create an identity of societal development along with information and bargaining power for a healthy and vibrant society, i.e.:

- Provides platform for the needy and poor to discuss and resolve problems.
- Helps to manage cash flow deficits (maintaining food intake and overcoming emergencies), leading to improvement in quality and productivity of their only capital/resource—human capital/resource.
- Helps the members to avoid moneylenders, especially to meet food and health emergencies.
- Helps the members to invest in asset creation, diversify their occupations, and improve their risk-bearing capacities.

- Helps the members to promote leadership qualities.
- Helps the members to foster women, even from conservative communities and regions, to interact with outsiders, particularly officials, including men.
- Helps the members to establish the linkage between banks and marginalised citizens, especially the women.

Critical Evaluation of SHG model of Microfinance Delivery in India

As shown in Table 1.4, though the cumulative number of SHGs linked to banks (financial inclusion) is impressive. However, what is worrisome is the percentage of repeat loans that have been extended to SHGs was just 21.3 per cent of the cumulative number of SHGs that were given. Was it sufficient to lift up the poor from one time loan? When the average amount of loan per family is Rs. 4,167 and Rs. 5,612, new and repeat loans respectively, as per the NABARD's reckonings (Table 1.4). The number of poor households covered was 4.95 crore, whereas the below poverty ratio at national level is 27.8 per cent as per the 61st National Sample Survey in 2004-05 data (*Economic Survey, 2007*). Accordingly so far, the SHG model could cover 16.9 crore (60 per cent of target) poor people (presuming family size 4.5 persons per family). And a large chunk—about 11 crore (40 per cent of target) people or about 3 crore poor households, are yet to be covered by this model. The gap should be bridged at the earliest on priority basis. Hence, it is required that efforts by all concerns should be geared up for financial inclusion of the excluded segment of the society for the better socioeconomic development in the near future.

Global Perspective

World Bank Report (2007) titled 'Microfinance in South Asia' puts the growth in microfinance in South Asia's perspective as follows:

- In South Asia, the modern microfinance movement was born in Bangladesh in the 1970s as a response to the prevailing poverty conditions among its vast rural population.
- Astonishing growth rates in Bangladesh, particularly during the 1990s, created a new dimension for microfinance worldwide as MFIs

grew to include millions of clients. For the first time, a substantial proportion of the low-income families of major developing countries were served by the activity.

- In India, a substantial microfinance system based on SHGs developed. Other countries of the region made slower and later starts but have since established active microfinance sectors.
- By 2005, microfinance covered at least 35 million of some 270 families in the region and met around 15 per cent of the overall credit requirements of low-income families. Coverage was particularly impressive in Bangladesh and Sri Lanka, where microfinance services reached more than 60 per cent of the poor.
- Moreover, this growth brought the women at the centre of the economic activities of the households.
- The start of organised sector finance in South Asia (particularly Bangladesh, India and Pakistan) can be traced to the Cooperative Credit Societies Act of 1904.
- It was an attempt, *albeit* very shallow, to reach out to those at peripheries of the formal financial system—farmers, artisans, and other persons of limited means. However, the cooperative model failed to make a visible impact and lacked scalability in the form it was implemented during the next seven decades. Eventually, in the 1970s, it led to nationalisation of commercial banks throughout the region, and the first attempts were made to launch microfinance as we know it today.

Financing Structures

MFIs essentially perform the role of intermediating financial resources and services between investors, banks, donors, depositors, and the poor. Like any other financial intermediary, MFIs need risk capital that can be leveraged to add to their funding base for operations and on-lending to low-income clients, either through debt finance or by raising additional deposits. Unlike commercial financial institutions, MFIs in South Asia/ India have evolved from non-profit entities. Due to higher transaction costs and small account sizes it typically has taken three to seven years for leading MFIs to become financially strong enough to attract commercial risk capital. Consequently, donor funding has had to play the key role of 'venture capital' in stimulating microfinance investment and promoting microfinance markets.

South Asia is a worldwide pioneer in the field of MFI ratings; the Microcredit Ratings International Limited (M-CRIL), based in India, is one of the first three international microfinance raters. Since then, two other corporate rating agencies have entered the microfinance business, one in India and one in Pakistan. This puts South Asia in a good position to further facilitate links between MFIs and investors.

Future Perspective

During the past 25 years, the microfinance movement has challenged conventional financial sector and government thinking, in the process fundamentally altering the financial landscape. Today, it provides most of the access to financial services available to low-income people in South Asia, but it is still largely a separate part of the financial system, with few examples of direct service provision to the poor by mainstream commercial institutions. Despite the growing discussion about the enthusiasm for developing a seamless and inclusive financial sector, there is little evidence that this has happened yet.

Over the next few years, most of the growth in microfinance will come from a few large, profitable, specialised institutions that might in some ways rival small banks. These institutions will make more use of commercial funding, both debt and equity from commercial banks and the growing number of social investment funds.

The Emergence of Microfinance Industry

The microfinance initiative in private sector can be traced to the initiative undertaken by Ms. Ela Bhatt for providing banking services to the poor women employed in the unorganised sector in Ahmedabad. Shri Mahila SEWA (Self Employed Women's Association) Sahakari Bank, set up in 1974 as an urban cooperative bank is providing banking services to the poor self-employed women working as hawkers, vendors, domestic servants etc. Though the MFI is making profit, yet the SEWA bank model of MFI has not been replicated elsewhere in the country.

After nationalisation of the banking sector, credit was recognised as a remedy for many of the ills of the poverty. Large number of credit-based programmes were introduced by the Central and state governments with large resource allocations.

While the underlying objectives were laudable and substantial progress was achieved, credit flow to the poor, and especially to poor women, remained low. This led to initiatives that were institution-led, which attempted to converge the existing strength of rural banking infrastructure and leverage this to better serve the unbanked poor. The pioneering efforts at this were made by NABARD.

The research studies conducted by NABARD during the early 1980s in association with MYRADA and also independently, revealed that a vast majority of the poorest of the poor was still at the periphery of the formal banking system. These studies indicated that the existing banking policies, systems and procedures, and deposit and loan products were perhaps not well-suited to meet the most immediate needs of the poor. It also appeared that what the poor really needed was a better access to these services and products, rather than cheap subsidised credit.

Against this background NABARD launched the pilot phase of the SHG-Bank Linkage programme in February 1992 aimed at promoting and financing 500 SHGs across the country. The SHG-informal thrift and credit groups of poor came to be recognised as bank clients under this programme.

The strategy involved forming small, cohesive and participative groups of the poor, encouraging them to pool their thrift regularly and using the pooled thrift to make small interest bearing loans to members, and in the process learning the nuances of financial discipline. Subsequently, bank credit also becomes available to the group, to augment its resources for lending to its members. NABARD, however, also took a conscious decision to experiment with other successful strategies such as replicating Grameen model, financing NGO-MFIs to enable them to on-lend to the groups.

Mainstreaming of SHG-Bank Linkage Programme

Based on recommendations of the Working Group on NGOs and SHGs, set up by the Reserve Bank of India in 1994, the RBI advised the banks to consider SHGs lending within their mainstream rural credit operations. In 1998, NABARD crystallised its vision for providing access to one-third of the rural poor through linking of one million SHGs by 2007. This was followed by massive scaling up of the training and capacity building awareness programmes by NABARD in partnership with NGOs, banks, government agencies and rural volunteers in SHG promotion, nurturing, appraisal and financing. The vision of linking one million SHGs was achieved in the year 2004.

Microfinance Service Providers

The microfinance service providers include apex institutions like NABARD, SIDBI and RMK. At the retail level, commercial banks, regional rural banks, and cooperative banks provide microfinance services. Today, there are about 60,000 retail credit outlets of the formal banking sector in the rural areas comprising 12,000 branches of district level cooperative banks, over 14,000 branches of the RRBs and over 30,000 rural and semi-urban branches of commercial banks, besides almost 90,000 cooperative credit societies at the village level. On an average, there is at least one retail credit outlet for about 5,000 rural people. This physical reaching out to the far-flung areas of the country to provide savings, credit and other banking services to the rural society is an unparalleled achievement of the Indian banking system.

Figure 1.3

Retail Credit Outlets of Formal Banking Sector in Rural Areas

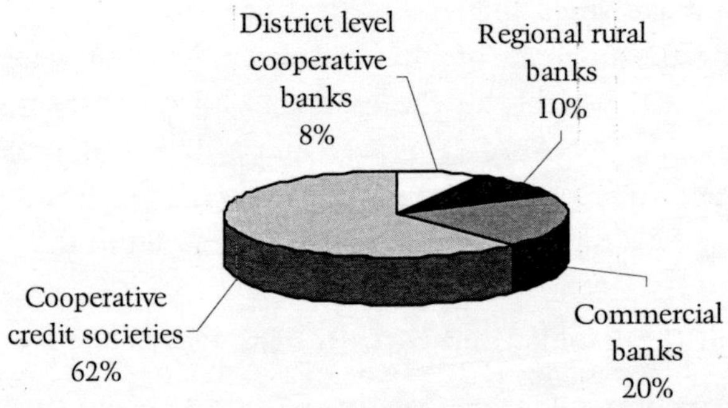

Source: Created on basis of NABARD Data.

2 Financial Exclusion

Inclusive growth is essential for long-term economic development of nation. The economic growth that equitably would facilitate sustainable economic development. Within the portfolio of inclusive growth, financial inclusion is more important as financial services are integral part of personal and societal growth and development. Financial 'exclusion' which is an impediment for equitable and inclusive growth of nation may be defined as a process by which specific segments of the population or a group of individuals is denied/deprived the access to basic formal financial system and financial services. Financial exclusion has gained importance during early 1990s in Europe where the geographers found that some definite pockets or regions of a particular nation were behind the others in utilising financial services. It was also found that these pockets or regions were poorer compared to regions which utilised more of financial services. The term secured a larger connotation in the late 1990s when it was expanded to refer to individuals who were denied access to financial system and inclusion rather than geographical areas. Financial exclusion may not mean a social exclusion in India as it does in the developed countries, but it is an issue that required to be addressed. The large presence of informal credit could avoid social exclusion but the legal validity of such financial services pose an obstacle for creating a modern globalising economy. Financial exclusion could pose hindrances to growth and development. Without a formal and a legally recognised financial system in which all sections of the population are an integral part of, it may not be possible even for the most efficient of the governments to reach out to all sections of the people in the society. A stable and healthy financial system promotes trust and confidence among the people about the economy and only with this trust and confidence (which has legal validity) could a robust, stable and an inclusive economy would evolve.

The world is moving at an astounding pace. The advances in technologies distances have become meaningless. Globalisation has enabled the rise of global trade leading to wealth generation in developed as well as developing countries. Wealth can be created in any part of the world with a single click of the mouse. Developing nations, like India have immensely benefited from the globalising economy. Wealth has been pouring into the country as investments (both direct and institutional). Wealth has been also generated by Indian companies from global trade. This has directly affected the lives of many citizens in our country. For many, there has been a dramatic increase in the disposable income. The savings, consumption and investment patterns have changed in the past few years. This has meant that there has been an increase in demand for many financial services from different financial firms.

The market has responded to the soaring demand with making attractive offers and services for the customers at affordable rates. The liberalisation of the economy in the 1990s has brought in new players into the field. This has not only brought in some much needed fresh air to the stagnant financial sector but also competition for the same market space which was relatively unknown in the financial sector till then. Since then, there have been progressive reforms in the financial sector allowing for better and easier facilities and options to the consumer. An increasing financially aware middle class have realised the importance of financial services. Banks have streamlined and rationalised themselves to meet up with the changing demands of the people. Banks have become partners in growth for many offering them a safer and secure future. However, not all the reforms in the financial services sector have still been able to bring in the other half of India's population who are yet to be banked. There are many reasons that are obvious for this kind of financial exclusion. The new surge in the economy has not yet percolated into the lower strata of the society. It is easy to blame the capitalist growth for this sort of income disparities; however, the inefficiencies and the inadequacies of the government and its policies are equally at fault for lack of reduction in poverty. Even after 60 years of Indian independence, one-third of our population is still illiterate (let alone financially literate) and at least 26 per cent of the population still lives under the poverty line. There are many statistics, which goes on to prove that for even a developing nation like India has a long way to go.

Most of the unbanked or financially excluded population of India lives in rural areas; nevertheless there is also a significant amount of the urban population of India who face the same situation even with easy access to banks. Many of the financially excluded in these areas are illiterates earning a meagre income just enough to sustain their daily subsistence needs. For such people, banking still remains an unknown phenomena or an elitist affair. It is easier for them to keep their money at their house or with some moneylenders and easily make immediate purchases (which make up most of their expenditure) rather than to follow the cumbersome process at banks. A lot of the financially excluded populations are at the mercy of moneylenders or pawnshop owners. They should be made a part of the formal banking structure so that they could also have the benefits that the others enjoy. By making them financially inclusive, the system is making their financial position less volatile. At the same time, we are treating them on an equal par with other members of the population so that they would not be denied of access to a basic service such as banking.

Backdrop

Nationalisation of banks in India in 1969 and 1980 marked a paradigm shift in the focus of banking from class banking to mass banking. The multi-agency approach consisting of cooperatives, regional rural banks (RRBs), commercial banks, non-banking financial institutions, etc., has played a key role in catering to the credit needs of rural population. Most of these agencies have been acting not merely as financial intermediaries but also playing a key developmental role. In the post-nationalisation era, launching of SHG-Bank linkage programme in 1992 and its success as one of the largest microcredit programmes in the world could be considered as a landmark programme and can be regarded as the most potent initiative since independence for delivering financial services to the poor in a sustainable manner.

Despite large-scale deepening and widening of formal as also informal credit delivery system, it is estimated that 45.9 million farmer households in the country (51.4 per cent), out of a total of 89.3 million households do not access credit, either from institutional or non-institutional sources. Further, despite the vast network of bank branches, only 27 per cent of total farm households are indebted to formal sources (or which one-third also borrow from informal sources). One of the benchmarks employed to access the degree of reach of financial services to the population of the country, is the quantum of deposit accounts (current and savings) held as a ratio to the adult population. In the Indian context, taking into the Census of 2001 (ignoring the incremental growth of the population thereafter), the ratio of deposit accounts (data available as on March 31, 2004) to the total adult population was only 59 per cent though this ratio in case of Karnataka (65 per cent) is above the national average, the fact remains that the formal financial institution in the state do not cater to these services or not doing enough.

Factors Responsible for Financial Exclusion

There are number of factors that are responsible for financial exclusion, these broadly include; socioeconomic system, development of financial system, infrastructure, poverty level, lack of income generating activities etc. Financial exclusion is mainly attributed to socio-economic standing of the individual in the society; yet, there are also other factors that have been leading to financial exclusion. These are:

a) Lack of income generating activities: Most of the poor have no access for perennial source of income. They are largely seasonal low-wage earners, for them opening an account and withdrawing money is seemingly not feasible. Most of the poor do not have high spending that would require borrowing of credit from a formal agency like bank. They would rather keep their daily income at their homes rather than in a bank.

b) Lack of financial awareness: The lack of financial awareness about the benefits of the banking and also illiteracy act as stumbling blocks to financial inclusion. The lack of financial awareness maybe the single most risk in financial inclusion as those who are newly included in the financial sector have to maintain within the formal financial sector.

c) Convenient access to alternative credit; For a good amount of low income people, the alternative credit provided by the moneylenders and pawnshop owners are far more attractive and hassle-free compared to getting a loan from a commercial bank. Some of the poor that do not have property find it impossible to get credit without the collateral. The uneducated poor would rather put their trust in moneylenders who provide easy non-collateral credit than on the well established commercial banks. There might also be cultural reasons for trusting a moneylender rather than a bank.

d) Lack of understanding of property rights: The concept of property rights are still not clearly understood in most parts of India. It was the Peruvian economist Hernando De Soto in the early 2000s who made the world aware of the concept of 'dead capital'. In most of the developing nations, the poor and the weaker sections of the society have little or no knowledge of property rights since most are uneducated. Since they do not possess the documents necessary for the collateral such people are denied credit. Their properties which they own, but have no legal authority over come under the extralegal system and therefore remain as 'dead capital'. This in turn helps in the rise of the informal economy which gives the alternative credit. In such a situation the property which has no 'legal' rights over it, would not provide any meaningful credit for the owner. This was the situation in the west prior to the advances in the 19th and the 20th century. The rapid development of property rights in these nations has meant that credit could be easily given to those who could prove that they were owners of some property. A formal acknowledgment of the property and its owner guarantees that the collateral is valid. The institutionalisation of the financial services whether one likes it or not demands this sort of formal acknowledgment. Property and property rights of the individual are extremely important since the financial agencies are dealing with individuals (includes businesses and other institutions) and not the society ultimately. Only by guaranteeing property rights through simpler procedures for ensuring the rights can the true financial inclusion start.

e) Indiffirence of commercial banks: There is a lot of criticism of the commercial banks because of their inherent tendency to think that poor people are not worthy of being banked. Banks are in business to make profit and would like to only indulge in activities that give them profit. Due to high transaction costs of smaller transactions and the speculated high risk in lending credit to the lower strata of the society, they see banking with poor as unviable. Even if banks are concerned with the poor, they do it in a manner of corporate social responsibility or social service and treat them differently instead of trying to bring them into the mainstream.

Unless banks see any incentive in banking with the weaker sections of the society, they would not be willing to do so.

f) Disincentives for the consumer: This point is closely related to the above one. The cost of maintaining an account (non-zero balance accounts) and procedural problems in accessing formal credit act as disincentives for consumers with weaker financial backgrounds. The consumers from the lower strata are likelier to ask for smaller credit which banks have no enthusiasm to give. It would rather give smaller number of large credits to middle and upper class individuals and institutions, due to the lower cost involved in banking with them. The banks and other financial service firms have fewer financial products which are attractive to the poor and the socially disadvantaged. All these act against the interest of a consumer from a poor background.

NSSO Survey Results (2003)

The Committee debated the various dimensions of inclusion and concluded that while aspects such as savings, remittance facilities, insurance, etc., were important, nevertheless exclusion was particularly germane from the standpoint of access to credit by vulnerable groups. The Committee accordingly scanned the data put out by the NSSO in the situation assessment survey on 'Indebtedness of Farmer Households' (2003). The Committee noted that the definition of indebtedness as adopted in the survey referred to farmer households having outstanding loans from 35 institutional or non-institutional sources in cash or kind having a value of Rs.300 or more at the time of transaction.

As per NSSO data, 45.9 million farmer households in the country (51.4 per cent), out of a total of 89.3 million households do not access credit, either from institutional or non-institutional sources. Only 27 per cent of total farm households are indebted to formal sources (of which one-third also borrow from informal sources). In other words, 73 per cent of farm households do not have access to formal credit sources. For purposes of this analysis, 'financially excluded' households will be defined as those not having any debt to formal credit sources. The various aspects of such exclusion among specific regions and population groups are indicated hereto:

Level of Non-Indebtedness: Across Regions

The farm households not accessing credit from formal sources as a proportion to total farm households is especially high at 95.91 per cent, 81.26 per cent and 77.59 per cent in the northeastern, eastern and central regions respectively. In terms of absolute numbers these regions taken together account for 64 per cent of farm households not accessing credit from formal sources (Table 2.1).

Table 2.1

Number of Farmer Households (HH) in Lakh

Region	*Total HHs*	*Indebted HHs*	*% to Total HHs*	*Non-Indebted HHs*	*% to Total HHs*	*Indebted to Formal Sources*	*% to Total HHs*	*Excluded by Formal Sources*	*% to Total HHs*
Northern	109.46	56.26	51.40	53.2	48.60	27.423	25.05	82.04	74.95
Northeastern	35.40	7.04	19.90	28.36	80.10	1.448	4.09	33.95	95.91
Eastern	210.61	84.22	40.00	126.39	60.00	39.467	18.74	171.14	81.26
Central	271.33	113.04	41.60	158.29	58.40	60.814	22.41	210.52	77.59
Western	103.66	55.74	53.70	47.92	46.30	45.586	43.98	58.07	56.02
Southern	161.56	117.45	72.70	44.11	27.30	69.072	42.75	92.49	57.25
Group of UTs	1.48	0.49	33.10	0.99	66.90	0.15	10.14	1.33	89.86
All-India	893.50	434.24	48.60	459.26	51.40	243.96	27.30	649.54	72.70
NE, C&E Regions*	517.34	204.30	39.49	313.04	60.51	101.73	19.66	415.61	80.34
Share to All-India (%)	57.90	47.05		68.16		41.70		63.99	

Note: * NE = northeastern region, C = central region, E = eastern region.
Source: NSSO, 2003.

The southern region, on the other end, exhibits relatively better levels of access to formal/non-formal sources (72.7 per cent) mainly on account of spread of banking habits and a more robust infrastructure.

Level of Non-Indebtedness: Across States

The proportion of non-indebted farmer households was most pronounced in Jammu & Kashmir (68.2 per cent) and Himachal Pradesh (66.6 per cent) in the northern region. Institutional sources include government, cooperative societies and banks, while non-institutional sources include agricultural/professional moneylenders, traders, relatives and friends, doctors, lawyers and other professionals etc. Also, all states in the northeastern region (61.2 per cent to 95.9 per cent) except Tripura, in Bihar (67 per cent) and Jharkhand (79.1 per cent) in eastern region, and Chhattisgarh (59.8 per cent), Uttar Pradesh (59.7 per cent) and Uttarakhand (92.8 per cent) in the central region, as per details see Table 2.2.

Table 2.2

Level of Non-Indebtedness of Farmers: Across States

State/Region	*Non-Indebted Farmer HHs @*		*State/Region*	*Non-Indebted Farmer HHs @*	
	Lakh	*%*		*Lakh*	*%*
Northern	**53.21**	**48.7**	West Bengal	34.53	49.9
Haryana	9.11	46.9	**Central**	**158.29**	**58.4**
Himachal Pradesh	6.03	66.6	Chhattisgarh	16.50	59.8
Jammu & Kashmir	6.43	68.2	Madhya Pradesh	31.09	49.2
Punjab	6.38	34.6	Uttar Pradesh	102.38	59.7
Rajasthan	25.26	47.6	Uttarakhand	8.32	92.8
Northeastern	**28.36**	**80.4**	**Western**	**47.92**	**46.3**
Arunachal Pradesh	1.15	94.1	Gujarat	18.20	48.1
Assam	20.51	81.9	Maharashtra	29.72	45.2
Manipur	1.61	75.2	**Southern**	**44.11**	**27.3**
Meghalaya	2.44	95.9	Andhra Pradesh	10.84	18.0
Mizoram	0.60	76.4	Karnataka	15.52	38.4
Nagaland	0.51	63.5	Kerala	7.82	35.6
Tripura	1.19	50.8	Tamil Nadu	9.93	25.5
Sikkim	0.36	61.2			
Eastern	**126.39**	**60.0**	**Group of UTs**	**0.99**	**66.9**
Bihar	47.42	67.0			
Jharkhand	22.34	79.1	**All India**	**459.26**	**51.4**
Orissa	22.09	52.2			

Note: @ refers to non-indebtedness to both levels of indebtedness to institutional.
Source: NSSO, 2003.

Derived data indicate that only 27.3 per cent of the total farm households were indebted to institutional sources as detailed in Table 2.3.

Table 2.3

Derived Data

Region	*Total No. of HHs (lakh)*	*Incidence of Indebtedness to both Formal and Non-Formal Sources*		*Indebtedness to Institutional Sources*	
		Lakh HHs	*(% to Total HHs)*	*Lakh HHs*	*(% to Total HHs)*
Northern	109.46	56.26	51.39	27.42	25.05
Northeastern	35.40	7.04	19.88	1.45	4.09
Eastern	210.61	84.22	40.01	39.47	18.74
Central	271.33	113.04	41.66	60.81	22.41
Western	103.66	55.74	53.77	45.59	43.98
Southern	161.56	117.45	72.70	69.07	42.75
Group of UTs	1.48	0.49	33.10	0.150	10.14
All-India	893.50	434.24	48.60	243.96	27.30

Source: NSSO, 2003.

Data disaggregated by states indicate that indebtedness among the more 'inclusive states' also exhibit high recourse to non-institutional sources of finance. In the states of the southern region this is particularly the case in Andhra Pradesh and Tamil Nadu. The state-wise levels of exclusion from formal sources are provided later in the NSSO Report (2003).

Level of Non-Indebtedness: Across Marginal/Small Farmer Households

It can be seen from Table 2.4 that 87 per cent of all non-indebted farm households belong to the marginal (70.6 per cent) and small (17.1 per cent) farmer categories. The NSSO estimates of the year 2003 show that only around 45 per cent of marginal farmer households (*viz.*, up to one ha.) had access to both institutional and non-institutional credit. There are no data to show the position of finance extended exclusively to marginal farmers by institutional sources. A major portion of the credit from financial institutions for weaker sections has supported small farmers. However, marginal farmers who account for 66 per cent of all farm holdings remain by and large excluded from the formal financial system and by rough approximation, only around 20 per cent of these households access credit from formal banking sources.

Table 2.4

Non-Indebtedness: Across Marginal/Small Farmer Households

Category of Farmer HH	*Size Class of Land Owned (Ha)*	*Total Farmer HHs (No. lakh)*	*Non-Indebted Farmer HHs (No. lakh)*	*Incidence of Exclusion by both Formal and Non-Formal Sources (%)*	*Proportion of Non-Indebted HHs (%)*
Marginal	<1.00	589.06	324.04	55.0	70.6
Small	1.01 – 2.00	160.60	78.68	49.0	17.1
Semi-medium	2.01 – 4.00	93.50	39.10	41.8	8.5
Medium	4.01 – 10.00	42.58	14.84	34.9	3.2
Large	10.00 +	7.76	2.60	33.6	0.6
All sizes	893.50	459.26	51.4	100.0	

Source: NSSO, 2003.

It is discernible that the proportion and level of inability to access credit increases with the decline in size of farm holdings.

Level of Non-Indebtedness: Across Social Groups

The highest levels of non-indebtedness to both formal and non-formal sources is observed among scheduled tribes (ST) with 63.7 per cent, followed by scheduled castes (SC) with 49.8 per cent as detailed below:

Table 2.5

Non-Indebtedness: Across Social Groups

Households	*Scheduled Tribes*	*Scheduled Castes*	*Other Backward Classes*	*Others*	*All*
Total no. of farmer HHs (lakh)	119.24	155.93	370.43	247.90	893.50
Non-indebted farmer HHs (lakh)	75.94	77.60	179.96	125.76	459.26
Proportion of non-indebted farmer HHs (%)	63.69	49.77	48.58	50.73	51.40

Source: NSSO, 2003.

Incidence of financial exclusion among all non-cultivator households was estimated at 78.2 per cent which comprises of 78.8 per cent of agricultural labourer households, 71.4 per cent of artisans and 79.7 per cent of other rural households. Out of 5.96 crore non-cultivator households about 4.66 crore were estimated to be financially excluded. The number of non-cultivator households affected by financial exclusion was the highest for 'others' category (2.44 crore), followed by agricultural labourer households (1.67 crore) and artisans (0.55 crore) as detailed below:

Table 2.6

Agricultural Labourers

Households	*Agricultural Labourers*	*Artisans*	*Others*	*Total Non-Cultivators**
Number of households (crore)	2.12	0.77	3.06	5.96
Number of households facing financial exclusion (crore)	1.67	0.55	2.44	4.66
Incidence of financial exclusion (%)	78.80	71.40	79.70	78.20

Source: NSSO, 2003.

3 Role of Microfinance in Financial Inclusion

'India is a rich country where poor people live' is an adage in vogue since long time. One of the important factors that is responsible for such kind of endorsement is lack of access for formal financial system and financial services to the poor. Of late the essence of including the excluded people into the formal financial system has been realised, which in the current days is called financial inclusion. The term financial inclusion could be described as being the opposite of financial exclusion. However financial inclusion is more of a process rather than a phenomenon. It is a process by which mainstream financial services are made accessible to all sections of the population. It is a conscious attempt at trying to bring the unbanked people into banking. Financial inclusion does not merely mean access to credit for the poor, but also other financial services such as insurance. Financial inclusion allows the state to have an easier access to its citizens. With an inclusive population, for e.g.: the government could reduce the transaction cost of payments like pensions, or unemployment benefits. It could prove to be a boon in a situation like a natural disaster, a financially included population means the government will have much less headaches in ensuring that all the people get the benefits. It allows for more transparency leading to curtailing corruption and bureaucratic barriers in reaching out to the poor and weaker sections. An intelligent banking population could go a long way by effectively securing themselves a safer future. More importantly financial inclusion is imperative for creating an inclusive economy at all fronts. This attains special importance at this stage of rising food and oil prices, without an inclusive economy the country's development will suffer. In the 2008 annual G8 meeting in Hokkaido, Japan, the World Bank chief, Robert Zoellick, reiterated the importance of creating an inclusive economy in an increasingly globalised world.

Figure 3.1

Proportion of Households Availing Banking Services

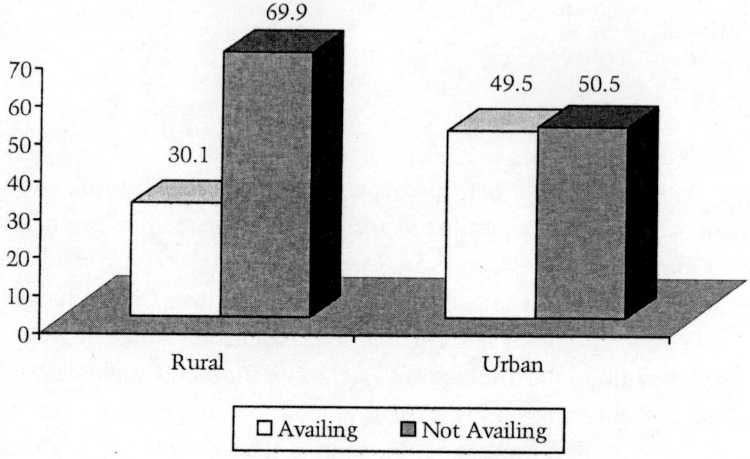

Source: RBI Data.

The Reserve Bank of India (RBI) has emphasised access to banking services for all sections of the society as a large segment of the population has been left outside the coverage of the formal banking sector. Census data revealed that in 2001, the proportion of rural households availing banking (deposit) services was 30.1 per cent, while for urban households, it was 49.5 per cent. The extent of exclusion was higher for specific population groups and regions. The NSSO (59th Round, 2003) data revealed that 45.9 million farmer households in the country, i.e., 51.4 per cent of the total of 89.3 million households do not access credit, either from institutional or non-institutional sources. Further, despite the vast network of bank branches, only 27 per cent of total farm households were indebted to formal sources (of which one-third also borrow from informal sources). Farm households not accessing credit from formal sources, as a proportion to total farm households, was especially high at 95.91 per cent, 81.26 per cent and 77.59 per cent in the northeastern, eastern and central regions, respectively. Thus, apart from the fact that exclusion in general is large, it also varied widely across regions, social groups and asset holdings. The poorer the group, the greater was the exclusion.

Concerns on financial inclusion also emanated from the results of the *All-India Debt and Investment Survey* (AIDIS), 2002, which revealed that over a period of 40 years, the share of non-institutional sources of credit for cultivator households declined sharply from about 93 per cent in 1951 to about 30 per cent in 1991, with the share of moneylenders declining from 69.7 per cent to 17.5 per cent. However, in 2002, the AIDIS revealed that the share of moneylenders again increased to 27 per cent and that of non-institutional sources overall rose to 39 per cent. In other words, notwithstanding the outreach of banking, the formal credit system has not been able to adequately penetrate the informal financial markets. Further, it may be noted that the rate of agricultural growth during the last decade slowed down, particularly in respect of food grains production.

What is Financial Inclusion?

Financial inclusion is providing financial services at an affordable cost to the vast sections of disadvantaged and low-income groups. Unrestrained access to public goods and services is indispensible for an open and efficient society. Banking services are in the nature of public good, it is essential that availability of banking and payment services to the entire population without discrimination is the prime objective of the public policy.

In general, the term financial inclusion is perceived in variety of ways in various contexts. There is a view that only access to credit is treated as financial inclusion whereas other view claims that it includes all the services extended by the financial institutions. All the same, financial inclusion by banks and other institutions must target, apart from personal/ private investment requirements of individuals and groups, the universal public investment requirements necessary for development of infrastructure, social sector services, public utilities and productive forces/ capacity building efforts, etc. Merely having a bank account may not be a good indicator of financial inclusion. Further, indebtedness as quantified in the NSSO, may also not be a fully reflective indicator. Hence, the ideal definition should look at people who want credit, but are denied the same. However, the bankers need not extend credit to everyone who approach them. If genuine claimants for credit are denied, then there is a case of exclusion. Therefore, it naturally means that all cases of denial of credit may not be exclusion. Further, the fact of denial of credit should be probed further. As this aspect raises the issue of creditworthiness or bankability, it was also deliberated on what could be done to make the 'institutionally excluded', bankable or creditworthy. Thus, financial inclusion may well be all about money and finance, but with the ultimate objective of directly abolishing the state of social exclusion in the economy.

Present Scenario

Financial inclusion, in the sense of extending banking products at an affordable cost to the vast sections of disadvantaged and low-income groups, is not new to India. For more than three decades after nationalisation of major commercial banks in 1969, Indian banking has shown tremendous growth in volume and outreach resulting in increase in the total number of branches of scheduled commercial banks (SCBs) from 8,321 in the year 1969 to 68,681 as at the end of March 2006 and reduction of the average population per branch office from 64,000 to 16,000 during the same period. Public sector banks (PSBs) were in the forefront of reaching out to sections that were once neglected and designing new, innovative loan products for agriculture and small-scale industries sectors is an outstanding example in this regard.

There are, however, concerns that banks have still not been able to reach a vast segment of the population and provide them with basic banking services. Growth has also not been uniform across all the regions/ states of the country and there still continue to be wide gaps in the availability of banking services in the rural areas. While from the policy angle none of the earlier measures aimed at broad-basing their clientele has been withdrawn, the banks might be laying somewhat less emphasis on inclusive practices in view of the thrust on profitability.

Scope of financial inclusion: The scope of financial inclusion can be expanded in two ways.

a) Through state-driven intervention by way of statutory enactments (for instance the US example, the Community Reinvestment Act (1977) and making it a statutory right to have bank account in France).

b) Through voluntary effort by the banking community itself for evolving various strategies to bring the large strata of society within the ambit of the banking sector.

When bankers do not give the desired attention to certain areas, the regulators have to step in to remedy the situation. This is the reason why RBI is placing a lot of emphasis on financial inclusion.

In India the focus of the financial inclusion at present is confined to ensuring a bare minimum access to a savings bank account without frills, to all. Internationally, the financial exclusion has been viewed in a much wider perspective. Having a current account/saving account on its own, is not regarded as an accurate indicator of financial inclusion. There could be multiple levels of financial inclusion and exclusion.

At one extreme, it is possible to identify the 'super-included', i.e., those customers who are actively and persistently courted by the financial services industry, and who have at their disposal a wide range of financial services and products. At the other extreme, we may have the financially excluded, who are denied access to even the most basic of financial products. In between are those who use the banking services only for deposits and withdrawals of money. But these persons may have only restricted access to the financial system, and may not enjoy the flexibility of access offered to more affluent customers.

The RBI, therefore, initiated policies focussing on financial inclusion from the year 2005. In simple terms, financial inclusion may be defined as delivery of banking services at an affordable cost to the vast sections of disadvantaged and low-income groups who tend to be excluded. Its broad approach to financial inclusion aims at 'connecting people' with the banking system and not just credit dispensation; giving people access to payments system and portray financial inclusion as a viable business model and opportunity. In consonance with the above approach, the RBI has undertaken a number of measures for bringing the financially excluded population into the structured financial system.

No-frills accounts: RBI advised the SCBs and regional rural banks (RRBs) in November 2005 to make available a basic banking 'no-frills' account with nil or low minimum balances as well as charges, that would make such accounts accessible to vast sections of the population.

Significant progress has been made by banks in this regard and the number of no-frills accounts opened by banks and, particularly, by PSBs increased sharply during the last few years (Table 3.1).

Table 3.1

Number of No-Frills Accounts

Bank Group	*As on*		
	31.03.2006	*31.03.2007*	*31.03.2008**
1	*2*	*3*	*4*
Public sector banks	332,878	5,865,419	13,925,674
Private sector banks	156,388	860,997	1,879,073
Foreign banks	231	5,919	33,115
Total	489,497	6,732,335	15,837,862

Note: * Provisional.
Source: RBI (*www.rbi.org.in*).

In the Annual Policy Statement for the year 2008-09 RBI advised banks to classify overdrafts up to Rs.25,000 (per account) granted against 'no-frills' accounts in rural and semi-urban areas as indirect finance to the agriculture sector under priority sector with immediate effect. The Reserve Bank advised the convener banks of the State Level/Union Territory Level Bankers' Committees (SLBC/UTLBC) in all states/union territories on April 28, 2006 to identify at least one suitable district in each state/union territory for achieving 100 per cent financial inclusion by providing a 'no-frills' account and issue of general credit card (GCC).

Use of intermediaries as agents: In January 2006, the Reserve Bank permitted banks to utilise the services of non-governmental organisations/ self-help groups (NGOs/SHGs), microfinance institutions (MFIs), other than regular non-banking financial companies (NBFCs) and other civil society organisations (CSOs) as intermediaries in providing financial and banking services through the use of business facilitator (BF) and business correspondent (BC) models. The BC model allows banks to do 'cash-in/ cash-out' transactions at a location much closer to the rural habitation, thus addressing the last mile problem. Banks are also entering into agreements with India Post for using the vast network of post offices as BCs, thereby increasing their outreach and leveraging on the postman's intimate knowledge of the local population.

The Reserve Bank has been encouraging the use of information and communication technology (ICT) solutions by banks for enhancing their outreach with the help of their BCs. The BCs carry hand-held devices, which are essentially smart card readers. Mobile phones have also been developed to serve as card readers. The information captured is transmitted to a central server where the accounts are maintained. These devices are used for making payments to rural customers and receiving cash from them. Account holders are issued smart cards, which have their photographs and finger impressions. Pilot studies have shown that the technology is practical, robust and also affordable. Scaling up is, at present, the challenge.

Who requires to be included: The essence of financial inclusion is in trying to ensure that a range of appropriate financial services is available to every individual and enabling them to understand and access those services. Apart from the regular form of financial intermediation, it may include a basic no-frills banking account for making and receiving payments, a savings product suited to the pattern of cash flows of a poor household, money transfer facilities, small loans and overdrafts for productive, personal and other purposes, etc. 'However, inclusive finance does not require that everyone who is eligible uses each of these services, but they should be able to choose to use them, if they so desired. To this end, strategies for building inclusive financial sectors have to be creative, flexible, appropriate to the national situation and if necessary, nationally owned.' For promoting financial inclusion, we have to address the issue of exclusion—of people who desire to use the financial services, but are denied access to the same. In countries with a large rural population like India, financial exclusion has a geographic dimension as well. Inaccessibility, distances and lack of proper infrastructure hinder financial inclusion. Vast majorities of population living in rural areas of the country have serious issues in accessing formal financial services.

Financial Inclusion Fund and Financial Inclusion Technology Fund

Pursuant to the announcement made by the Union Finance Minister in his Budget Speech for the year 2007-08, a Financial Inclusion Fund (FIF) and Financial Inclusion Technology Fund (FITF), with an overall corpus of

Rs. 500 crore each, has been set up with NABARD, with initial funding to be contributed by the Government of India, the Reserve Bank and NABARD in a ratio of 40:40:20. The funding would be contributed in a phased manner over a maximum period of five years, depending upon utilisation of funds. The FIF/FITF would be in operation until financial inclusion to the extent of 100 per cent of rural families in all districts is achieved, over a period of five years from the date of commencement of the Fund or for such enhanced period as may be decided by the government.

The objective of the FIF is to support 'developmental and promotional activities' with a view to securing greater financial inclusion, particularly among weaker sections, low-income groups and in backward regions/ hitherto unbanked areas.

The objectives of the FITF is to enhance investment in information communication technology (ICT) aimed at promoting financial inclusion, stimulating the transfer of research and technology in financial inclusion, increase the technological absorption capacity of financial service providers/ users and encourage an environment of innovation and cooperation among stakeholders.

The programme sanction, implementation, monitoring and administration of the FIF/FITF shall vest with NABARD. The interest accrued/income earned from the FIF/FITF shall be ploughed back into the FIF/FITF as per the investment policy approved by the Advisory Board.

Modalities of Inclusion

Microfinance and financial inclusion: Provision of microfinance through self-help groups (SHGs) since the early 1990s through the SHG-Bank Linkage Programme and the emergence of NGOs as facilitators have been major developments in the field of rural finance. The strategy of linking SHGs to banks, initially through savings and later through loan products, has been able to ensure financial inclusion of the hitherto excluded sections of the society to a certain extent.

Cumulatively, the number of SHGs linked to banks aggregated over 2.2 million as at the end of March 2006, which translates into an estimated 33 million poor families brought within the fold of formal banking services. It is important to note that about 90 per cent of the groups linked with banks are exclusive women's groups.

There are several MFIs which normally have the organisational form of societies, trusts, cooperatives, NBFCs and not-for-profit companies set up under Section 25 of the Companies Act, 1956, which supplement the efforts of banks in providing financial services to the poor. The experience of the formal banking system partnering with such MFIs has been quite encouraging in several places.

Role of lead banks: The mechanics of financial inclusion would largely depend on the profile of the excluded population, as also the institutional framework available for the purpose. In the context of the multi-agency approach to rural banking in India, financial inclusion could involve several steps and the role of the coordination mechanism in the form of the lead bank in the district or the convener of the State Level Bankers' Committee (SLBC) at the state level assumes critical importance. The policy announcement of the Reserve Bank has envisaged an active role for the convener banks of the SLBCs in all states, who have been given the responsibility of reaching 100 per cent financial inclusion in at least one district in their area of operation. Illustratively, the convener of the SLBC has to undertake the following steps for ensuring financial inclusion in the pilot areas in the state:

Step 1: Allocation of villages to the banks in the area.

Step 2: Undertaking village/ household surveys involving banks/ NGOs/SHGs etc.

Step 3: Assessment of the need for financial products.

Step 4: Preparation of Action Plan in terms of targets for different products, e.g., opening of no-frills accounts, issue of kisan credit cards (KCCs) and general credit cards (GCCs), offering overdraft facilities in no-frills accounts, setting up of SHGs, providing microinsurance, etc.

Step 5: Review and evaluation based on experience gained, other areas in the state may be covered in a time bound manner. On a priority basis, the districts covered under the National Rural Employment Guarantee Programme (NREGP) may also be taken up for financial inclusion, in particular, opening of 'no-frills' accounts which would facilitate credit of drafts issued in favour of the beneficiaries, and formation of SHGs to support microenterprise-linked livelihoods on a sustainable basis.

Basic 'no-frills' bank accounts: At the first stage, there is a need for lowering the entry barriers to the banking system and simplifying procedures. Thanks to developments in microfinance, one of the myths held earlier by the banking system that the poor cannot save, has been demolished. Experience has shown that the poor can and do save, may be by way of thrift, and all they need is an appropriate product and access to the banking system. Holding a savings product to a substantial extent reduces financial exclusion. Moreover, the act of saving, however little it may be, reinforces longer-term thinking and a sense of responsibility for one's future. Keeping in view the need for the banking system to take urgent steps to bring about financial inclusion in the country, RBI, in the *Mid-Term Review of the Annual Policy* for the year 2005-06, exhorted banks to make available a basic banking 'no frills' account either with nil or very low balances as well as charges that would make such accounts accessible to vast sections of the population. The nature and number of transactions in such accounts would be restricted and would be made known to customers in advance in a transparent manner. Several banks, both in the public and private sectors, have responded positively to this to this measure and devised no-frills accounts for the lower-income groups.

Although such basic bank accounts are generally considered unprofitable, provision of such deposit accounts has been accepted the world over as a stepping stone to financial inclusion. In a somewhat different way, this requires bank branches to be aware of the surrounding areas in which they work and promotes a more outward-looking, customer-centric model to work alongside their usual profit-driven model. A basic 'no-frills' account is just the beginning of a relationship and can pave the way to the customer availing of a variety of savings products and loan products for consumption, housing etc. The account can be used for sanctioning small overdraft facilities and making small value remittances at low cost. The same banking account can also be used by state governments to provide social security services like health and calamity insurance under various schemes for the disadvantaged. Having such social security cover makes the financing of such persons less risky from the bank's point of view and they can be financed for various purposes. Further, holders of the no-frills accounts who would be beneficiaries of the Employment Guarantee Scheme of the Government of India, can also be customers of banks over a longer time horizon.

General Credit Cards (GCCs): It is almost a cliché that rural credit should adhere to the basic requirements of timeliness, adequacy and hassle-free delivery, apart from taking care of the financial needs of the customer in a holistic manner, including consumption credit. To address these issues, several 'credit card' schemes have been devised and implemented by banks over the past. Such schemes have the flexibility of use and they fulfil the above requirements to a substantial extent. But all these schemes have so far been activity-specific, i.e., for farmers, artisans etc. The latest in the line is the general credit card (GCC) which does not target any specific functional group, but has the potential to address the credit needs of persons with small means having some income-generating activity, without bothering so much about the nature of the activity. Banks have flexibility in fixing the limit based on the assessment of income and cash flow of the entire household. The borrowers are eligible for availment of the credit facilities provided under GCC as per their requirement without any insistence on security and the purpose or end-use of the credit. To provide an incentive to banks for issuing the GCCs, 50 per cent of credit outstanding under GCC up to Rs. 25,000 has been made eligible for being treated as indirect agricultural finance under the priority sector lending. While several banks have put in place schemes for issuing GCCs, the progress will have to be accelerated. As done earlier in the case of KCC scheme, issue of GCC too can be made part of the corporate plans of all banks.

Microinsurance: More than credit, the poor need access to some form of insurance, as they are the most vulnerable to various types of risk to both life and property. They need suitably designed schemes offering health, life or property insurance: limited protection at a somewhat low contribution. It is heartening to know that insurance companies are coming up with schemes aimed at poorer sections of the population and designed to help them cover themselves collectively against risks, the delivery channels being banks, NGOs and SHGs working in rural areas. There is also a possibility of providing some kind of microinsurance to holders of the GCCs, on the lines of the personal accident insurance cover available to KCC holders.

Financial education: Financial inclusion mean the capacity to have familiarity with and understanding of financial market products, especially rewards and risks in order to make informed choices. Viewed from this standpoint, financial education primarily relates to personal financial education to enable individuals' to take effective actions to improve overall well-being and avoid distress in matters that are financial. People have been responsible for managing their own finance on a day to day basis spend on a holiday or save for new furniture; how much to put aside for a child's education or to set them in life. But recent development have made financial education awareness increasingly important for financial well-being. For one thing, the growing sophistication of financial markets means consumers are not just choosing between interest rates on two different bank loans or savings plans, but are rather being offered a variety of complex financial instrument for borrowing and saving with a large range of options. At the same instrument for borrowing and saving with the large range of options. At the same time, the responsibility and risk for financial decisions that will have a major impact on an individual's future life, notably pensions are shifted increasingly to workers and away from government and employers. As life expectancy is increasing, the pension question is particularly important as individuals will be enjoying longest period of retirement.

Issues: One of the major hindrances in the way of delivery of financial services to the poor is the lack of basic knowledge and lack of awareness of the products and services available. In fact, education is a great facilitator. The delivery of financial education would include:

- increasing knowledge of financial matters,
- developing understanding of financial products, and
- building skills in financial management.

One of the pioneers in promoting the concept of financial inclusion, the United Kingdom, has established a Financial Inclusion Task Force, which has emphasised 'access to free face-to-face money advice' as an important component of financial inclusion, apart from access to banking and access to affordable credit. A FIF has also been established there to promote financial inclusion.

Poverty is a well-known problem in most developing countries. But what is needed is development of mechanisms that ensure that poverty is not exacerbated by lack of access to financial services. People need information and advice when they get into debt. Such information and guidance can best be delivered by appropriate mechanisms and if such effective mechanisms are put in place, they in turn would reinforce the demand for credit. Some banks have on their own take steps to provide such education, as in the case of the debt counselling cells (DSCs) recently set up by some banks. However, any large scale delivery of financial education has to leverage on the presence of other agencies, such as private entities, NGOs, CSOs, outlets of the corporate sector etc., apart from government initiatives. The use of information technology (IT) offers a lot of promise in providing financial literacy and education and experience in several parts of the country through the use of kiosks, mobile vans, etc., and has shown to what extent IT can be leveraged to provide information on various products and services, production processes and markets for the products. While provision of connectivity for facilitating communication services in rural areas is still an issue, recent developments in wireless technology holds out a lot of promise for evolving an IT-based information dissemination system.

Institutions and Financial Inclusion

Financial institutions, both large and small have an important role to play in financial inclusion. With their organised structure and effective management larger financial institutions could act as mentors for small financial services firm by ensuring a strong financial backing.

Commercial banks: Commercial banks could act as an important part of the process to achieve full financial inclusion. Especially with simplified savings bank accounts (including no-frills account), relaxed know your customer (KYC) procedures, primary sector lending and even microfinance.

Cooperative banks: The urban and rural cooperative banks could cater to populations that are generally neglected by the commercial banks. Their position allows them to reach out to the people far easier than the more formal commercial banks. Since they are operated by the members of the banks themselves, there would be more involvement from the people of such cooperatives.

Regional rural banks: Through priority sector lending, KCCs and GCCS, the RRBs could ensure a steady flow of credit to the rural poor especially the marginal farmers. The RRBs like the commercial banks can deal with the agencies like NGOs who are interested in helping out the poor and the weaker sections.

Non-banking financial companies (NBFCs): The NBFCs could include both large and small financial firms which provide financial services. They could offer specific financial products to the poor and low income people such as microinsurance, microcredit, etc. The NBFCs could create financial awareness among the people by not only offering alternative financial services but also spreading financial literacy by providing financial advices.

Microfinance institutions (MFIs): They are created with the specific aim of extending financial services to the poor and the weaker sections of the populations. A MFI could be independent or as in most cases are promoted by NGOs, government agencies, NBFCs, commercial banks and other institutions. MFIs have so far been the most successful at ensuring basic financial services to the unbanked sections of the populations. Along with the SHG movement, the MFIs has enabled the wealth generation in many underdeveloped rural as well as neglected urban areas in India.

Post office savings bank (POSB): These along with their extensive network could offer wide variety of small and microfinancial services to the people. The POSBs could utilise their staff to deliver door-to-door service to the people.

Non-governmental organisations (NGOs): NGOs could provide financial assistance to the poor and the weaker sections through NGO promoted MFIs or by providing financial advice. NGOs working for the poor and the economically deprived can more closely analyse their spending patterns and credit requirements. Commercial banks and other large financial agencies can work closely with NGOs to ensure that the dealings with the poor and the weaker sections turn out to be a fruitful activity not only for the people but also for the lending agencies.

Microfinance and Financial Inclusion

The concept of microfinance was championed in the 1970s and since then has become a global phenomenon. The concept of microlending existed in different forms in the past and still does exist in many parts of the world. (Chit funds in India are a form of microlending). Microfinance is the process by which diverse financial services are made available to the poor and the low-income people. MFIs include NGOs, private commercial banks, NBFCs, cooperative societies. It has had far-reaching impacts in the developing world especially Latin America, South and Southeast Asia. It along with the SHG movement in India (for e.g.: Kudumbashree in Kerala) has ensured microcredit to women entrepreneurs. Microfinance through its innovative dealing has achieved to some extent the target of 'helping people help themselves'. It has also successfully debunked the myth that poor people are not worthy of being banked upon because of the low defaulting by the debtors especially women. The 2006 Nobel Peace Prize being awarded to the Bangladeshi economist Muhammad Yunus (for Gramin Bank) shows the success and relevance of a concept like microfinance.

However, financial inclusion is a paradigm shift from microfinance to inclusive finance. Financial inclusion acquires a broader definition since it is not limited to MFIs. Financial Inclusion aims at bringing into the mainstream those people who had not had the chance of being financially included while at the same time looking at the comparative advantages for the banks. Although the terms microfinance and financial inclusion are closely inter-related, there is some difference between the two. Till now, through microfinance we have only allowed the people access to microfinancial services provided mostly by small agencies. Financial inclusion aims at bringing the unbanked citizens into the financial mainstream. With initiatives the previously excluded section of the population could have access to financial facilities. They should be made aware of the advantages of remaining with a formal financial agency. The financial inclusion is therefore a step by step process involving the people as well as the respective agencies. Financial inclusion takes the process of microfinance a step further by not just treating them as different or poor but by considering them as creditworthy citizens and bankable consumers. Financial inclusion aims to bring into contact the poorest of the poor with the big banks who have so far been hesitant to deal with them.

The valuable experience of microfinance has shown that the doubts of poor consumers defaulting payment of credit might not be valid after all. MFIs have been a big success because they have been able to come up with financial products that the populations in the lower economic strata want. However, there still remains to be seen how the transaction costs on the large number of small credit can be lowered.

India has around 59 per cent of the people who are in the financial system; the country has a poverty rate of around 26 per cent (2000: *www.inafiindia.in*). The rest are outside the financial system due to low incomes or lack of pre-owned collaterals. There are around 40 per cent landless and another 30 per cent marginal landholders in India, access to financial access still remains a distant reality for many of them. Financial inclusion may not be 100 per cent even in many of the developed nations but the high level of access to financial services do explain the necessity of a sound and inclusive financial sector. Thus, by creating a strong and inclusive financial sector the country would be better at distributing the development and help achieve equity.

RBI and Financial Inclusion

As the central bank of the country, the RBI has taken steps to ensure financial inclusion in the country. It has tried to make banking more attractive to citizens by allowing for easier transactions with banks. In 2004 RBI appointed an internal group to look into ways to improve financial inclusion in the country. It came out with a report in July 2005 (H.R. Khan Committee) and subsequently RBI issued a circular in 2006 allowing the use of intermediaries for providing banking and financial services. Through such policies the RBI has tried to improve financial inclusion. Financial inclusion offers immense potential not only for banks but for other businesses. Through an integrated approach the businesses, the NGOs, the government agencies as well as the banks can be partners in growth. RBI has realised that a push is needed to kick-start the financial inclusion process. Some of the steps taken by RBI include the directive to banks to offer no-frills account, easier KYC norms, offering GCCs to the poor, better customer services, promoting the use of IT and intermediaries, and asking SLBCs and UTLBCs to start a campaign to promote financial inclusion on a pilot basis. So far the campaign for 100 per cent financial inclusion has been said to be a success with many states now reaching near-total financial inclusion.

Policy Initiatives by RBI

Keeping in view the tremendous scope for improving financial coverage, the RBI as a proactive measure, has taken several initiatives to promote financial inclusion:

No-frills accounts: The RBI in its annual policy statement for the year 2005-06 and also in the *Mid-Term Review of the Annual Policy* (2005-06), exhorted the banks, with a view to achieving greater financial inclusion, to make available a basic banking 'no-frills' account either with nil or very minimum balances as well as charges that would make such accounts accessible to vast sections of the population. The nature and number of transactions in such accounts would be restricted and made known to customers in advance in a transparent manner. All banks have been urged to give wide publicity to the facility of such 'no-frills' accounts. Banks are required to make this available in print used by retail customers in the concerned regional language.

Simplification of KYC norms: In order to ensure that persons belonging to low-income group in urban and rural areas do not face difficulty in opening accounts, KYC norms have been simplified for those persons with balances not exceeding Rs. 50,000 and credits in the accounts not exceeding Rs. 1,00,000 in a year.

Overdraft facilities in no-frills accounts: RRBs have been specifically advised to allow limited overdraft facilities in 'no-frills' account without any collateral or linkage to any purpose. The idea is that provision of such overdraft facility provides a ready source of funding to the account holder who is thereby induced to open such accounts.

One-time settlement (OTS): For all borrowers where the principal amount is less than Rs.25,000/-, banks have been asked to offer a one-time settlement scheme. As there is large number of such very small no-frills accounts with banks, offer of such an OTS was expected to restore borrowing relationship with the formal system and thereby obviate the need to go back to the informal system in case where the loans are under government sponsored schemes.

What is a 'no-frills' account? It is a basic savings account either with 'nil' or very low minimum balance as well as charges that would make such accounts accessible to vast sections of population. The nature and number of transactions in such account could be restricted, but made known to the customer in advance in a transparent manner. The state level banker's committee (SLBC) was expected to evolve a suitable policy.

General purpose credit card (GCC): Banks have been advised by RBI to provide a GCC facility at their rural and semi-urban branches. The credit facility extended under the scheme will be in the nature of revolving credit. The GCC-holder will be entitled to draw cash from the specified branch of bank up to the limit sanctioned. Banks would have flexibility in fixing the limit based on the assessment of income and cash flow of the entire household, without insistence on security or purpose. However, the total credit facility under GCC for an individual should not exceed Rs.25,000/-. It is expected that banks will come out with their own schemes to popularise this product amongst the rural client.

Business facilitators and correspondents: With the objective of ensuring greater financial inclusion and increasing the outreach of the banking sector, banks were permitted to use the services of NGOs/SHGs, MFIs and other CSOs as intermediaries in providing financial and banking services through the use of business facilitator and correspondent models.

Broader definition of financial inclusion: RBI subsequently observed that a family satisfying the following conditions also would be treated as financially included:

a) member of SHG;

b) member of a primary agriculture cooperative society (PACS);

c) if having a post office savings account; and

d) member covered under government schemes.

International Experience in Promoting Financial Inclusion

An interesting feature which emerges from the international practice is that the more developed the society is, the greater the thrust on empowerment of common person and low-income groups. It may be worthwhile to have a look at international scenario in tackling the problem of financial exclusion so that we can learn from their experience.

United Kingdom

The financial Inclusion Task Force in UK has identified three priority areas for the purpose of financial inclusion, *viz.*: (i) access to banking, (ii) access to affordable credit, and (iii) access to free face-to-face money advice. UK has established a Financial Inclusion Fund to promote financial inclusion and assigned responsibility to banks and credit unions in removing financial exclusion. Basic bank 'no-frills' accounts have been introduced. An enhanced legislative environment for credit unions has been established, accompanied by tighter regulations to ensure greater protection for investors. A post office card account (POCA) has been created for those who are unable or unwilling to access a basic bank account. The concept of a 'Savings Gateway' has been piloted. This offers 50p from the state for every £1 low-income groups invest, up to a maximum of £25 per month. In addition the community finance learning Initiatives (CFLIs) were also introduced with a view to promoting basic financial literacy among housing association tenants.

United States

A civil rights law, namely Community Reinvestment Act (CRA) of 1977 in United States prohibits discrimination by banks against low and moderate income neighbourhoods. The CRA imposes an affirmative and continuing obligations on banks to serve the needs for credit and banking services of all the communities in which they are chartered. In fact, numerous studies conducted by Federal Reserve and Harvard University demonstrated that CRA lending is a win-win proposition and profitable to banks. In this context, it is also interesting to know the other initiative taken by state of New York in United States. Apart from the CRA experiment, armed with the sanction of Banking Law, the State of New York Banking Department, with the objective of making available the low-cost banking services to consumers, made mandatory that each banking institution shall offer basic banking account and in case of credit unions the basic share draft account, which is in the nature of low-cost account with minimum facilities. Some key features of the basic banking account are worth mentioning here.

a) The initial deposit amount required to open the account shall not exceed US $25.

b) The minimum balance, including any average balance, required to maintain such account shall not exceed US $0.10.

c) The charge for periodic cycle for the maintenance of such accounts to be declared upfront.

d) The minimum number of withdrawal transactions which may be made during any periodic cycle at no charge to the account holder must at least be eight.

e) A withdrawal shall be deemed to be made when recorded on the books of the account holder's banking institution except, as provided below, an account holder shall not be restricted as to the number of deposits which may be made to the account without incurring any additional charge.

f) The banking institution may charge account holders for transactions at electronic facilities which are not operated by the account holder's banking institution as well as other fees and charges for specific banking services which are not covered under the basic banking account scheme.

g) Very periodic statement issued for the basic banking account should invariably cover on it or by way of separate communiqué, maximum number of withdrawals permitted during each periodic cycle without additional charge and the consequences of exceeding such maximum and the fee if any, for the use of electronic facilities which are not operated by the account holder's banking institution.

h) An interesting feature of basic banking account scheme is the element of transparency i.e., the banking institution should, prior to opening the account, furnish a written disclosure to the account holder describing the main features of the scheme i.e., the initial deposit amount required to open the account, minimum balance to be maintained, charge per periodic cycle for use of such account, maximum number of withdrawal transactions without any additional charge and other charges imposed on transactions for availing electronic facility not operated by the account holder's banking institution, etc.

Indian Scenario

The bank nationalisation in India marked a paradigm shift in the focus of banking as it was intended to shift the focus from class banking to mass banking. The rationale for creating RRBs was also to take the banking services to poor people. The branches of commercial banks and the RRBs have increased from 8,321 in the year 1969 to 68,282 branches as at the end of March 2005. The average population per branch office has decreased from 64,000 to 16,000 during the same period. However, there are certain underbanked states such as Bihar, Orissa, Rajasthan, Uttar Pradesh, Chhattisgarh, Jharkhand, West Bengal and a large number of northeastern states, where the average population per branch office continues to be quite high compared to the national average. As we all are aware, the new branch authorisation policy of Reserve Bank encourages banks to open branches in these underbanked states and the underbanked areas in other states. The new policy also places a lot of emphasis on the efforts made by the bank to achieve, *inter alia*, financial inclusion and other policy objectives.

One of the benchmarks employed to assess the degree of reach of financial services to the population of the country, is the quantum of deposit accounts (current and savings) held as a ratio to the adult population. In the Indian context, taking into account the Census of 2001 (ignoring the incremental growth of population thereafter), the ratio of deposit accounts (data available as on March 31, 2004) to the total adult population was only 59 per cent (details furnished in Appendix Table A-3.1). Within the country, there is a wide variation across states. For instance, the ratio for the state of Kerala is as high as 89 per cent while Bihar is marked by a low coverage of 33 per cent. In the northeastern states like Nagaland and Manipur, the coverage was a meagre 21 per cent and 27 per cent, respectively. Northern region, comprising the states of Haryana, Chandigarh and Delhi, has a high coverage ratio of 84 per cent (Appendix Table A-3.1). Compared to the developed world, the coverage of our financial services is quite low. For instance, as per a recent survey commissioned by British Bankers' Association, 92 to 94 per cent of the population of UK has either current or savings bank account.

Financial Inclusion and Urban Areas

Although it is true that urban areas are better-off when it comes to bank connectivity and use of financial services compared to rural areas, a good share of the urban population however remain financially excluded. The difference between the rural-urban poverty rates in many of the states is not much. In at least 11 states the percentage of urban poverty was higher than the rural poverty. The plight of the urban poor is augmented by the high cost of living in urban areas and the lack of resources. With increasing prosperity on one side and incrementing poverty on the other the urban divide between the poor and the prosperous is widening. Agriculture which could have provided them some level of sustenance cannot be practiced in urban areas; this is the same with many of the activities. Slums have come up in all the major cities of India characterised by the low levels of sanitation and living conditions. The increasing urbanisation will only deteriorate the present situation. According to the 43rd round of NSS, it was found that at least 41.8 million people were below the poverty line (the actual numbers could be much higher!). Therefore an urgent plan is needed to tackle the problems in the slums. The rise of informal slums makes it hard for the authorities to plan development for the cities. In cities like Mumbai almost half of the population now live in slums.

The slum dwellers have come to the cities from villages looking for better opportunities and live on meagre or no income. The unskilled and the uneducated poor have no other choice but to go for menial jobs, sometimes into crime, or remain unemployed. Most of the slum dwellers are poor and therefore are excluded from the financial system, and have to depend on informal credit. Reaching out to them would take more time and perseverance compared to reaching out to people in the rural areas. Most of the slum dwellers do not hold proper identification cards, legal documents, etc., which might be necessary to open an account even with the relaxed KYC norms.

Table 3.2

Comparison of Rural and Urban Poverty Rates in Some States (2004-05)

Name of the State	*Rural Poverty (%)*	*Urban Poverty (%)*	*Total (%)*
Andhra Pradesh	11.2	28.0	15.8
Bihar	42.1	34.6	41.4
Chhattisgarh	40.8	41.2	40.9
Gujarat	19.1	13.0	16.8
Haryana	13.6	15.1	14.0
J&K	4.6	7.9	5.4
Jharkhand	46.3	20.2	40.3
Kerala	13.2	32.43	15.0
Madhya Pradesh	36.9	42.1	38.3
Maharashtra	29.6	32.2	30.7
Orissa	46.8	44.3	46.4
Rajasthan	18.7	32.9	22.1
Tamil Nadu	22.8	22.2	22.5
Uttar Pradesh	33.4	30.6	32.8
All-India	28.3	25.7	27.5

Source: Government of India Press Information Bureau "Poverty Estimates for 2004-05" on March 2007, (URP Consumption).

Funding

The Committee recognised that there is a cost involved in providing credit plus services and technology applications. Such costs may come down over a period of time with the resultant business expansion. Banks are expected to meet a part of the costs. However, in the initial stages some funding support through specially constituted funds may be extended to them. This funding support, envisaged as a mechanism to reduce costs, may be provided to the banks on two counts: (i) promotional and developmental initiatives that will lead to better credit absorption capacity among the poor and vulnerable sections, and (ii) application of technology for facilitating the mandated levels of inclusion.

Financial Inclusion Funds

The Committee proposes the constitution of two funds—the Financial Inclusion (Promotion & Development Fund), with NABARD, for meeting the cost of developmental and promotional interventions indicated below and the Financial Inclusion Technology Fund (FITF), with NABARD, to meet the costs of technology adoption. Each fund will have an initial corpus of Rs. 500 crore, with a start-up funding of Rs. 250 crore each, to be contributed in equal proportion by GoI/RBI/NABARD and with annual accretions thereto. Banks will be eligible for support from the funds on a matching contribution of 50 per cent from the fund in regard to districts other than tribal districts and 75 per cent in case of branches located in tribal districts identified under the Tribal Sub-Plan.

Financial Inclusion Promotion and Development Fund

The Financial Inclusion Promotion and Development Fund will focus on financing the following interventions:

Farmers' service centres (FSC): With the creation of and support to FSCs a host of financial and farm advisory services are to be provided to the new/hitherto excluded customer segments. The centres will network on the technology front with agricultural universities/KVKs, farmers clubs, the formal extension machinery of the state governments, technical staff of banks, portals of national level commodity exchanges etc. Such FSCs can be financed by the banks on the pattern of agri-clinics. In the 50 initial stages, it may be necessary to provide them some support by way of viability gap funding.

Promoting rural entrepreneurship: Commercial banks may consider setting up institutions like farmer training centres and Rural Development and Self-Employment Training Institutes (RUDSETI) for developing skills among farmers/rural entrepreneurs for effectively managing the assets financed.

Self-help groups: The process of financial inclusion can be greatly facilitated through the medium of linking SHGs with the formal sector. It was observed in the NABARD's Report on Financial Inclusion that the SHG movement is yet to catch up on a big scale in regions manifesting high levels of exclusion (central, eastern and northeastern regions). The funding support for promotion, nurturing and credit linking of SHGs can be extended.

Developing HR: Addressing attitudinal issues through training—Different studies have corroborated that lending to the poor raises a number of issues ranging from sources and reliability of their incomes to lack of suitable bank projects for them to the elitist approach of the formal institutional credit delivery apparatus. These factors are the outcome of attitudes towards the poor, as generally not viable and profitable customers of the bank. Experience indicates that the poor, if guided properly, not only succeed as entrepreneurs, but are also good 'repayers'. However, changing this attitude or mindset is a challenge. However in the recent past the attitudes of bank branch managers have been changed, due to training and education programmes conducted for bank managers, now they are positive at lending to the poor.

In addition to facilitating members of established SHGs to graduate to microenterprises, it helps in ensuring long-term sustainability of SHGs for which promotion resources centres are also required. The cost of setting up such centres can be met out of this Fund and/or the MFDEF. Funding support for capacity building, on priority basis, to be extended to specialised institutions which provide capacity building inputs to BFs/BCs.

Nodal branches (ADB model): considering the fact that the marginal and sub-marginal farmers require credit plus services in the form of extension services, in all districts identified as having the largest number of excluded people, it may instituted that one branch of the lead bank or the bank having the largest presence at the block/*taluka* level may be categorised as the nodal branch to address the issue of exclusion. Lead banks or banks having the largest presence may strengthen these nodal branches with technical staff to provide agricultural/business development services in the farm and non-farm sectors respectively, comprising technical inputs and extension services to the banks/farmers. These could either be provided by regular officers of the bank or local consultants/practitioners/agri-business clinics on a retainer basis. As the services of the nodal branch would be available to all other branches in the vicinity, an appropriate cost sharing arrangement may be worked out between various banks.

Annexure Table A-3.1

Coverage of Banking Services (Ratio of Demand Deposit Accounts to the Adult Population)

Region/State/ Union Territory	*Current Accounts*	*Savings Accounts*	*Total Population*	*Adult Population (Above 19 Years)*	*Total No. of Accounts*	*No. of Accounts Per 100 of Population*	*No. of Accounts Per 100 of Adult Population*
Northern region	4215701	52416125	132676462	67822312	56631826	43	84
Haryana	572660	8031472	21082989	11308025	8604132	41	76
Himachal Pradesh	134285	2433595	6077248	3566886	2567880	42	72
Jammu & Kashmir	277529	3094790	10069917	5379594	3372319	33	63
Punjab	1156137	13742201	24289296	14185190	14898338	61	105
Rajasthan	689657	12139302	56473122	28473743	12828959	23	45
Chandigarh	80607	1126696	900914	546171	1207303	134	221
Delhi	1304826	11848069	13782976	7929589	13152895	95	166
Northeastern region	476603	6891081	38495089	19708982	7367684	19	37
Arunachal Pradesh	10538	209073	1091117	544582	219611	20	40
Assam	378729	5071058	26638407	14074393	5449787	20	39
Manipur	12514	200593	2388634	1222107	213107	9	17
Meghalaya	24305	458779	2306069	1088165	483084	21	44
Mizoram	3441	117885	891058	476205	121326	14	25
Nagaland	13819	195452	1988636	995523	209271	11	21
Tripura	33257	638241	3191168	1784212	671498	21	38
Eastern region	1814219	47876140	227613073	122136133	49690359	22	41
Bihar	464511	13225242	82878796	40934170	13689753	17	33
Jharkhand	166007	5834341	26909428	13737485	6000348	22	44
Orissa	228160	7030004	36706920	21065404	7258164	20	34
Sikkim	4097	125365	540493	288500	129462	24	45
West Bengal	942733	21544753	80221171	45896914	22487486	28	49
Andaman & Nicobar Islands	8711	116435	356265	213660	125146	35	59
Central region	2202217	64254189	255713495	129316677	66456406	26	51
Chhattisgarh	192067	3346898	20795956	11209425	3538965	17	32
Madhya Pradesh	553381	11731918	60385118	31404990	12285299	20	39
Uttar Pradesh	1324509	45804350	166052859	82229748	47128859	28	57
Uttarakhand	132260	3371023	8479562	4472514	3503283	41	78
Western region	3178102	49525101	149071747	86182206	52703203	35	61
Goa	81551	1584177	1343998	891411	1665728	124	187
Gujarat	955964	16220262	50596992	28863095	17176226	34	60
Maharashtra	2127240	31568184	96752247	56207604	33695424	35	60
Dadra & Nagar Haveli	6076	69308	220451	122765	75384	34	61
Daman & Diu	7271	83170	158059	97331	90441	57	93
Southern region	4666014	83386898	223445381	135574225	88052912	39	65
Andhra Pradesh	1156405	23974580	75727541	44231918	25130985	33	57
Karnataka	1086662	19147819	52733958	30623289	20234481	38	66
Kerala	600065	17669723	31838619	20560323	18269788	57	89
Tamil Nadu	1786514	22052812	62110839	39511038	23839326	38	60
Lakshadweep	491	22997	60595	33686	23488	39	70
Pondicherry	35877	518967	973829	613971	554844	57	90
All-India	16552856	304349534	1027015247	541031553	320902390	31	59

Source: Leeladhar (2005).

4 Indian Financial System and Emergence of Microfinance

Economic development of a nation rely on the soundness of that nation's financial system. It induces generation and transformation savings into an entrepreneurial efforts. Indian financial system is undergoing restructuring process for efficient mobilisation and allocation resources and can be segmented into organised, unorganised semi-organised systems. The organised system has money and capital markets as major components and also set of facilitators catering to financial intermediation. That supports increasing capital accumulation through the institutionalisation of savings and investment. The Banking sector is a major player in the system concentrating its business in organised and urban sector. Strategic alliance with postal department financial services division and swiftly emerging semi-organised sector can result in covering the uncovered. The emergence of new institutions and bodies is contributing to effective and efficient functioning of the system.

Financial system (Teki, 2001) acts as a nerve system of a nation's economy. A nation's economic development largely relies on the effective and efficient financial system of that nation. The financial system consists of many subsystems like financial services, banks, financial institutions etc. Developing countries' financial system is also in the process of development.

In any economic society all individuals and organisations earn and spend money. Sometimes few individuals\organisations will have earnings more than spending and vice-versa. Those units whose income exceeds their spending are denoted as surplus spending units/savers of money. On the other hand whose spending exceeds earnings they are called as deficit spending units/borrowers of money. Hence, an inherent need raised to coordinate between surplus spending units and deficit spending units. Therefore a system which shoulders this responsibility was needed to be developed which is rightly called as 'financial system'. Precisely describing, it is the backbone of a country's economy. Financial system also helps in providing means of payment and medium of exchange.

Financial system is the system, which induces generation of savings, transfer of those savings into an entrepreneurial effort and stimulates an entrepreneur to undertake various business ventures. It is a key weapon in monitoring the economic progress of any country, because eventually all efforts and resources are measured in financial terms.

The financial system (Chandra, 1998) consists of a variety of institutions, markets, and instruments that are related. It provides the principal means by which savings are transformed into investment. Given its role in the allocation of resources, the efficient functioning of the financial system is of critical importance to a modern economy.

The financial system provides services that are indispensible to all industries in the economy. In this context financial activities are complementary to all other economic activities. It does particular acute functions for the economy, which consist of up-keeping a perfect system, collection and allocation of the savings of society and creation of variety of stores of wealth to suit the preferences of individual savings.

In any given period of time there are some people whose current expenditure are less than their current incomes. While there are others whose current expenditure exceed their current incomes. In the appropriate terms the former is known as savers who is in a position to lend money to the needy ones, and later is called as borrower, who can source out the savings from the lender to deploy those savings for productive activities. The existence of various financial assets (financial services like bank saving account, a financial instrument like equity share or bond), which can be bought with savings is warranted to inculcate and stimulate savings habits of individuals/organisations. It is true that in the absence of such a facility of physical capital formation the savings (vital resource for economic development) would remain idle and take the form of hoarding. With the opportunities to earn income through financial investment these savings are activated. In addition, the possibility of earnings and income may lead in many cases to an increase in the volume of savings. Since, savers differ in their attitude to risk, return and liquidity. The greater the diversified portfolio of financial assets which the financial system can offer, the greater is its efficiency in generating and transferring savings to a deficit spending unit for productive operations/activities.

The experience of successfully developed countries indicates that the rapid growth required sustained effort in mobilising savings and deploying these in various ways, which encourage efficient production.

The financial system of today is enabling not only physical capital formation but also consumption expenditure. Similarly, it now handles financial flows not only between individual savers/investors but also between institutional savers/investor. Further, the financial system effects the transfer of savings not only merely for new production, but also provides facilities for financial investment so as to earn income on the surplus. In other words it performs financial and non-financial functions, and also provides facilities for financial investment so as to earn income on the surplus. It is also to be noted that while financial markets aid development, they in turn grow along with the developments. The relationship between them is not that of one preceding the other. The positive relationship between the level of economic growth of the country and that of the financial system proves this point.

The original and the expanding role of the financial system is succinctly expressed in the following quotation from Schumpeter. 'The money market is always the head quarter of the capitalist system, from which order got out to its individual division, and that which is debated and decided there is always in essence the settlement of plans for further development. All kinds of credit requirements come to this market all kinds of economic projects are first brought relation with each other and contend for their realisation in it all kinds of purchasing power flow and then it is to be sold. This gives rise to a number of arbitral operation and intermediating maneuver which may easily veil the fundamental things.'[1] Thus, the main function of the money or capital market is trading in credit for the purpose of financing development. Development creates and nourishes this market. In the course of development it becomes the market for sources of income themselves.

The structure of the financial system: The Indian financial system mainly embodies financial markets (both money and capital markets).

1. *http://www.scribd.com/doc/26804098/Management-of-Financial-Institutions*

Players in these markets can be largely segmented into: a) savers/funds providers, b) borrowers/funds utilisers, c) merchant middlemen, and d) agent middlemen. The number and different types of institutions spreading from grassroot level village pawnshops, moneylender, landlord to banks, insurance companies, asset management companies, financial institutions (domestic including microfinance institutions, and foreign), sophisticated stock exchanges. Financial instruments like equity shares, debentures, fixed deposits, warrants, bonds, securitisation etc., used. And also employs financial services, like factoring, bill discounting, merchant banking, lease financing, venture capital, credit card, ATM etc.

The Indian (Sarathi, 1999) financial system is being restructured to improve the efficiency of the resource mobilisation and allocation mechanism. Many reforms are being introduced in the money market, the government securities market, the equity market and the foreign exchange market. These measures are aimed at removing the barriers to movement of funds across market segments. If the reforms achieve their desired objective of increasing the extent of integration between the major segments of the Indian financial system, one expects to find substantial spillovers between these financial market segments.

The structure of the financial system (Desai, 1996) the financial system consists of many institutions, instruments, and markets. Financial institutions range from pawnshops and moneylenders to stock exchanges. Financial instruments ranging from the common-coins, currency notes, and cheques to the futures and swaps of high finance. Markets from stock markets to capital market.

Metamorphosis in Indian financial system: Indian financial system traditionally was largely divided into two main segments *viz.*: a) organised sector consisting banks, insurance companies, stock markets, financial institutions etc., (select chronology in development in the Indian Financial system is given in Annexure Table A-4.1); b) unorganised sector includes, village grocery shops, indigeneous banker, chit fund, moneylender, landlords, traders (dealing with advancing money against the harvest of local food grain, natural resource like non-timber forest products) inter-lending by relatives and friends etc. And the recent third segment: c) semi-organised sector including microfinance institutions (MFIs) that is emergent in India for the last one and half decades or so, mainly consists of self-help groups (SHGs) and alike subsystems.

Figure 4.1

Indian Financial System

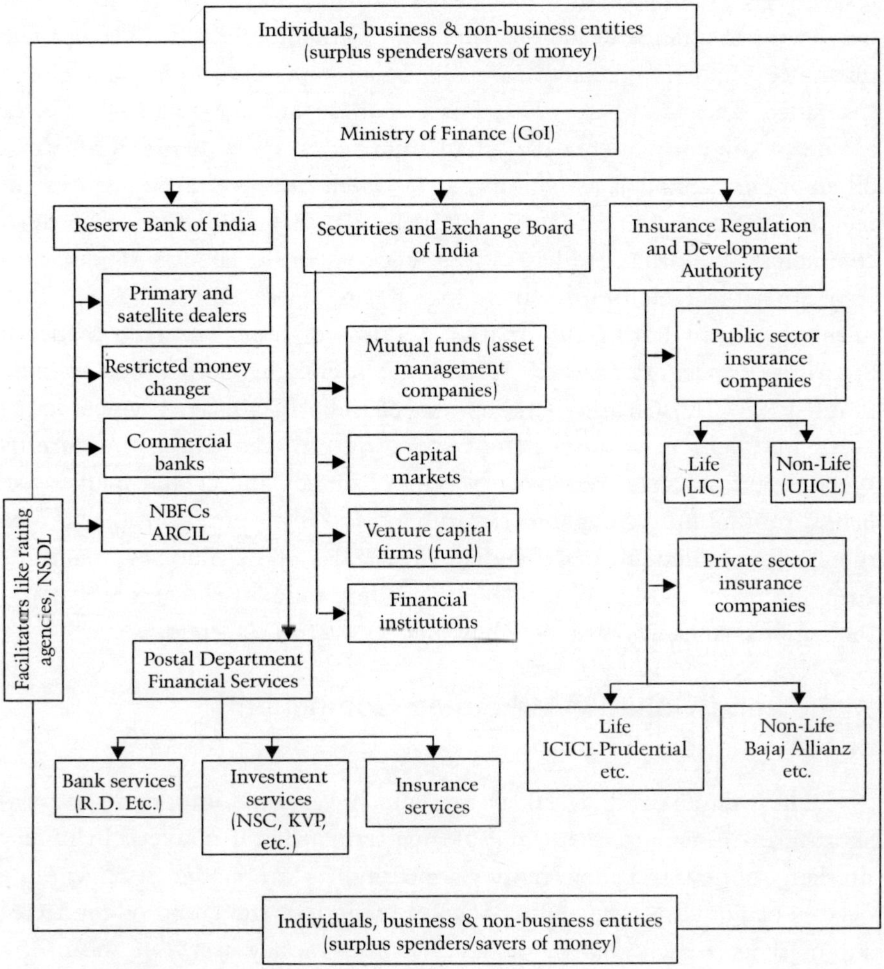

Note: NSDL: National Securities Depository Ltd.
NSC: National Savings Certificate.
KVP: Kisan Vikas Patra.
ARCIL: Asset Reconstruction Company (India) Ltd.
NBFC: Non-Banking Financial Company.
LIC: Life Insurance Corporation.
UIICL: United India Insurance Company Ltd.

As shown in Figure 4.1, the Indian financial system (organised sector) consists at the top the Ministry of Finance (Government of India) that directly or indirectly supervises the overall system. The two statutory bodies *viz.*, Reserve Bank of India (RBI) and Securities and Exchange Board of India (SEBI) regulate and supervise money markets and capital markets respectively. Insurance sector, a swiftly evolving sector, comes under the purview of Insurance Regulation and Development Authority (IRDA). The insurance sector is regulated, controlled and supervised jointly under the Insurance Act and IRDA, 1999. The Postal Department financial services is one of the components of Indian financial system. It offers all three different services such as banking, investment and insurance services. In fact it would be wise to say that this would be the future modern commercial bank that can have widest network in the country. The system also consists of facilitators including Rating agencies like CRISIL Ltd. (formerly Credit Rating Information Services of India Limited), National Securities Depository Limited (NSDL), Stock Holding Corporation of India Limited (SHCIL), Clearing Corporation of India (CCIL) etc., which act as agent middlemen between deficit spending units/borrower and surplus spending units/savers. While the players of money and capital market like banks, mutual fund companies, venture capital firms etc., considered to be merchant middlemen in the Indian financial system. The savers/surplus spending units and borrowers/deficit spending units at the extreme end of the entire system works as coupling link between these ends.

Money and Capital Markets as Components of the Financial System

The financial (Teki, 2001) markets have two components *viz.*: a) short-term (money market), and b) long-term (capital market). In money market, money and near money instruments are traded with varying degrees of liquidity. The money market comprises the group of connected sub-markets, which deal in money and near money assets of short-term lending institutions which borrow and lend for short terms and have more liquidity. Various instruments like call money, treasury bills and bills of exchange, factoring savings bank accounts, term deposits etc., are transacted in this market. Whereas capital market consists of longer-term lending institutions which borrow and lend for long terms and deal in lower liquidity instruments such as equity shares, debentures fixed deposits and bonds, government debt and private debt etc. The nature of the financial system is determined by such variables as the nature and the number of financial institutions, the structure and variety of financial assets, the volume of trading in these assets etc.

According to a Report published in *Economic Times*–1996, India's financial system and physical infrastructure have been found to be deficient as compared to several other Asian countries. It reveals the following facts.

Graded on scales from 0 to 10, with zero representing the best situation possible and 10 the worst. The survey disclosed that India ranking 10th in financial system with the rating of 6.29 while it ranked 9th with a rating of 6.93 in physical infrastructure.

Financial intermediary—the core functions of financial system: It is a channel in which funds are mobilised from a lender who is surplus spender and willing to offer his surplus to a person or organisation who is in need of funds in turn who will employ those funds for the productive activities. In simple words, financial intermediary refers to the activity of channeling funds between those who wish to lend (people or institution with surplus money) and those who wish to borrow (people or organisations with deficit funds).

But the foregone explanation is rather restrictive & suffers with the following shortcomings.

1) Synchronisation of desire to save and willing and need to borrow very seldom occur.
2) The surplus available with lender may not be matching with borrower's deficit, and quite often it is found that surplus is less or more than the deficit. Barely match is a very remote possibility.
3) Lack of awareness, the surplus units and deficit units may be located in different geographical areas and no communication perhaps be made.
4) The risk which is born by the lender in this case is very high, there may be every possibility to non-recovery or absolute loss.
5) Thc return expected by the lender and the time period may differ from both of their views.

6) The liquidity facility to lender may not be available when he directly lends to ultimate borrower. Because ultimate borrower's project maturity time may be larger than the lender's required time period.
7) Lack of information about borrowers creditworthiness or asymmetric information, by lenders can result in high risk-premium included interest rates or credit rationing. Financial intermediaries reduce those types of market imperfections.

The above stated shortcomings clearly reveals that there should be someone, who can reconcile the things between the surplus spending (lender) and deficit spending (borrower) units. Thus it is indispensible to have financial intermediation, which will recoup the above stated shortcomings and acts as a catalyst between lender and borrower to mobilise the required funds for economic development of the nation. Now the definition of financial intermediary can be revised in the following words:

Financial intermediary is a person/organisation, which seeks funds from surplus spending units and providing the funds so collected to the ultimate borrower who is in a position to use and employ the funds for the productive purposes.

Figure 4.2

Financial Intermediation Process

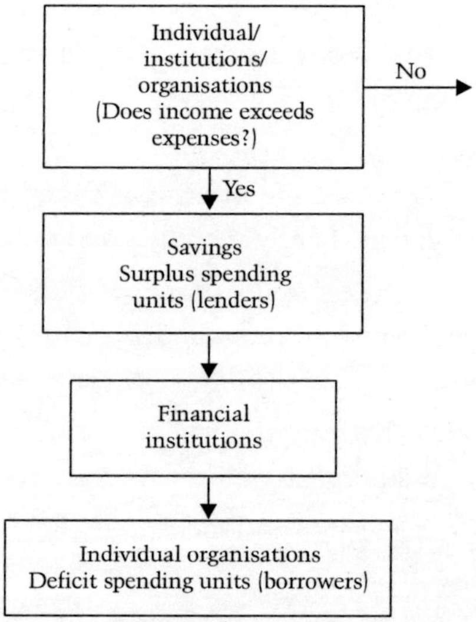

The process of financial intermediary shown in Figure 4.2 discloses the appropriate financial intermediation from the surplus spending and then lending those funds to deficit spenders (Teki, 2001). This is quite different from direct flow of funds from lender to borrower. Hence, the financial intermediary seeks funds from the ultimate lender, thus creating liability for himself and also assets by lending to the ultimate borrower. As far as the liquidity position is concerned, the financial intermediary's assets have less liquidity than his corresponding liability because the ultimate lender can demand his money back when and as he required, thus giving a flexible privilege to the surplus spending units.

This system posse the following benefits.

To the lender:

a. lender's risk has dwindled substantially;
b. liquidity position is improved;
c. return is certain on his savings (either fixed or variable);
d. lender gets impetus to save;
e. he will get accurate information from specialised financial institutions; and
f. lender's botheration with respect to selecting a prompt borrower is reduced.

To the borrower:

a. borrower certainty in raising funds is soared;
b. he makes less effort and needs minimum time in questing for an ultimate lender;
c. in whatsoever fashion he needs funds he can procure; and
d. he can seek professionals and specialised assistance from a specialist in the field.

The process of financial intermediation supports increasing capital accumulation through the institutionalisation of savings and investment (Rangarajan, 2001). The gains to the real sector of the economy, therefore, depend on how efficiently the financial sector performs this basic function of financial intermediation.

Major Institutional Players in the Financial Intermediation

There are varieties of financial intermediaries in Indian financial system, classification of which may not be an easy task due to their peculiar criterion and their functioning system. However here an attempt is made to classify these financial intermediaries from a narrow glance/point of view. All the financial intermediaries (merchant middlemen) are broadly segregated as follows:

1. Banking financial institutes (RBI, commercial banks and co-operative banks).
2. Development banks (all India financial institutes like IDBI, IFCI).
3. Investment financial institutes: (LIC), General Insurance Corporation (GIC), Unit Trust of India (UTI). Since 2000, private insurance companies like SunLife, Bajaj Allianz, ICICI Prudential etc.).
4. Non-banking financial institutes (SBI capital services, merchant banking companies, hire-purchase companies, etc.).
5. Postal department financial services (recurring deposits, NSC, KVP, Postal Life Insurance etc.).

1. Banking financial institutes: The magnitude of banking financial institutions in the process of economic development and growth has been given due importance from time to time by the luminaries in the economic field. These institutions play a vital role in a country's economy. It is indeed unthinkable how a country's economic system could function effectively and efficiently in the absence of these institutes. These banks are nodal points of a nation's financial structure. These banks play pivotal role in seeking out the savings of individuals and organisations and purveying these gleaned savings to the productive purposes. They encourage the individuals and organisations to save money and provide them various profitable avenues for their savings. In the absence of these banks the entire economic system remains inanimate. It includes commercial cooperative banks etc. RBI plays a very crucial role not only as regulatory of entire banking system—an indispensible subsystem of Indian financial system—but also as a banker to government and banks. Indian Banking system is shown in Figure 4.3.

Figure 4.3

The Indian Banking System

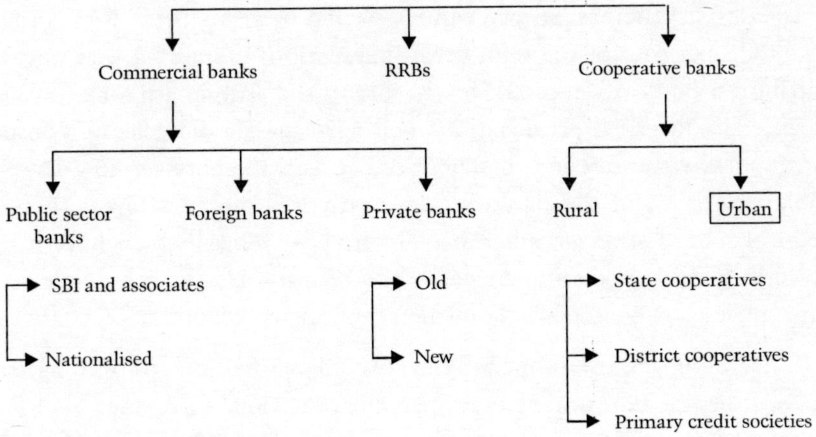

Source: RRBs: Regional rural banks.

Table 4.1

Scheduled Commercial Banks (SCBs) Credit and Deposits by Population during 2001-02

Population Segment	*Total Population (Yr. 2001)**		*Credit*		*Deposits*	
	Million	*%*	*(Rs. Crore)*	*% Share in Total Credit*	*(Rs. Crore)*	*% Share in Total Credit*
Rural	741.7	72.22	87712.9	13.37	159423.5	14.19
Semi-urban	285.4	27.78	90156.3	13.74	214990.4	19.14
Urban			123757.0	18.87	748979.5	66.67
Metropolitan			354366.9	54.02		
Total	1027.1	100.0	655993.1	100.00	1123393.4	100.0

Source: Compiled from Centre for Monitoring Indian Economy (2003). "Money and banking", December, pp.151; * *www.censusindia.net.* , as reproduced in India 2004, pp.15.

From Table 4.1 it can be stated that 72.2 per cent of the Indian population (year 2001) is living in the rural area and the remaining 27.8 per cent in urban area. The SCBs during 2001-02 received 85.8 per cent deposits from semi-urban (19.1%), urban and metropolitan areas (66.6%), and the rest of 14.2 per cent was from rural sector. The same situation with just 1 per cent variation observed in SCBs credit extension. It can be inferred that though 72 per cent of population live in rural area but they are accounting for only about 14 per cent of total bank deposits and credit transactions. Whereas 86 per cent of SCBs' total business was cornered around 28 per cent of the semi-urban population. It shows a very unevenly distributed banking network of the organised Indian financial system. Hence, all concerned organisations and agencies should gear up efforts to narrow down the unequal distribution of banking services in India. For viable extension of the banking services to remote rural areas, banking sector can have strategic alliance with the post offices which have a huge network in every nook and corner of the country. Hence, the public sector banks have to play crucial role in the economic development.

2. Development banks: The core idea of development banking depends on the assumption that apparent provisions of finance alone may not necessarily bring about entrepreneurial progress and development (IDBI Report on Development Banking in India, 1999). In fact development banks play a pivotal role in raising mobilising resources efficiently and effectively to uplift the development needs of the nation. It is difficult to envisage the course of economic progress and growth which have taken place in the world without the substantial contribution rendered by the financing institutions. Their catalytic vitality must not be overlooked in any case. They have been able to make an impact on employment, societal development and have also encouraged small scale and medium enterprises. As experience is gained by these agencies, they are themselves developing and are capable of taking new venture to widen the further growth and development.

Development banks as they appear today, they are having a very flexible nature without any fixed pattern, shape and have taken many norms. There are varying structures and forms of organisation, irrespective of private sector, public sector, joint sector, or number of variations of these categories. The organisation of development banks and the pattern of their financing all over the developing world, present a kaleidoscopic variety, with regard to ownership of the initial equity capital by the government, government agencies and non-governmental agencies. Eventually the form of these banks are not very important, what is important is the spirit, stimuli, their functioning and the dedication of the executives to attain their basic development objectives.

A well integrated network of financial institutions has been developed over the years in India providing a variety of financial products and services for industrial development. The network comprises institutions at the national level like Industrial Development Bank of India (IDBI) and the state level financial institutions like State Industrial Development Corporation (SIDC). Among the All-India Development Banks (AIDBs)—IDBI and Industrial Reconstruction Bank of India (IRBI) provide financial assistance to medium and large enterprises whereas Small Industries Development Bank of India (SIDBI) extends assistance to the small and tiny industries. The AIDBs also undertake promotional and developmental activities of the specialised financial institutions (SFIs). Risk Capital and Technology Finance Corporation Ltd. (RCTC) and Technology Development and Information Company of India (TDICI) and other private venture capital firms provide risk capital, venture capital and technology development finance. State Financial Corporations (SFCs) provide financial assistance mainly to small and medium enterprises, whereas SIDCs cater to the needs of medium enterprises and small industry in their respective states. Apart from providing financial assistance SFCs and SIDCs also undertake promotional and developmental activities. The AIDBs have been providing financial assistance to industry in the form of term loans, underwriting, and direct subscription to share\debentures and guarantees for nearly four decades. Evolving with the years, the institutions have developed and introduced several innovative products and services to meet the growing needs of the corporate sector. Besides expanding the scope of their funding activity the institutions have diversified into newer fee-based services offering a variety of services such as debenture trusteeship and forex service.

3. *Investment financial institutions:* Investment financial institutions are those institutions whose major business is gleaning of the savings of individuals and organisations and mobilising these sources to productive purposes. The network of these institutions in India, include life and non-life insurance which were exclusively in the public sector till 2000, is now opening up to private sector. Life insurance comes under public sector like LIC, and non-life insurance include GIC, Indian Reinsurance Company (IRC), National Insurance Company Ltd. (NIC), United India Insurance Company of India Ltd. (UIIC), the New India Assurance Company Ltd.

(NIAC), the Oriental Insurance Company Ltd. (OIC), Export Credit Guarantee Corporation Ltd. (ECGC), and the latest entrant Agriculture Insurance Company of India Ltd. (AIC) which mobilises the savings of the society through sale of units and channel them into corporate investments. In the private sector as many as 12 companies (Annexure Table A-4.2) are already in business. In non-life segment so far eight private sector companies (Annexure Table A-4.3) have entered the swiftly growing market. The investment institutions are major players in the secondary market. They also extend assistance to the corporate sector by way of term loan, underwriting, direct subscription, to equity and debenture.

4. Non-banking finance companies (NBFCs): During the past (IDBI Report) decade, NBFCs have emerged as significant contributors to the Indian economic progress and growth by strengthening the efforts of banks and other development financial institutions (DFIs). They indeed play a vital role in the direction of savings and investment. In the light of swift industrial development and liberalisation of the financial sector the entrepreneurs, corporate sector and also the major financial institutions have diversified their activities to cater to the needs of the economy. In this regard, the major financial institutions and professionals have promoted financial institutions to crate a diversified and competitive financial system.

The NBFCs are different and distinguished from those of commercial and cooperative banks. These companies render intermediary services between the savers and the investors. The NBFCs in advanced countries have grown phenomenally and they are venturing into developing countries in a big way. The various types of the NBFCs include loan companies, investment companies, hire-purchase finance companies, equipment leasing companies, mutual benefit finance companies, merchant banking companies, bill discounting and factoring companies, venture capital funds, depositories etc.

Currently NBFCs are entangled with hazardous problems and havoc, due to continuous failures caused by reforms in financial sector, misconceived philosophy of business practices, management's fallacious perceptions, lack of long-term perspective and bias regulation of Reserve Bank of India towards NBFCs (Satynarayana, 2003).

5. *Postal department financial services:* The Indian Postal Department also offers a portfolio financial services including banking—savings bank account, national savings certificates, post office monthly income scheme, recurring deposits, KVPs, post office time deposits etc., postal life insurance, money order, international money transfer, mutual fund, electronic money transfer, corporate money order, dematerialised NSC/KVP, etc. In fact these financial services are offered far and wide in the country. There is no other institution/organisation which has the network of delivery of financial services at par with Postal Department in India. This is the only institution which is more proximate formal financial institution to a remotely living common man in India.

Reforms in the 1990s

The 1990s were characterised by fundamental changes in monetary/ fiscal coordination as part of the macro-economic reform programme (Mohan, 2004). This was largely facilitated by the conscious efforts of the government to launch a comprehensive programme of economic reform in July 1991 with fiscal correction as its key element. The agenda of fiscal correction focussed on both tax reform and expenditure management and the containment of non-plan expenditures in order to enhance pubic spending in productive sectors and thereby to provide a stimulus to economic growth. Although the progress in reducing the fiscal deficit was interrupted and even suffered a reversal, the fiscal retrenchment experienced facilitated a more conducive environment for undertaking some path-breaking measures to strengthen fiscal/monetary coordination as well as financial sector reform.

The reforms in the financial sector since, 1991, have brought about a radical change in the outlook and functioning of the financial institutions. Each institution has been adapting itself to the needs of the changing environment. In October 1994, the IDBI act was amended to enable IDBI to restructure its capital, and raise equity from the public. It reconstituted its board of directors and attain greater operational flexibility. Consequently IDBI made its first public issue of equity in July, 1995, the largest ever in the Indian capital market.

Financial System (Intermediation) in Unorganised Sector

Unlike in organised sector the financial intermediation in unorganised sector is less hassle some, more efficient but greater prevalence of borrowers' exploitation. As shown in Figure 1.1 (Chapter 1) the financial intermediation process in unorganised sector starts with 'felt-need' mainly by poor people who often have meagre income generating activities within their vicinity to earn sufficiently to finance their requirements. Therefore, out of sheer need the poor people have to knock the doors of moneylender/ local trader/friends and relatives for financing their needs. The accessibility is easy—with or without any written deeds they can get easy finance but what is problematic is the interest which is exorbitantly high and/or often required to give physical collateral, things like ornaments, utensils, land, house and other fixed assets. The unorganised sector is mostly concentrated in rural India which still accounts for 72 per cent of the total population. Very less rural people have accessibility to the organised financial system, it should be a great concern for the nation.

The Importance of Unorginsed Sector in Terms of Employment

As per the survey (India 2004) carried by the National Sample Survey Organisation (NSSO) in the year 1999-2000, the total employment in both organised and unorganised sectors in the country was of the order of 39.7 crore, i.e., around 2.8 crore in the organised sector and the 36.9 crore (about 92%) in the unorganised sector. Out of this 92 per cent of unorganised sector employees very few people are having access to organised financial system in our country. It is essential to extend the sphere of organised financial system to the fullest extent possible.

From the above, it can be stated that during 1994-95 the unorganised sector contribution accounted for 63 per cent of net domestic product (NDP). But the share of unorganised sector in NDP has dwindled to 59 per cent in 2000-01. This can be inferred that the transactions in unorganised sector have been shifting to the organised sector. This might be due to graduation of reforms in financial sector that helps transforming unorganised sector to organised sector thereby extending the sphere of the organised financial system. This is also hypothetically believed that the extension of organised sector eventually lead to balanced economic growth.

Financial System of Semi-Organised Sector

The system is about one and half decades old in India. As discussed above, in one hand, the organised sector that is highly structured, regulated

Figure 4.4

Financial System of Semi-Organised Sector

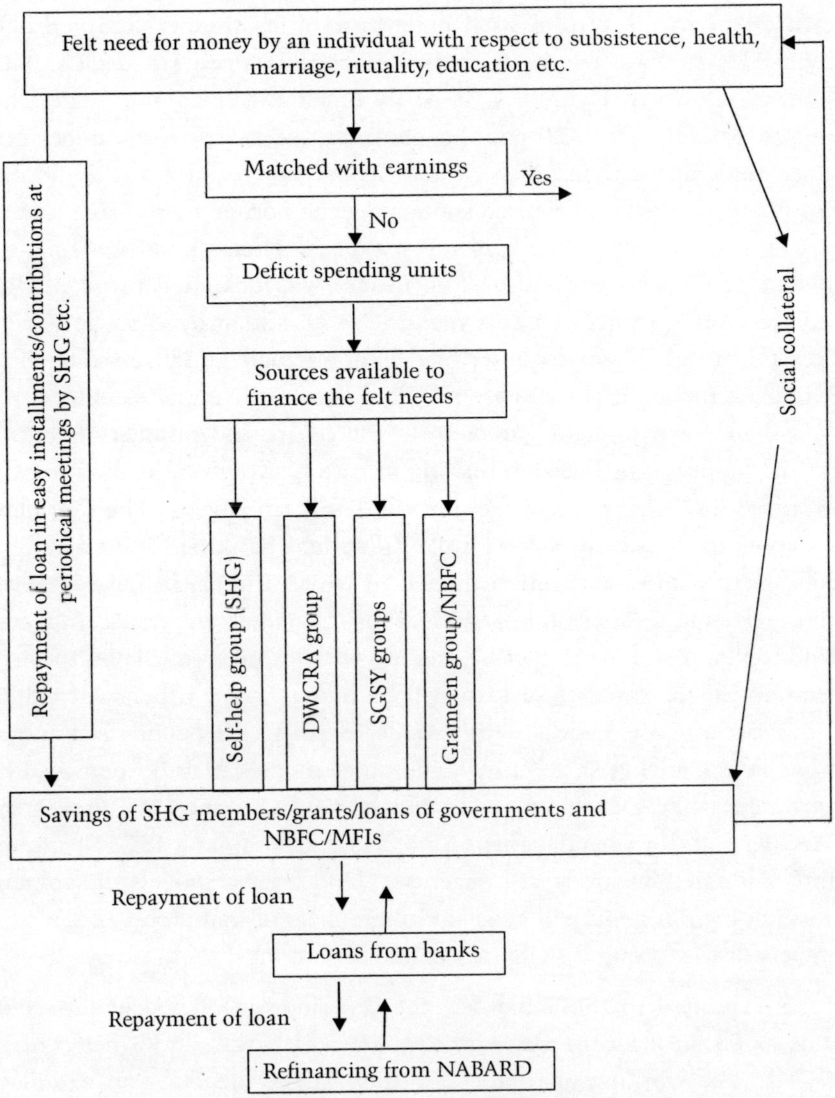

and controlled by government and its agencies, on the other hand, unorganised financial system which is unstructured and not regulated by government and its agencies. Both are catering to different segments of the society. It is a known fact that the unorganised sector is exploitative and anti-poor in nature but indispensible especially in rural and urban slum areas.

The concern of governments, national and international developmental agencies for these poor people paved a way for semi-organised financial system with buzzwords microfinance and self-help groups (SHGs) that have been emergent in India since late 1980s. This system as shown in Figure 4.4, is partly organised in nature. Under this system a group of 10 to 20 poor people come together to save money and finance their needs themselves. If the SHGs survive for 6 to 12 months successfully after saving required sum as per the norms, these SHGs can be linked to formal commercial banks to get loans. This is known as linkages between SHGs and the bank. The model was designed by NABARD through a pilot project in the year 1990-91 and proved to be a very successful model. There are other models of microcredit delivery including: a) Grameen model, it is more of individual loaning, five members form the group, then seven to eight groups form the centre and number of centres form the branch. The decision-making in case of Grameen bank is not de-centralised and always facilitated by the bank employees. The Grameen bank model is basically a model of 'Individual banking—joint liability' model, b) the cluster/federation model, in which the banks have linkages with the federation or cluster of SHGs, thus can reduce the transaction cost substantially. Since, they will be dealing with number of SHGs through federation/cluster and size of loan will be much higher which will reduce the transaction cost. However, this model is yet to get popularised and at present is in evolving stage only. Some other models mainly sponsored by governments like Development of Women and Children in Rural Areas (DWACRA) and Swarnajayanti Gram Swarozgar Yojana (SGSY) groups mainly animated by government agencies. Under these models the amount in form of loan or grant will be given to members of that group and in turn members of that group distribute the amount amongst themselves.

As exhibited in the Table 4.2, the contribution of household sector stands at 93.75 per cent GDS in 2001-02 which was 76.95 per cent in 1991-92. The working of financial system largely depends on extent of savings and generation and allocation of savings in turn induced by prevalence of efficient financial system. This can be inferred that during the last decade Indian financial system underwent sea change, the result of which reflected in the increased contribution of household sector to GDS from 77 per cent to 94 per cent.

Table 4.2

Contribution of Household Sector in the Indian Financial Sector

Particulars	*Year 1991-92 (at Current Prices)*		*Year 2001-02 (at Current Prices)*	
	Rs. Crore	*As % GDS*	*Rs.*	*As % GDS*
Contribution to gross domestic savings (GDS)	110736	76.95	515565	93.75
Contribution to gross capital formation (GCF)	48635	33.95	258918	50.27

Source: Compiled from National Income Statistics, January 2004, Centre for Monitoring Indian Economy, pp.139, 219.

As per the National Income Statistics (NIS) during the 2001-02 almost 50 per cent household sector savings were deployed in physical assets. The trend since 1991-92 (as per the figures given in the reference) more or less same with an average 5 per cent variation upwards to financial savings. Hence, this can be inferred that the Indian financial system needs to be more effective, efficient and conducive to attract household savings towards deployment in financial instruments. This would be the real sign of maturity of the financial system and economic development of the nation.

Emergence of New Institutions/Bodies in the Indian Financial System in the Recent Past

Securities and Exchange Board of India (SEBI): The birth of SEBI was necessitated during early 1990s due to vulnerable scams in the stock market. The SEBI, which was initially set up as an administrative body (Mohan, 2004), later received statutory status in 1992 after the SEBI Act established it as the regulatory body for the promotion of orderly development of the capital market. SEBI has also been since vested with concurrent/delegated powers regarding the provisions under the Companies

Act, 1956 and Securities Contracts (Regulation) Act, 1956. SEBI governs all stock exchanges and securities transactions in India. Besides, all stock brokers, share transfer agents, bankers to an issue, trustees of trust deed, registrars to an issue, merchant bankers, underwriters, portfolio managers, investment advisers and such intermediaries who are associated with the securities market are obliged to register with the SEBI. The RBI has been acting as regulator and controller of banking system (money markets), as there was no specific regulatory/controller in the capital market system prior to SEBI's establishment. Both RBI and SEBI have been functioning as regulatory cum controller in money markets and capital markets respectively.

National Securities Depository Limited (NSDL): Although India had *(www.nsdl.co.in)* a vibrant capital market which is more than a century old, the paper-based settlement of trades caused substantial problems like bad delivery and delayed transfer of title till recently. The enactment of Depositories Act in August 1996 paved the way for establishment of NSDL, the first depository in India. This depository promoted by institutions of national stature responsible for economic development of the country has since established a national infrastructure of international standard that handles most of the trading and settlement in dematerialised form in Indian capital market.

Clearing Corporation of India Limited (CCIL): Establishment of CCIL is an important (*www.ccilindia.com*) milestone in the Indian financial market serving as an important link in the Payment & Settlement system. Promoted by leaders in India's financial sector, CCIL provides an electronic, efficient, transparent, risk-mitigated clearing and settlement platform to its members in guilds and foreign currency markets. Operating in close tandem with RBI, it endeavours to constantly enhance market transparency and efficiency in India's money, debt and forex markets.

Asset Reconstruction Company (India) Limited (Arcil): The Arcil is the first (*www.arcil.co.in*) asset reconstruction company (ARC) to commence business in India. ARCs are established to acquire non-performing assets (NPAs) from financial institutions and banks with the objective of focussed management of these assets and maximisation of recovery. Relieving institutions and banks of the burden of NPAs should allow them to focus on core activities. Arcil has been set up to fulfill these objectives in the Indian banking landscape.

Adopting a bank-based model of ARC, Arcil has been sponsored, *inter alia*, by the significant players in the Indian financial sector, namely State Bank of India (SBI), ICICI Bank Ltd., Industrial Development Bank of India (IDBI), Housing Development Finance Corporation Ltd. (HDFC) and HDFC Bank Ltd. Arcil is set up as a private sector entity with 51 per cent of its equity capital being held by the private sector banks, thus facilitating flexibility in its operations.

Arcil is registered under Reserve Bank of India (RBI) under Section 3 of the Securitisation and Reconstruction of Financial Assets and Enforcement of Security Interest (SARFAESI) Act 2002 as a securitisation company (SC) and reconstruction company (RC) to commence business with effect from August 29, 2003 and is considered as a public financial institution within the meaning of section 4A of the Companies Act, 1956. Arcil is also an associate member of Indian Banks' Association (IBA).

Arcil has already acquired a few financial assets from the institutions and banks creating the history of becoming the first ARC to acquire financial assets in India.

Emerging Issues in the Indian Financial System

Financial disintermediation: In post-liberalised era disintermediation is one of the emergents. Prior to liberalisation almost all of the corporate houses used to finance their short-term and long-term commits through banks and financial institutions. But after liberalisation most of the major corporate houses are having their own financial companies who are providing the required funds to their parent houses.

Microfinance, the semi-formal banking facility to the non-bankable people is yet another emergent. The financial system earlier had very stipulated sphere of extension to almost all poor people. They were deprived from the benefits of an integrated financial system. Evolution of microfinance can address this segment.

Evolution of financial super markets or universal banking is redefining the role and nature of a commercial banker. Before this evolution commercial banks used to cater the short-term (working capital) financial needs and industrial developmental financial institutions like IDBI and ICICI used to render long-term financial assistance to business houses. But the concept of universal banking is (e.g., ICICI bank, Kotak Mahindra bank etc.) a confluence of both these short-term and long-term funds provider. The emergence of this universal bank (where short-term as well as long-term services/instrument traded) system is now bringing both money market (short-term funds) and capital market (long-term funds) closer. In such case who will take the place of regulator/controller, whether RBI or SEBI or together? If they together have to shoulder the responsibility, there may be a possibility of giving conflicting guidelines, which eventually proves to be a suffering for the clients. To avoid any such undesirable situation, what transitions are required in the existing Indian financial system is a food for thought at least in the academic world.

Research studies show that the formal financial system is accessible to only about 12 per cent of the total population in states like Jharkhand and northeastern region. This is a great concern for the financial system, that too for banking sector. The emergent semi-organised microfinance sector has done a lot in reaching the unreached so far. The financial sector scenario of the northeastern region (NER) indicates that much more remains to be done. Outstanding deposits of scheduled commercial banks (SCBs) in the NER as at end-March 2003 formed only 1.5 per cent of the all-India level (RBI, 2003). The share of bank credit to industry showed a modest rise in some states but there were noticeable declines in states of Mizoram and Meghalaya. This problem of covering only 12 per cent can be solved to a great extent by way of evolving strategic alliance between commercial banks and post offices which have wide network throughout every nook and corner of the country. As post offices are the only formal wide network that offers some sort of financial services can also be assigned with more functions of commercial banks. A viable *modus operandi* can be developed between commercial banks and post offices at least by nationalised banks initially.

The commercial banks have been also striving to reach the unreached through microfinance channel linking SHGs with banks, MFIs etc. But efforts should be geared up to cover the uncovered segments of the society at the earliest, as we are in 21st century.

A large part of the Indian insurance market that deals in pension plans and insurance as an investment option is not yet freed from tariff and administered price regime. The hype of competitive market like in banking and telecom sectors especially in pricing of insurance products has not yet emerged. If this happens the sphere of insurance sector will certainly reach the unreached and will result in tapping of the 80 per cent population who are yet to come under insurance cover. This would positively impinge the economic security of the Indian people.

The Indian financial system that is indispensible for economic development of the nation is undergoing numerous evolutions especially since the 1990s that are rendering as lubricants to the fast economic development. Banking sector is a major component of the financial system liberalised in early 1990s, but presently also public sector banks together account for 78 per cent deposits and 74 per cent of advances of banking business in India. Hence, these banks have to play a very crucial role in extending the banking services to so far not reached segment especially states like Jharkhand and northeastern region where only 12 per cent of the total population have access to bank services. Despite 72 per cent of population live in rural area, they account for about 14 per cent of total bank deposits and credit transactions. This uneven distribution of banking can be addressed by way of evolving strategic alliance with post offices which have a network in every nook and corner of the country to offer more banking services. The contribution of unorganised sector to NDP (2000-01) was 59 per cent only. The organised/formal financial system is mainly concentrated in organised sector but it is equally important to cover unorganised sector for a balanced economic growth. Almost 50 per cent of the householding savings are committed to investing in physical assets, hence, the financial system needs to be more effective, efficient and conducive to attract household savings towards deployment in financial instruments. That would be a real sign of maturity of the financial system and economic development of the nation. Efforts should also be augmented to extend the sphere of formal financial system's accessibility to the poorest of the poor through semi-organised financial system.

Annexure Table A-4.1

Select Chronology of Developments in the Indian Financial System

Year	Event
1770	Bank of Hindustan, the first bank in India on modern lines established.
1818	Oriental Life Insurance Company started by Europeans.
1850	First general insurance company established.
1875	Bombay Stock Exchange started formal trading.
1921	Three Presidency banks, Bank of Bengal, Bank of Madras and Bank of Bombay, merged into Imperial Bank.
1926	Establishment of Hilton-Young Commission to suggest a central bank for the country.
1935	Establishment of Reserved Bank of India as the central bank.
1947	Control of Capital Issues Act imposed restrictions on issues of capital.
1948	Establishment Industrial Finance Corporation, the first DFI.
1955	Imperial Bank taken over by State Bank of India.
	Establishment of Industrial Credit and Investment Corporation of India.
1956	Life Insurance Company of India came into effect; Securities Contract (Regulation) Act impacted directly and indirectly on securities trading, running of stock exchanges and prevention of undesirable transaction.
1962	Deposit Insurance Corporation established.
1963	Insertion of new Chapter in RBI Act, 1934 to effectively supervise, control and regulate deposit-taking activities of NBFCs.
1964	Establishment of Industrial Development Bank of India.
1966	Deposit insurance extended to cooperative banks.
1969	Nationalisation of 14 largest commercial banks.
1973	Nationalisation of general insurance companies; Foreign Exchange Regulation Act (FERA) was promulgated which provided an opportunity to develop India equity market.
1975	Establishment of Regional Rural Banks.
1980	Second round of nationalisation of six commercial banks.
1982	Establishment of National Bank for Agriculture and Rural Development; First credit rating agency established in India.
1990	Establishment of Small Industries Development Bank of India.
1991	Report of the Committee on the Financial System, which provided the blueprint for first generation financial sector reforms.
1992	Introduction of prudential norms for income recognition and asset classification; SEBI obtained statutory powers to promote orderly development of capital market; Incorporation of National Stock exchange (NSE) as the first screen-based and transparent trading platform for investors; Introduction of auction system for Government securities.

contd...

...contd...

Year	*Event*
1993	Introduction of depositories.
1994	Board for Financial Supervision, an autonomous body under the aegis of RBI, established; New guidelines for entry of new private sector banks announced; Wholesale debt market operations initiated by NSE.
1996	Establishment of Institute for Development and Research in Banking Technology; Depositories Act was passed which allowed for holding of securities in dematerialised form. The enactment of Depositories Act in August 1996 paved the way for establishment of NSDL.
1997	Promulgation of RBI (Amendment) Act for intensified regulation deposit-taking NBFCs; Termination of automatic magnetisation of Government deficit; Bank rate activated as a signaling rate; Statutory Liquidity Rate (SLR) reduced to 25 per cent (legal minimum).
1999	Insurance Regulation and Development Act passed allowing new players/joint ventures to undertake insurance business; Detailed guidelines on risk management in banks announced; Standing committee on International Financial Standards and codes set up to evolve sound standards based on recognised best practices.
2000	Guidelines issued regarding interest rate swaps and forward rate agreement to enable financial entities to hedge interest rate risk; New guidelines for categorisation valuation of banks' investment portfolio announced; Foreign Exchange Management Act, replacing the earlier FERA introduced.
2001	Establishment of Credit Information Bureau of India Ltd; Cleaning Corporation of India Limited (CCIL) incorporated.
2002	Revised guidelines announced for entry of new private banks; Enactment of SARFAESI Act (Securitisation and Reconstruction of Financial Assets and Enforcement of Security Interest) for enforcement of security interest for secured creditors; Establishment of first universal bank in the country; Clearing Cooperation of India Limited became operational; Consolidated guidelines issued on FDI in banking; Asset Reconstruction Company India Limited (Arcil) is registered under Reserve Bank of India (RBI) under Section 3 of the SRFAESI Act 2002 as a securitisation company (SC) and reconstruction company (RC).
2003	Central listing Authority was constituted; Arcil commence business with effect from August.

Source: Compiled from, Reserve Bank of India Bulletin, Februry, 2003, pp-151. *www.ccilindia.com*, *www.arcil.co.in*, *www.nsdl.co.in*, Proceedings of the XIV Insurance Congress of Developing Countries (ICDC) 2004 and *Economic Times,* March 9, 2004 p.4, New Delhi Edition.

Annexure Table A-4.2

List of Private Sector Companies (Life Insurance Segment)

1)	Aviva Life Insurance Company Private Limited.
2)	ICICI Prudential Life Insurance Company Limited.
3)	Om Kotak Mahindra Life Insurance Company Limited.
4)	Allianz Bajaj Life Insurance Company Limited.
5)	Birla Sun Life Insurance Company Limited.
6)	Ing Vysya Life Insurance Company Limited.
7)	Metlife India Life Insurance Company Limited.
8)	AMP Sanmar Assurance Company Limited.
9)	HDFC Standard Life Insurance Company Limited.
10)	Max New York Life Insurance Company Limited.
11)	SBI Life Insurance Company Limited.
12)	Tata AIG Life Insurance Company Limited.

Source: Proceedings of the XIV Insurance Congress of Developing Countries (ICDC), 2004 and *Economic Times*, March 9, 2004, New Delhi Edition.

Annexure Table A-4.3

List of Private Sector Companies (Non-Life Insurance Segment)

1)	Cholamandalam MS General Insurance Company Limited.
2)	ICICI LOMBARD General Insurance Company Limited.
3)	IFFCO-TOKIO General Insurance Company Limited.
4)	Royal Sundaram Alliance Insurance Company Limited.
5)	Bajaj Allianz General Insurance Company Limited.
6)	Reliance General Insurance Company Limited.
7)	Tata AIG General Insurance Company Limited.
8)	HDFC-CHUBB General Insurance Company Limited.

Source: Proceedings of the XIV Insurance Congress of Developing Countries (ICDC), 2004 and *Economic Times*, March 9, 2004, New Delhi Edition.

5 Role of Banks in Financial Inclusion

Traditionally agriculture sector had been the backbone of Indian economy, as more than 60 per cent of our country's population, today also, rely on agriculture for employment and livelihood. Within the financial system, banking sector plays an instrumental role in economic growth and development. The banking sector is envisaged to be the heart of the Indian financial system. The role of banks *viz.*, commercial banks (CBs), regional rural banks (RRBs) and cooperative banks is indispensible for financial inclusion, without which it is perhaps not possible to achieve desired level of financial inclusion. The financial services like savings, credit, remittances and insurance, that are required in the initial stage of financial inclusion can be rendered by only banks as they are not only specialised in these important financial services that are pivotal for initial stage of financial inclusion but also have huge integrated network of 33,553 rural and semi-urban branches of commercial banks, 13,932 rural and semi-urban branches of RRBs, 1.09 lakh primary cooperatives, with state-of-the-art technology and experienced human resources. Therefore, the role of banks in financial inclusion is enormous and indispensible for it. This chapter outlines the role of banks (CBs, RRBs and cooperatives) in financial inclusion.

Role of Commercial Banks

Evolution and growth in outreach (1951-1991): The commercial banking system was one of the oldest subsystems of Indian financial system. In India, the Bank of Hindustan, the first commercial bank on modern lines, was established in 1770. In 1921 three presidency banks—Bank of Madras (1843), Bank of Bengal (1809) and Bank of Bombay (1840) merged into Imperial bank, made a landmark in Indian banking annals. Establishment of Reserve bank of India in 1935, set leadership for the banking sector. In 1955, taking over of the Imperial Bank by State Bank of India (SBI) was a big stimuli to growth and development of banking in

India. Nationalisation of banks in 1969 and 1980, remarkable strides in the growth and development of banking sector in general. The establishment of National Bank for Agriculture and Rural Development (NABARD) was indeed instrumental in outreach of banking system to the rural credit and it was a foundation stone for financial inclusion.

From the position prevalent in 1951-52, commercial banks came a long way with a substantial network with 32,224 branches in rural and semi-urban areas spread over every nook and corner of country, comprising 68 per cent of their total outlets as on 31 March 1991. The outstanding deposits of such branches at Rs.67,855 crore as on the same date constituted around 35 per cent of their total deposits, while loans outstanding at Rs. 43,797 crore comprised 36 per cent of outstanding credit. The agricultural advances of the commercial banking system aggregated Rs. 16,687 crore and constituted 14 per cent of total advances in March 1991. The rural and semi-urban branches of commercial banks covered 17.6 crore deposit accounts while the number of loan accounts serviced aggregated 3.7 crore. The period since 1991-92 has seen a fairly rapid expansion of credit to agriculture. Available data indicate that the flow of credit to agriculture by commercial banks and RRBs taken together increased to Rs. 60,022 crore in 2003-04. This implies a compounded annual growth rate (CAGR) of 22.2 per cent. In fact, as compared with commercial banks (including RRBs), the flow of credit from the cooperative sector was much slower through this period. The CAGR of credit for agriculture from cooperative institutions was only 13.7 per cent. Further, the proportion of agriculture credit to total credit came down because of the rapid growth in non-agriculture credit. The Government took some major initiatives during the period to boost agriculture production and productivity through enhanced credit flow and by way of building agricultural infrastructure, particularly irrigation and connectivity in rural areas. Special Agricultural Credit Plan (SACP) was introduced by RBI for public sector commercial banks (PSCBs) in 1994-95. Credit growth for agriculture and allied sectors under this caption reflected a CAGR of 36.45 per cent during 2001-02 to 2005-06.

SACP has since been extended to private sector commercial banks from 2005-06. The SHG–Bank Linkage Programme was started as a pilot project by NABARD in 1992. It led to the evolution of a set of RBI approved guidelines to banks to enable SHGs to transact with banks. Initially there was slow progress in the programme up to 1999 as only 32,995 groups were credit-linked during the period 1992 to 1999. Since then the programme has been growing rapidly and the cumulative number of SHGs financed increased from 4.61 lakh on 31 March 2002 to 10.73 lakh on 31 March 2004 and further to 29.25 lakh groups as on 31 March 2007. Rural Infrastructure Development Fund (RIDF) was set up in NABARD by Government of India (GoI) during 1995-96 with an initial corpus of Rs.2,000 crore, to accelerate the completion of 47 on-going projects of rural infrastructure. Banks which did not fulfill the priority sector credit requirement and agriculture credit mandate were required to contribute to this Fund. The fund has been strengthened every year with additional allocations in the Union Budget. A large number of irrigation and rural connectivity projects could get completed under RIDF. RBI scaled down its contribution to the rural credit funds with NABARD to a token amount of Rs.1 crore per annum since 1993-94. However to enable NABARD to have reasonably strong leverage for accessing market funds, the share capital of NABARD was strengthened and increased to Rs.2,000 crore (paid up) from Rs.100 crore at the time of its formation in 1982. Contributions to enhanced share capital have come from GoI and RBI. By prudent funds management, the institution has also built a strong base of reserves and has been using it in its business operations judiciously to keep lending rates to rural financial institutions at significantly lower than market costs.

Developments post-2003-04: Since 2003-04, there has been a substantial increase in the flow of credit to agriculture through commercial banks. Disbursements have increased from Rs. 52,441 crore in 2003-04 to Rs. 1,16,447 crore in 2005-06, reaching an annual growth of 43 per cent each year. As envisaged in the GoI's strategy for 'doubling of credit', 95 lakh new farmers have been brought under the institutional fold and 1,383 agri-clinics opened. Commercial banks have also played a major role in the promotion of the SHG–bank linkage movement with more than 11.88 lakh groups being linked to banks for provision of credit. Reforms in the commercial banking system include removal of procedural and transactional bottlenecks including elimination of service area approach (SAA), reducing margins, redefining overdues to coincide with crop cycles, new debt restructuring policies, one time settlement and relief measures for farmers indebted to non-institutional sources.

The task ahead: Commercial banks are now slowly coming to appreciate the business potential in financial inclusion and also the need for better involvement. RRBs who are expected to function with the social heart of cooperatives and financial acumen of commercial banks have a significant role to play in financial inclusion, especially in the post-amalgamation scenario. The vast postal network, leveraging on their immense outreach, could also be an effective vehicle for supplying financial services. While, there is evidence that commercial banks have been cognisant of their social responsibility in regard to small farmers, their focus on marginal and submarginal farmers, tenants, share croppers, oral lessees and non-cultivator households, *viz.*, the very poor and disadvantaged sectors has been found wanting. In the circumstances, there is a need to evolve conscious strategies for providing easier access to affordable credit to the marginal, submarginal and other disadvantaged groups in the rural sector. Such strategies should combine using a variety of delivery channels, intermediaries and IT solutions apart from the traditional brick and mortar branch network.

Product innovation: The excluded segments of the population require products which are customised, taking into consideration their varied needs. Their banking requirements being small, the issue of servicing and delivery in a cost-effective manner assumes significance. The need for savings by these groups require special attention, e.g., for meeting life cycle needs, creating assets, repaying high cost borrowings, meeting emergencies etc. The saving products offered at present do not effectively meet these needs. The services offered are also not suitable because of the spatial spread of the excluded people and also the small quantum of finance involved.

(a) *Savings:* Savings products to meet the specific requirements of the poor need to be evolved. One way of meeting this would be to utilise SHGs for tapping the small savings by providing incentives to the SHGs with suitable back-end technology support. The banks can develop medium and long-term savings instruments by issue of pre-printed deposit receipts to the SHGs which in turn can be sold to the SHG members. Banks could be given the freedom to develop their own products, suiting local requirements and felt needs of the poor.

(b) *Credit:* With regard to credit products, the savings linked financing model can be adopted for these segments. The approach should be kept simple which should guarantee the beneficiaries a credit limit, subject to adherence to terms and conditions. The credit within the limit can be made available in 2-3 tranches, with the second and subsequent tranches disbursed based on repayment behaviour of the first tranche. This is to ensure that the vulnerable groups do not get into a debt trap; it also ensures good credit dispensation.

(c) *Insurance:* Banks can play a vital role in this regard—by distributing suitable microinsurance products. Incentivising human resource—measurable performance indicators like lending to low-income groups and increasing financial inclusion need motivated bank staff. Such motivation is a function of attitudes and beliefs as also a system of incentives/disincentives put in place by the bank's management for special efforts/failures to achieve desired levels of financial inclusion.

(d) *Promoting rural entrepreneurship:* Commercial banks may consider setting up institutions like farmer training centres and rural development and self employment training institutes (RUDSETIs) for developing skills among farmers/rural entrepreneurs for effectively managing the assets financed.

(e) *Self-help groups:* Technology applications for greater financial inclusion—Extending outreach on a scale envisaged under National Rural Financial Inclusion Plan (NRFIP) would require the application of low-cost technology solutions. This may also call for certain levels of funding support for rolling out such IT-based inclusive financial sector plan.

Cooperative Banks

The modern banking system in India initially had failed to impress the rural people to a stipulated extent due to its inherent bottlenecks. But importance of bank services to people in their survival and growth is inseparable. Hence, in quest of providing banking services to the rural people— the cooperative bank system's foundation is based on the principle of 'one for all and all for one' and democracy. Thus, the evolution of cooperative banking system had begun in 1900 in India. Cooperative banking system in India was *ab initio* considered as a mechanism to put together the resources of people with small and marginal means and offering them access to various financial services especially savings and loan products. The evolution of cooperative banking system was also envisaged in the beginning as a vivid tool for converting degraded waste lands into cultivable lands, enhancing productivity, creating direct and indirect employment opportunities, promoting food security, warranting socioeconomic justice to the poor and down-trodden people. Coverage of cooperative banks: as per the statistics of National Federation of State Cooperative Banks Ltd. (NAFSCOB)-2005, there were nearly 1.09 lakh primary agricultural credit societies (PACSs), 368 district central cooperative banks (DCCBs) with 12,858 branches and 30 state cooperative banks (SCBs) with 953 branches or a total of 122,590 service outlets. On an average, there is one PACS for every six villages; with a total membership of more than 12 crore rural people and about 2.6 crore (as on March 2007) microfinance clients, witnessing it as one of the largest rural financial systems on this planet.

Achievement of Rural Cooperative Credit Institutions

Primary agricultural credit societies (PACSs): These are the credit institutions at the grassroot level dealing directly with individual members/clients. A large proportion of PACSs also serve as outlets for inputs and for the public distribution system (PDS) for food and other essential items. As shown in Table 5.1, the total membership of PACSs as on 31 March 2005 aggregated to 1,274 lakh, of which, the borrowing members at 451 lakh constituted around 35 per cent. The total as well as borrowing members of PACS declined during 2004-05. Deposits and borrowings of PACS increased by 5 and 17 per cent, respectively, as on 31 March 2005 over the previous year. The loans issued increased by 12 per cent during 2004-05 as compared to an increase of 3.3 per cent during 2003-04, over the previous year. As per the data available with NAFSCOB, small and marginal farmers constitute nearly 70 per cent of total membership of PACS at the national level, while SCs/STs constitute 34 per cent.

In Table 5.2 wide regional variations can be observed—while western and southern regions have a greater proportion of small farmers as

Table 5.1

Performance of PACS

Particulars (31st March)	PACS 2003	2004	2005
No. (lakh)	1.12	1.06	1.09
Members (No. cr)	12.36	13.54	12.74
Borrowers (No. cr)	6.39	5.13	4.51
Owned funds (Rs. cr)	8198	8397	9197
Deposits (Rs. cr)	19120	18143	18976
Borrowings (Rs. cr)	30278	34257	40429
Loans issued (Rs. cr)	33996	35119	39212

Source: NAFSCOB.

Table 5.2

PACS: Region-wise Performance

Region	Total No. of PACSs	Total Membership (No. '000)	Average Membership/ PACS	Total Borrowing Membership (No. '000)	Average Borrowing Membership/ PACS	Credit Potential Available (No./PACS) (col. 3– col. 5/ col. 2)
Central	13723	8322.68	606	6810	496	110
Eastern	28928	38952.94	1347	11989	414	933
Northeastern	3628	3835.62	1057	330	91	966
Northern	16819	17084.63	1016	7191	428	588
Southern	15349	45832.06	2986	14484	944	2042
Western	30332	13378.49	441	4266	141	300
Total	108779	127406.42	1171	45070	414	757

members, eastern and central regions have nearly half of their members belonging to SC/ST category. The average membership per PACS (all-India) is 1,171 persons. Southern region has the highest average at 2,986 persons, while western has the lowest at 441 persons. The average borrowing membership per PACS (all-India) is 414 persons. While the southern region has the highest average at 944 persons, northeastern region has only 91 borrowing members, on an average. The gap between the average membership (NABARD, 2008) and the average borrowing membership can be presumed as the credit potential available. Viewed thus, there is a huge potential for extending credit outreach by the cooperatives, especially in the southern region. Though the network of commercial banks and RRBs has spread rapidly and they now have nearly 50,000 branches, their reach in the countryside both in terms of the number of clients and accessibility to the small and marginal farmers and other poorer segments is far less than that of cooperatives. In terms of number of agricultural credit accounts, the STCCS (Short Term Rural Cooperation Structure) has 50 per cent more accounts than the commercial banks and RRBs put together. Directly or indirectly, it covers nearly half of India's total population.

RRBs: Their role is instrumental in the process of financial inclusion. RRBs can play a vital role than scheduled commercial banks (SCBs) in attaining the integrated goal of financial inclusion for inclusive grwoth. The essence of the banking sector in general and rural banking in particular, in the economic growth and development of the nation should be considered as vital tool. Mahatma Gandhi, rightly put that, 'real India lies in villages,' as village economy is the backbone of Indian economy and rural banking system is the heart of village economy. The objective of inclusive growth and financial inclusion can be achieved when rural people economy is improved. The real economic growth and development largely depend on freeing rural masses from vicious poverty, unemployment, and weak socioeconomic status of being rural poor. Keeping this in mind, since First Five Year Plan period (1951-1956), a variety of socioeconomic and welfare strategic programmes like Integrated Rural Development Programme (IRDP), District Rural Development Agency (DRDA), self-employment schemes etc., have been activated to address the problem. All these strategic programmes could attain the desired results up to some extent. But, the government's quest for alternative endeavours is a continous process. This in turn paved a way to the concept of accessibility of formal financial system to the rural poor. Therefore, RRBs have come into existence as low-cost institutions having a rural ethos, local feel and pro-poor focus to extend the formal financial system cover to rural masses. In fact the current concern of inclusive growth and financial inclusion were very well thought over and conceived long time ago, under the provisions of an Ordinance promulgated on the 26th September 1975 and the RRB Act, 1976 with an objective to ensure sufficient institutional credit for agriculture and other rural sectors. The RRBs mobilise financial resources from rural/semi-urban areas and grant loans and advances mostly to small and marginal farmers, agricultural labourers and rural artisans. The area of operation of RRBs is limited to the area as notified by GoI covering one or more districts in the state. However, RRBs could achieve desired results to stipulated extent in the first phase of RRB evaluation, but it is indeed true that any evaluation is a gradual process and takes time to fructify. The importance of financial inclusion further gained prominence during 1990s when the movement of microfinance alongwith SHGs was emerging in India, since late 1980s. This evolution has been proving to be result-oriented and effective, and changing the classical phenomenon that says, 'poor people in India born in debt, survive in debt and die in debt'. RRBs certainly have to play a crucial role in extending important financial services including, savings products, credit, remittances and insurance for the achievement of current Five Year Plan (2007-2012) goal of financal inclusion and inclusive growth.

Present and future roles of RRBs: RRBs have been playing an integral role in achieving their core objective of providing formal financial services to the rural poor. During present five year plan period and future to come, the role of RRBs is instrumental for long-term sustainable inclusive economic development. Toward this end government has initiated the process of structural consolidation of RRBs by amalgamating RRBs sponsored by the same bank within a state as per the recommendations of the Vijay Shankar Vyas Committee (2004).[1] The amalgamated RRBs were expected to face emerging challenges and provide better customer service due to better infrastructure, computerisation of branches, pooling of experienced work force, common publicity/marketing efforts, etc., and also derive the benefits of a large area of operation, enhanced credit exposure limits and more diverse banking activities. As a result of the amalgamation, the number of RRBs were reduced from 196 to 133 as on 31 March 2006 and to 96 as on 30 April 2007. Post-merger RRBs represent a powerful instrument for financial inclusion.

Their outreach *vis-à-vis* other scheduled commercial banks particularly in regions and across population groups facing the brunt of financial exclusion is impressive, as observed from an analysis of *Basic*

1. Report of the Advisory Committee on Flow of Credit to Agriculture and Related Activities from the Banking System. *http://rbidocs.rbi.org.in/rdocs/PublicationReport/Pdfs/55259.pdf*

Statistical Returns of the RBI and indicated in the following paragraphs. With merger infusing the much needed financial strength in RRBs coupled with the local feel and familiarity they command, RRBs are in a unique position to play a decisive role in financial inclusion.

Coverage: In rural areas, RRBs account for a substantial 37 per cent of total offices of all scheduled commercial banks (SCBs). In semi-urban areas, their share comes to 15 per cent. It indicates that financial exclusion is more severe in rural areas.

Table 5.3

Offices of Scheduled Commercial Banks: Population Group and Bank Group-wise (March 2005)

Bank Group	*Rural Offices*		*Semi-Urban Offices*		*Urban/Metro Offices*		*Total*	
	No.	*% to Total*	*No.*	*% to Total*	*No.*	*% to Total*	*No.*	*% to Total*
RRBs	11824	37	2284	15	537	2	14645	21
SCBs other than RRBs	20143	63	13335	85	21846	98	55324	79
Total	31967	100	15619	100	22383	100	69969	100

Source: NABARD (2008).

Moping of savings: At national level, RRBs account for 12 per cent of all deposit accounts of scheduled commercial banks and a meagre 3.5 per cent of deposit amount. However, in rural areas, RRBs share in deposit accounts is a significant 31 per cent and that in deposit amount 19 per cent. This reveals that the average deposit amount is lower in RRBs than other commercial banks, thus corroborating that RRBs' outreach is better.

Table 5.4

Deposits of Rural Branches of Scheduled Commercial Banks: Bank Group-wise (March 2005)

Bank Group	*No. of Accounts*		*Deposit Amount*	
	No. ('000)	*% to Total*	*Amount (Rs. crore)*	*% to Total*
RRBs	43540	31	40957	19
SCBs other than RRBs	98368	69	172147	81
Total	141908	100	213104	100

Source: NABARD (2008).

Credit services performance: At national level, RRBs account for 18 per cent of loan accounts of all SCBs and 3 per cent of loans outstanding. Whereas the share of RRBs' loan accounts is 38 per cent in rural areas. Important point here is, besides the account for 38 per cent of all loan accounts, RRBs' share is 21 per cent of total credit outstanding in rural areas, which confirms the better outreach of the RRBs in rural areas.

Table 5.5

Credit Disbursed by Rural Branches of Scheduled Commercial Banks: Bank Group-wise (March 2005)

Bank Group	No. of Accounts		Credit Outstanding	
	No. ('000)	% to Total	Amount (Rs. crore)	% to Total
RRBs	10913	38	23017	21
SCBs other than RRBs	18155	62	86959	79
Total	29068	100	109976	100

Source: NABARD (2008).

From the above paras on deposit (savings) and credit (loan) data reveals that RRB branches in rural areas have delivered effectively in comparision to other SCB branches. This shows the important role RRBs play in financial inclusion as RRBs' branches are proximate and more concerned with extending outreach to distant and interior countryside. Hence, it can be concluded that RRBs are in a position to render a major role in financial inclusion, including in the areas where the financial exclusion is high. It is hoped that the RRBs continue to maintain the present pace and spirit and would only strive for continous improvement in reaching the non-hitherto, unreached poor masses for the eventual goal of uplifting of the poor from the vicious cycle of poverty and for long-term sustainable inclusive growth and economic development of the nation.

6 Microfinance Institutions

A range of institutions in public sector as well as private sector offers the microfinance services in India. They can be broadly categorised into two categories namely, formal institutions and informal institutions. The former category comprises apex development financial institutions (AFIs), commercial banks, regional rural banks (RRBs), and cooperative banks that provide microfinance services in addition to their general banking activities and are referred to as microfinance service providers. On the other hand, the informal institutions that undertake microfinance services as their main activity are generally referred to as microfinance institutions (MFIs). While both private and public ownership are found in the case of formal financial institutions offering microfinance services, the MFIs are mainly in the private sector.

Microfinance Service Providers

The microfinance service providers include apex institutions like National Bank for Agriculture and Rural Development (NABARD), Small Industries Development Bank of India (SIDBI), and Rashtriya Mahila Kosh (RMK). At the retail level, commercial banks, RRBs and cooperative banks provide microfinance services. Today, there are about 60,000 retail credit outlets of the formal banking sector in the rural areas comprising 12,000 branches of district level cooperative banks, over 14,000 branches of the RRBs and over 30,000 rural and semi-urban branches of commercial banks besides almost 90,000 cooperatives credit societies at the village level. On an average, there is at least one retail credit outlet for about 5,000 rural people. This physical reaching out to the far-flung areas of the country to provide savings, credit and other banking services to the rural society is an unparalleled achievement of the Indian banking system. In this chapter, an attempt is made to deal with various aspects relating to emergence of private microfinance industry in the context of prevailing legal and regulatory environment for private sector rural and microfinance operators.

The Emergence of Private Microfinance Industry

The microfinance initiative in private sector can be traced to the initiative undertaken by Ela Bhatt for providing banking services to the poor women employed in the unorganised sector in Ahmedabad city of Gujarat. Shri Mahila SEWA (Self-Employed Women's Association) Sahakari bank was set up in 1974 by registering it as a urban cooperative bank. Since then, the bank is providing banking services to the poor self-employed women working as hawkers, vendors, domestic servants etc. As on March 2003, the MFI had a membership of 30,000, 70 per cent of whom are from urban area. The deposit and loan portfolio stood at Rs 623.9 million ($13.86 million) and Rs.133.6 million ($2.97 million) respectively. Though the MFI is making profit, yet the SEWA bank model of MFI has not been replicated elsewhere in the country.

In the midst of the apparent inadequacies of the formal financial system to cater to the financial needs of the rural poor, NABARD sponsored an action research project in 1987 through an NGO called MYRADA. For this purpose a grant of Rs. 1 million ($22,222) was provided to MYRADA for an R&D programme related to credit groups. Encouraged by the results of field level experiments in group based approach for lending to the poor, NABARD launched a Pilot Project in 1991-92 in partnership with non-governmental organisations (NGOs) for promoting and grooming self-help groups (SHGs) of homogeneous members and making savings in existing banks and within the existing legal framework. Steady progress of the pilot project led to the mainstreaming of the SHG-Bank Linkage Programme in 1996 as a normal banking activity of the banks with widespread acceptance. The Reserve Bank of India (RBI) set the right policy environment by allowing savings bank accounts of informal groups to be opened by the formal banking system. Launched at a time when regulated interest rates were in vogue, the banks were expected to lend to SHGs at the prescribed rates, but the RBI advised the banks not to interfere with the SHGs' management of affairs, particularly on the terms and conditions on which the SHGs disbursed loans to their members.

The uniqueness of the microfinance through SHG is that it is a partnership based approach and encouraged NGOs to undertake not only social engineering but also financial intermediation especially in areas where banking network was not satisfactory. The rapid progress achieved in

SHG formation, which has now turned into an empowerment movement among women across the country, laid the foundation for emergence of MFIs in India.

MFIs and Legal Forms

With the current phase of expansion of the SHG–Bank Linkage Programme and other microfinancial initiatives in the country, the informal microfinance sector in India is now beginning to evolve. The MFIs in India can be broadly sub-divided into three categories of organisational forms as given in Table 6.1. While there is no published data on private MFIs operating in the country, the number of MFIs is estimated to be around 800. However, not more than 10 MFIs are reported to have an outreach of 100,000 microfinance clients. An overwhelming majority of MFIs are operating on a smaller scale with clients ranging between 500 to 1,500 per MFI. The geographical distribution of MFIs is very much lopsided with concentration in the southern India where the rural branch network of formal banks is excellent. It is estimated that the share of MFIs in the total microcredit portfolio of formal and informal institutions is about 8 per cent.

Table 6.1

Legal Forms of MFIs in India

Types of MFIs	*Estimated Number**	*Legal Acts under which Registered*
1. Not for profit MFIs a) NGO–MFIs	400 to 500	Societies Registration Act, 1860 or similar Provincial Acts Indian Trust Act, 1882
b) Non-profit companies	10	Section 25 of the Companies Act, 1956
2. Mutual benefit MFIs a) Mutually aided cooperative societies (MACSs) and similarly set up institutions	200 to 250	Mutually Aided Cooperative Societies Act enacted by State Government
3. For profit MFIs a) Non-banking financial companies (NBFCs)	6	Indian Companies Act, 1956 Reserve Bank of India Act, 1934
Total	700 to 800	

Note: * The estimated number includes only those MFIs, which are actually undertaking lending activity.

Source: Article presented at the APRACA seminar at Manila in July 2004 by K. Maralidhar Rao CM, NABARD, Mumbai.

NGO-MFIs: There are a large number of NGOs that have undertaken the task of financial intermediation. Majority of these NGOs are registered as Trust or Society. Many NGOs have also helped SHGs to organise themselves into federations and these federations are registered as Trusts or Societies. Many of these federations are performing non-financial and financial functions like social and capacity building activities, facilitating training of SHGs, undertaking internal audit, promoting new groups, and some of these federations are engaged in financial intermediation as well. The NGO-MFIs vary significantly in their size, philosophy and approach. Therefore these NGOs are structurally not the right type of institutions for undertaking financial intermediation activities, as the byelaws of these institutions are generally restrictive in allowing any commercial operations. These organisations by their charter are non-profit organisations and as a result face several problems in borrowing funds from higher financial institutions. The NGO-MFIs, which are large in number, are still outside the purview of any financial regulation. These are the institutions for which policy and regulatory framework would need to be established.

Non-Profit Companies as MFIs: Many NGOs felt that combining financial intermediation with their core competency activity of social intermediation is not the right path. It was felt that a financial institution including a company set up for this purpose will do a better banking function. Further, if MFIs are to demonstrate that banking with the poor is indeed profitable and sustainable, it has to function as a distinct institution so that cross-subsidisation can be avoided. On account of these factors, NGO-MFIs are, of late, setting up a separate non-profit companies for their microfinance operations. The MFI is prohibited from paying any dividend to its members. In terms of RBI's Notification dated 13 January 2000, relevant provisions of RBI Act, 1934 as applicable to NBFCs will not apply for NBFCs: (i) licensed under Section 25 of Companies Act, 1956, (ii) providing credit not exceeding Rs. 50,000 ($ 1,112) for a business enterprise and Rs.1,25,000 ($ 2,778) for meeting the cost of a dwelling unit to any poor person, and (iii) not accepting public deposits.

Mutual Benefit MFIs: The State Cooperative Acts did not provide for an enabling framework for emergence of business enterprises owned, managed and controlled by the members for their own development. Several state governments therefore enacted the Mutually Aided Cooperative Societies (MACS) Act for enabling promotion of self-reliant and vibrant cooperative societies based on thrift and self-help. MACSs enjoy the advantages of operational freedom and virtually no interference from government because of the provision that societies under the Act cannot accept share capital or loan from the state government. Many of the SHG federations, promoted by NGOs and development agencies of the state government, have been registered as MACSs. RBI, even though they may be providing financial service to its members, does not regulate MACSs.

For Profit MFIs: NBFCs are companies registered under Companies Act, 1956 and regulated by RBI. Earlier, NBFCs were not regulated by RBI but in 1997 it was made obligatory for NBFCs to apply to RBI for a certificate of registration and for this certificate NBFCs were to have minimum net owned funds of Rs.25 lakh and this amount has been gradually increased. RBI introduced a new regulatory framework for those NBFCs who want to accept public deposits. All the NBFCs accepting public deposits are subjected to capital adequacy requirements and prudential norms. There are only few MFIs in the country that are registered as NBFCs. Many MFIs view NBFCs a more preferred legal form and are aspiring to be NBFCs but they are finding it difficult to meet the requirements stipulated by RBI. The number of NBFCs having exclusive focus on microfinance is negligible.

Capital Requirements

NGO-MFIs, non-profit companies MFIs, and mutual benefit MFIs are regulated by the specific act in which they are registered and not by the RBI. These are therefore not subjected to minimum capital requirements, prudential norms etc. NGO-MFIs to become NBFCs are required to have a minimum entry capital requirement of Rs.20 million ($0.5 million). As regards prudential norms, NBFCs are required to achieve capital adequacy of 12 per cent and to maintain liquid assets of 15 per cent on public deposits.

Foreign Investment

Foreign investment by way of equity permitted in NBFC-MFIs is subject to a minimum investment of $500,000. In view of the minimum level of investment, only two NBFCs are reported to have been able to raise the foreign investment. However, a large number of NGOs in the development-empowerment are receiving foreign fund by way of grants. At present, over Rs.40,000 million ($889 million) every year flows into India to NGOs for a whole range of activities including microfinance. In a way, foreign donors have facilitated the entry of NGOs into microfinance operations through their grant assistance.

Deposit Mobilisation

Not for profit MFIs are barred by the RBI from mobilising any type of savings. Mutual benefit MFIs can accept savings from their members. Only NBFC-MFIs rated by approved credit rating agencies are permitted to accept deposits. The quantum of deposits that could be raised is linked to their net owned funds.

Borrowings

Initially, bulk of the funds required by MFIs for onlending to their clients were met by apex institutions like NABARD, SIDBI and RMK. In order to widen the range of lending institutions to MFIs, the RBI has roped in commercial banks and RRBs to extend credit facilities to MFIs since February 2000. Both public and private banks in the commercial sector have extended sizeable loans to MFIs at interest rate ranging from 8 to 11 per cent per annum. Banks have been given operational freedom to prescribe their own lending norms keeping in view the ground realities. The intention is to augment flow of microcredit through the conduit of MFIs. In regard to external commercial borrowings (ECB) by MFIs, not for profit MFIs are not permitted to raise ECB. The current policy effective from 31 January 2004, allows only corporates registered under the Companies Act to access ECB for permitted end-use in order to enable them to become globally competitive players.

Interest Rates

The interest rates are deregulated not only for private MFIs but also for formal banking sector. In the context of softening of interest rates in the formal banking sector, the comparatively higher interest rate (12 to 24 per cent per annum) charged by the MFIs has become a contentious issue. The high interest rate collected by the MFIs from their poor clients is perceived as exploitative. It is argued that raising interest rates too high could undermine the social and economic impact on poor clients. Since most MFIs have lower business volumes, their transaction costs are far higher than that of the formal banking channels. The high cost structure of MFIs would affect their sustainability in the long run.

Collateral Requirements

All the legal forms of MFIs have the freedom to waive physical collateral requirements from their clients. The credit policy guidelines of the RBI allow even the formal banks not to insist on any type of collateral and margin requirement for loans upto Rs. 50,000 ($1,100).

Regulation and Supervision

India has a large number of MFIs varying significantly in size, outreach and credit delivery methodologies. Presently, there is no regulatory mechanism in place for MFIs except for those that are registered as NBFCs. As a result, MFIs are not required to follow a standard rule and it has allowed many MFIs to be innovative in its approach particularly in designing new products and processes. But the flip-side is that the management and governance of MFIs generally remain weak, as there is no compulsion to adopt widely accepted systems, procedures and standards. Because the sector is unregulated, not much is known about their internal health. Following Committees have examined the roadmap for regulation and supervision of MFIs:

- Task Force (appointed by NABARD) *Report on Regulatory and Supervision Framework for MFIs* (1999).
- Working Group (constituted by Government of India) on Legal & Regulation of MFIs (2002).
- Informal Groups (appointed by RBI) on microfinance which studied issues relating to: (i) structure & sustainabilty, ii) funding (iii) regulations and (iv) capacity building (2003).
- Advisory Committee (appointed by RBI) on Flow of Credit to Agriculture and Related Activities from the Banking System (2004).

To address the issue of need for a differential regulatory framework, the latest Committee[1] sought answers to the following questions and concerns facing private MFIs in the country:

(i) Is non-existence of a separate differential regulatory framework a critical bottleneck hindering the growth of the sector?

(ii) Will MFIs be sustainable in medium-term? If so, will they continue to focus on the poor?

(iii) Is access to public/member deposit the key for their sustainability?

(iv) Can MFIs finance loans for income generation at interest rates, which are sustainable by the rural poor?

(v) Is it possible to evolve commonly agreed standards for MFI sector covering performance, accounting and governance issues, which can open up possibilities of self-regulation?

(vi) Has the sector reached a critical mass where regulation becomes important?

The Committee observed that while a few of the MFIs have reached significant scales of outreach, the MFI sector as a whole is still in evolving phase as is reflected in wide debates ranging around: (i) desirability of NGOs taking up financial intermediation, (ii) unproven financial and organisational sustainability of the model, (iii) high transaction costs leading to higher rates of interest being charged to the poor clients, (iv) absence of commonly agreed performance, accounting and governance standards, (v) heavy expectations of low cost funds, including equity and the start up costs, etc.

The current debate on development of a regulatory system for the MFIs focusses on three stages. Stage one—to make the MFIs appreciate the need for certain common performance standards, stage two—making it mandatory for the MFIs to get registered with identified or designated institutions, and stage three—to encourage development of network of MFIs which could function as quasi self-regulatory organisations (SROs) at a later date or identifying a suitable organisation to handle the regulatory

1. Advisory Committee (appointed by RBI) on Flow of Credit to Agriculture and Related Activities from the Banking System (2004).

arrangements. The Committee recommended that while the MFIs may continue to work as wholesalers of microcredit by entering into tie-ups with banks and apex development institutions, more experimentation is needed to be be sure about the sustainability of the MFI model. Such experimentation needs to be encouraged in areas where banks are still not meeting adequate credit demand of the rural poor.

In regard to offering thrift products, the Committee felt that, while the NGO-MFIs can continue to extend microcredit services to their clients, they could play an important role in facilitating access of their clients to savings services from the regulated banks. As regards allowing NGO-MFIs to access deposits from public/clients, the Committee considers that in view of the need to protect the interests of depositors, they may not be permitted to accept public deposits unless they comply with the extant regulatory framework of the RBI. As no depositors' interest is involved where they do not accept public deposits, the RBI need not regulate MFIs.

As regards the high interest rates being charged by the MFIs, the Committee felt that the lenders to MFIs may ensure that these institutions adopt a 'cost-plus–reasonable-margin' approach in determining the rates of interest on loans to clients.

Private MFIs in India, barring a few exceptions, are still fledgling efforts and therefore unregulated. Their outreach is uneven in terms of geographical spread. They serve microfinance clients with varying quality and using different operating models. Regulatory framework should be considered only after the sustainability of MFI model as a banking enterprise for the poor is clearly established. Experimentation of MFI model needs to be encouraged especially in areas where formal banks are still not meeting adequate credit demand of the rural poor.

7 Emerging Innovative and Creative Approaches for Financial Inclusion

Business Facilitators and Business Correspondents

It is a fact that access to financial services is indispensible for inclusive growth and poverty reduction. One of the major role players in extending financial services accessibility to the poor is the banker. But the banker has certain limitations in extending financial services to the poor due to commercial viability. Opening a bank branch in village or cover some villages may not give sufficient business to the banker. As the clients of microfinance seekers are scattered over remote and distant places and the size of the business they have are constraining to the banker in offering financial services conveniently and cause hindrances to the process of extending financial services to the poor. This is also a universal truth that 'where there is a problem there is a solution(s) always!'. When all concerned stakeholders especially, bankers, development thinkers, NGOs and policymakers together brainstormed, and a vivid and feasible strategy emerged i.e., to rope in post offices which have wide and huge network covering every nook and corner of the country. Perhaps which was underutilised for extending financial services, despite post offices too offering important financial services like, recurring deposits (RD), money orders, insurance, trading of long-term financial securities like National Saving Certificates (NSCs), Kisan Vikas Patra (KVP) etc. The post office system is one of the viable options to provide financial services to the poor. Apart from post offices, retired government employees, school teachers, army personnel, NGOs, etc., who can play an instrumental role in extending financial services to the poor. This whole process ultimately led to a system *viz.*, business facilitators (BF) and business correspondents (BC) model for extending microfinancial services to the poor. The RBI has evolved framework and *modus operandi* for BFs and BCs which is outlined below.

Under the 'business facilitator' model, banks may use intermediaries, such as, NGOs/farmers' clubs, cooperatives, community based organisations, IT enabled rural outlets of corporate entities, post offices, insurance agents, well functioning *panchayats*, village knowledge centres, agri clinics/agri business centres, krishi vigyan kendras (KVKs) and Khadi & Village Industries Commission/Board (KVIC/KVIB) units, depending on the comfort level of the bank, for providing facilitation services. Such services may include: (i) identification of borrowers and fitment of activities; (ii) collection and preliminary processing of loan applications including verification of primary information/data; (iii) creating awareness about savings and other products and education and advice on managing money and debt counselling; (iv) processing and submission of applications to banks; (v) promotion and nurturing self-help groups (SHGs)/joint liability groups (JLGs); (vi) post-sanction monitoring; (vii) monitoring and handholding of SHGs/JLGs/credit groups/others; and (viii) follow-up for recovery.

As these services are not intended to involve the conduct of banking business by business facilitators, no approval is required from RBI for using the above intermediaries for facilitation of the services indicated above.

Business Correspondent Model: Eligible Entities and Scope of Activities

Under the 'business correspondent' model, NGOs/MFIs set up under Societies Registration Act (1860)/Indian Trust Act (1882), Mutually Aided Cooperative Societies Act, and Section 25 of Companies Act (1956), registered NBFCs not accepting public deposits and post offices may act as business correspondents. Banks may conduct 'thorough due diligence' on such entities keeping in view the indicative parameters given in Annex 3.2 of the RBI *Report of the Internal Group to Examine Issues Relating to Rural Credit and Micro-Finance* (July 2005). In engaging such intermediaries as business correspondents, banks should ensure that they are well established, enjoying good reputation and having the confidence of the local people. Banks may give wide publicity in the locality about the intermediary engaged by them as business correspondent and take measures to avoid being misrepresented.

In addition to activities listed under the business facilitator model, the scope of activities to be undertaken by the business correspondents will include: (i) disbursal of small value credit, (ii) recovery of principal/ collection of interest, (iii) collection of small value deposits, (iv) sale of microinsurance/mutual fund products/pension products/other third party products, and (v) receipt and delivery of small value remittances/other payment instruments.

The activities to be undertaken by the business correspondents would be within the normal course of the bank's banking business, but conducted through the entities indicated above at places other than the bank premises. Accordingly, in furtherance of the objective of increasing the outreach of the banks for microfinance, in public interest, the Reserve Bank hereby permits banks to formulate a scheme for using the entities indicated in paragraph above as business correspondents. Banks should ensure that the scheme formulated and implemented is in strict compliance with the objectives and parameters laid down in this circular.

Payment of Commission/Fees for Engagement of Business Facilitators/Correspondents

Banks may pay reasonable commission/fee to the business facilitators/ correspondents, the rate and quantum of which may be reviewed periodically. RBI Master Circular DBOD.Dir.5/13.07.00/2005-06 dated July 1, 2005 may be treated as modified to that extent. The agreement with the business facilitators/correspondents should specifically prohibit them from charging any fee to the customers directly for services rendered by them on behalf of the bank.

Other terms and conditions for engagement of business facilitators and correspondents: As the engagement of intermediaries as business facilitators/correspondents involves significant reputational, legal and operational risks, due consideration should be given by banks to those risks. They should also endeavour to adopt technology-based solutions for managing the risk, besides increasing the outreach in a cost-effective manner. In formulating their schemes, banks may be guided by the recommendations made in the H.R. Khan Group Report as also the draft outsourcing guidelines released by Reserve Bank of India on December 6, 2005.

The arrangements with the business correspondents shall specify: Suitable limits on cash holding by intermediaries as also limits on individual customer payments and receipts, the requirement that the transactions are accounted for and reflected in the bank's books by end of day or next working day, and all agreements/contracts with the customer shall clearly specify that the bank is responsible to the customer for acts of omission and commission of the business facilitator/correspondent.

Redressal of grievances in regard to services rendered by business facilitators/correspondents: Banks should constitute grievance redressal machinery within the bank for redressing complaints about services rendered by business correspondents and facilitators and give wide publicity about it through electronic and print media. The name and contact number of designated grievance redressal officer of the bank should be made known and widely publicised. The designated officer should ensure that genuine grievances of customers are redressed promptly.

The grievance redressal procedure of the bank and the timeframe fixed for responding to the complaints should be placed on the bank's website. If a complainant does not get satisfactory response from the bank within 60 days from the date of his lodging the compliant, he will have the option to approach the Office of the Banking Ombudsman concerned for redressal of her/his grievance/s.

Compliance with know your customer (KYC) norms: Compliance with KYC norms will continue to be the responsibility of banks. Since the objective is to extend savings and loan facilities to the underprivileged and unbanked population, banks may adopt a flexible approach within the parameters of guidelines issued on KYC from time to time. The KYC guidelines issued (vide RBI circulars dated November 29, 2004 and August 23, 2005; *www.rbi.org.in*) provide sufficient flexibility to banks. In addition to introduction from any person with whom KYC guideline has been reached, banks can also rely on certificates of identification issued by the intermediary being used as banking correspondent, block development officer (BDO), head of village *panchayat*, postmaster of the post office concerned or any other public functionary, known to the bank.

Rangarajan Committee recommendations on BCs and BFs: Originally, only individuals who were insurance agents could act as BFs while no individuals could be placed as BC. This was later on widened to include retired officials, *viz.*, government servants like postmasters, school teachers and headmasters, who were considered eligible by RBI to act as BF. These people have a social standing in the local community and provide the needed comfort level to the banks. The banks may make use of this relaxation and use individuals as indicated above as BFs. Ex-servicemen in rural areas have the comforting support, not only of the institutionalised ex-servicemen's fraternity but also of their regional centres. These centres act as guide and monitor both serving and retired armed forces personnel. During discussions with the Committee, it was indicated that ex-servicemen would volunteer to act as BCs in selected districts having a high concentration of ex-servicemen. The Committee is of the view that, initially, banks may appoint ex-servicemen and retired bank staff as their BFs. Further, after identification and placement of BFs, the banks should ensure that the banking awareness created and potential identified by BFs get translated into business propositions by providing suitable banking services in the area. This could be attempted through mobile outlets, which could visit the various locations, as per a scheduled programme, so as to purvey banking services to the excluded. To facilitate easy roll-out of this mobile banking model, banks should simplify and rationalise back-end processes and front-end procedures so that banking operations are made more customer-friendly.

Business correspondents: With increasing competition, banks are getting to be quite wary of the reducing margins available to them on financial intermediation. Banks are, therefore, hesitant to opt for increasing their physical presence in upcountry/remote locations entailing considerable capital/operating costs. Under the present dispensation, small value clients (depositors) in remote locations get very little preference in accessing financial services. It is, therefore, imperative to have in place an arrangement which can cater to a large number of clients having irregular and low value transactions ensuring at the same time full protection of the interests of depositors. Such an arrangement is possible only by having a

BC touchpoint in each of the six lakh plus villages serving as a customer interface at the front-end and backed by appropriate technology for its integration with the mainframe banking at the bank level.

Keeping this in view, the following recommendations for the BC model are made:

- In addition to the institutions presently allowed by RBI to function as BCs, individuals like locally settled retired Government servants like postmasters, school teachers, ex-servicemen and ex-bank staff whose relationship with the banking system, through a pension account, has already been established, may be permitted to act as BCs. Further, MF-NBFCs may be allowed to act as limited BCs of banks for only providing savings and remittance services. The Committee recognises the fact that technology has to be an integral part in sustaining outreach efforts through the BC model. Ultimately, banks should endeavour to have a BC touchpoint in each of the six lakh villages in the country. (This is discussed in detail later in the Report.) With a view to encouraging the BCs to widen their client-base, a suitable incentive mechanism may be formulated by the banks, appropriately linked to the number of accounts opened/transactions put through by the BCs. This will go a long way in stabilising the arrangement between the banks and the BCs. Further, banks may consider identifying BCs even in areas where they have their own branches, so as to supplement their efforts in widening outreach and addressing access issues. The Committee also observed that certain banks have already put in place intermediaries in the form of loan agents, who are akin to the BCs, (for undertaking loan disbursements and recovery) but in addition, also partake a certain element of risk/responsibility in case of loan defaults. In the initial stages, the BC model as envisaged by RBI could be implemented widely. In due course, when the BCs reach a higher level of turnover, they should bear commensurate financial responsibilities. Banks may, at their discretion, appoint any individual/institution of its choice as business correspondent, after exercising due diligence. This will facilitate greater acceptance of the BC model by banks. Funds may be provided to specialised institutions which provide capacity building inputs to BCs. Such funding support could be extended on priority basis to most excluded areas/sectors of the society and met out of the Financial Inclusion Promotion & Development Fund (FIPF).

- State Level Bankers' Committee (SLBC) convener banks may initiate discussion with their respective state governments regarding routing government payments through BCs using the smart card or other relevant technology on a pilot basis. SLBCs may undertake a study to identify organisations having the capacity to serve as customer service points and BC. In states like Andhra Pradesh and Kerala the village organisations (VOs) and Kudumbashree structures already exist and these can be used as customer service points. Training modules for BFs/BCs may be prepared in vernacular and in culture sensitive pictorial forms.

8 Role of NGOs in Financial Inclusion

Non-governmental organisations (NGOs) are an integral part of development process, they act as agents to create awareness, educate the poor, tag them into groups, nourishes them, stand along with them till the group stands and can sustain their business on their own. NGOs are efficient in rendering services, due to their inherent strengths like commitment to serve the poor, availability, professional acumenship of the personnel to serve the needy, and their network and accessibility to the poor makes them offer cost-effective services that are important for financial inclusion. An NGO in common terms may be defined as a body of people who come together to provide help to those who fail to accumulate sufficient resources to survive. In its most ambitious form, an NGO is a private, not-for-profit institution dedicated to influencing the working structure of government and ensure the greater welfare of all citizens.[1]

Non-Governmental Organisations

Definitions

According to Willets (2002) the term non-governmental organisation or NGO was accepted in 1945 in order to differentiate between, in UN Charter, intergovernmental specialised agencies and international private organisations. 'There is as yet no universally acceptable definition of non-governmental organisations. Yet defining non-governmental organisations is fundamentally less important and useful than understanding what they do, who their members are, and where their money comes from' (Simmons, 1998: 85).

---

1. Mustafa *et al.* (2000).

Willets (2002) agree with Simmons (1998) that there is no generally accepted definition of NGOs and concludes that the term has different connotations in different circumstances. He points out that the most significant characteristic of NGOs is their independence from any direct governmental control. In addition to that, Willets states that NGOs cannot be constituted as a political party or a criminal (in particular violent) group and that they are non-profit making organisations.

A United Nations document defines NGO as 'non-profit entity whose members are citizens or associations of citizens of one or more countries and whose activities are determined by the collective will of its members in response to the needs of the members of one or more communities with which the non-governmental organisations cooperate' (Simmons, 1998: 83).

According to D'Cruz (2002), NGOs are values-based organisations run by activists dedicated to their institution's values. He also (2002) points out those NGOs that have political nature and focus on advocacy, campaigning, direct action and the mobilisation of committed followers. In the opinion of Manuel Balza Duran and Davor Radojicic in the book titled *Corporate Social Responsibility and Nongovernmental Organizations* (2004), this definition is rather descriptive since it emphasises NGOs' characteristics and functions.

NGOs can also be defined as 'self-governing, private, not-for-profit organisations that are geared to improving the quality of life of disadvantaged people' (Vakil in Doh and Guay, 2003: 3). I found this definition the most appropriate because it points out that the rights of disadvantaged people is the main concern of these NGOs.

According to Simmons (1998) the ultimate goal of NGOs is to change societal norms, improve understanding, influence agendas, influence and implement policies and to solve problems in absence of adequate government action in order to give benefit to the public and private interests and interests of the 'non-represented' (future generations and planet).

Simmons also points out that advocacy, information gathering and analysis, information dissemination, generation of ideas and recommendation, monitoring, service delivery, mediation/facilitation, financing and grant making are the main functions of NGOs. He has summed up some of the most important features of an NGO such as goals, membership, personnel, funding and activities (see Table 8.1). In my opinion, the author provides an easy way to summarise the non-governmental issues.

Table 8.1

Profile of NGOs

Goals	*Membership and Personnel*	*Funding*	*Activities*
Ultimate goal? Change societal norms; improve understanding; influence agendas; influence policies; implement policies; solve problems absent adequate government action? For what/ whose benefit? Public interest (for single purpose or broad social benefit); private interests of members or groups of firms; interests of the 'non-represented' (future generations, planet)?	Members? Individuals, organisations? Quasy-governmental, voluntary, open to everyone, etc.? Geographic range? Community, subnational, national, regional, transnational personnel? Undifferentiated (voluntary), expert and professional, invited, elected, managerial?	Sources? Dues/assessments, donations, foundations, governments (grants or contracts), intergovernmental organisations (IGOs)?	Function? Advocacy, information gathering and analysis; information dissemination; generation of ideas and recommendations; monitoring and watching role; service delivery; mediation/ facilitation; financing and grant making? Area of operation? Community, subnational, national, regional, international? Targets? Public, consumers, governments, IGOs, non-state actors (including other NGOs, private actors)?

Above, has been briefly discussed many interpretations of the definition of non-governmental organisations. Vakil's (in Doh and Guay, 2003: 3) defintion: 'self-governing, private, not-for-profit organisations that are geared to improving the quality of life of disadvantaged people', is the most suitable. Hence, it could be of interest to have a brief discussion regarding NGO.

History of Non-Governmental Organisations

According to Skjelsbaek in Spar and La Mure (2003) the roots of NGOs can be traced to the 16th century and Rosicrucian Order (Egyptian educational organisation) that was characterised with resource mobilisation, information provision and activism to advocate for changes. Spar and La Mure (2003), also consider anti-slavery groups in the 1770s as NGOs.

According to Simmons (1998: 84), 'Non-governmental organisations have long played a key role in forcing leaders and policymakers to pay attention'. He further points out that British and Foreign Anti-Slavery Society in the early 1800s played an important role regarding government action on the slave trade and that Anglo-Oriental Society for the Suppression of the Opium Trade contributed to the antidrug movement in the early 1900s.

According to Simmons (1998) NGOs were largely responsible for inserting human rights issues in the UN Charter in 1945. Clark (1995) states that the formal NGOs achieved consultative status in the Economic and Social Council (ECOSOC) in 1946 as a concession to US NGOs and the Roosevelt administration that wanted to increase the support for the United Nations. Clark also states that NGOs proliferated in the second half of the past century. Their zenith of NGOs was reached in 1997 when one of the NGOs received the Nobel Prize for the conclusion of banning landmines treaty despite the opposition of the United States.

van Tuijl (1999) acknowledges that NGOs influenced the formulation of many United Nations treaties and conventions such as Convention on the Elimination of All Forms of Discrimination against Women (CEDAW) in 1979 and the Convention on the Rights of the Child (CRC) in 1989. He opines that NGOs' role was particularly significant in the past 25 years regarding issues such as poverty, gender equality, peace, sustainable development and human rights. According to him there were 50,000 NGOs worldwide in 1993. According to Simmons (1998), more than 1,500 NGOs were accredited at the United Nations Conference on the Environment and Development in Rio de Janeiro in 1992.

Classification of Non-Governmental Organisations

Gordenker/Weiss in Doh and Guay (2003) classify NGOs into two main groups: (i) operational NGOs that provide social services such as education, health or human relief, and (ii) advocacy NGOs that lobby governments, multinational companies and intergovernmental organisations. According to van Tuijl (1999) this approach differentiates social, economic and cultural rights from civil and political rights.

Vakil in van Tuijl (1999) uses the level of operations of NGOs as the base for the distinction between international, national, regional and community-based NGOs.

Simmons (1998) classifies NGOs as community-based, subnational, national, regional and transnational according to the geographic range of membership and personnel and the area of operation of their activities.

In my opinion, it is not an important issue to classify NGOs. The most important task is to investigate what they actually do. This matter will be further discussed below.

Non-Governmental Organisations' Role

As Simmons (1998: 84) put it, 'Until recently, non-governmental organisations clustered in developed and democratic nations; now groups sprout from Lima to Beijing: They are changing societal norms, challenging national governments, and linking up with counterparts in powerful transnational alliances.' He emphasises that NGOs are present in the areas previously dominated by the state such as arms control, banking and trade.

Simmons (1998) points out that NGOs' significant role is to translate international agreements and norms into domestic realities. He uses the example of Amnesty International and its capacity to draw attention to violations of the United Nations Declaration of Human Rights.

Van Tuijl (1999) summarises NGOs' support of the development of the United Nations system of human rights in these three functions: standards setting, monitoring and implementation. According to him, NGOs pressured the World Bank to create the World Bank's Inspection Panel in 1993 that monitored the Bank's activities and projects.

As per Fri (1992), 'Non-governmental organisations identify issues that belong on the official agenda, define policies to treat with these issues, and organise to bring pressure to bear on the system to pay attention to their ideas'. He points out that NGOs act as action agents to deliver programmes that officialdom cannot manage. Clark (1995) perceives

Amnesty International (AI), the International Commission of Jurists (ICJ), the International Committee of the Red Cross (ICRC) and Human Rights Watch (HRW) as organisations that try to influence governments by applying general human rights principles.

According to Doh and Guay (2003) few research efforts have been directed toward exploration of the influence NGOs have on corporate conduct. These authors propose a typology to classify NGOs' involvement in international labour and environmental standards and they identify four broad types of codes, classified by their principal sponsoring organisations: (1) international agreements signed by governments; (2) international codes sponsored by intergovernmental organisations; (3) international codes sponsored by corporate groups; and (4) international codes sponsored by not-for-profit NGOs.

Doh and Guay (2003) describe the role of NGOs in the formulation of international codes sponsored by government (i.e., North American Free Trade Agreement (NAFTA), World Trade Organization (WTO), Free Trade Agreement of the Americas (FTAA)) as less and their role in agreement compliance as moderate. They also view the role of NGOs regarding the formulation of international codes sponsored by intergovernmental organisations (UN Global Compact, ILO declaration of Principles concerning Multinational Enterprises and Social Policy, OECD Guidelines for Multinational Enterprises) as low and their role regarding agreement compliance as low to moderate.

According to Doh and Guay (2003: 9), 'The role of non-governmental organisations in formulation of codes and agreements sponsored by corporate and industry associations are difficult to generalise. If we consider these associations themselves as non-governmental organisations, then the role is high. If we consider only non-corporate non-governmental organisations, the role is probably moderate. In either case, the non-governmental organisations role in agreement compliance is, in many cases, moderate-high, since the role of advocacy non-governmental organisations is to serve as an oversight check on corporations' compliance with their own publicly-touted standards and commitments'. They use World Business Council for Sustainable Development (WBCSD), Global Environmental Management Initiative (GEMI) and ISO 14000 as examples of international codes sponsored by industrial and corporate associations.

Finally, Doh and Guay (2003) give examples of Social Accountability International (SAI) SA8000, Rugmark and Forest Stewardship Council (FSC) as international codes sponsored by not-for-profit NGOs and describe the role of NGO in agreement formulation and agreement compliance as high. According to these authors SA8000 is a human rights organisation that addresses child labour, forced labour, health and safety issues, compensation and working hours, discrimination, discipline, free association and collective bargaining.

They further point out, 'A partnership among development and human rights non-governmental organisations, companies exporting carpets from India, the Indo-German Export Promotion Council, and UNICEF-India set up a project to devise and regulate a special label for hand-knotted carpets made without the use of child labour. The Rugmark process includes loom and factory monitoring, consumer labeling, and running schools for former child workers. By agreeing to adhere to Rugmark's "no child labour" guidelines, and by permitting random inspections of carpet looms, manufacturers receive the right to put the Rugmark label on their carpets, which provides assurance that a carpet was not produced by children. As an non-governmental organisations, Rugmark almost single-handedly developed and implemented this code.'

India has been experimenting since 1960s with flexible systems, giving a lot of freedom to the NGOs to set up self-help groups (SHGs). The Seventh Five Year Plan (1985-1990) had emphasised the need to closely associate NGOs with rural development programmes, particularly poverty alleviation. A pilot project for linking SHGs with banks was introduced in 1992 by National Bank for Agriculture and Rural Development (NABARD)[2] to encourage thrift and savings amongst the rural poor and to supplement their credit needs through the banking system.

Women, especially those belong to the weaker sections of society have limited access to resources or employment opportunities. They live in conditions that do not permit them to meet bare consumption needs. Even the money earned by them from hard physical labour is not controlled by them. Institutional credit is difficult to access as women rarely have any property rights to mortgage or collateral to offer, and they have to depend

2. National Bank for Agriculture and Rural Development (1999).

on moneylenders for their production-cum-consumption needs. This entraps them into a vicious cycle of perpetual poverty and indebtedness. The men do not welcome NGOs/SHGs working for the upliftment of women as an economically independent woman is perceived a threat to their male dominance. That a woman's savings/earnings are generally used for the family is conveniently forgotten!

Table 8.2

International Codes

International Government Agreements	*International Codes Sponsored by IGOs*	*International Codes Sponsored by Industrial and Corporate Associations*		*International Codes Sponsored by Not-for-Profit NGOs*
Examples	North American Free Trade Agreement, World Trade Organization, Free Trade Agreement of the Americas	UN Global Compact, ILO Declaration of Principles concerning Multinational Enterprises and Social Policy, OECD Guidelines for MNEs	World Business Council for Sustainable Development (WBCSD), Global Environmental Management Initiative (GEMI), ISO 14000	Social Accountability International SA8000, Rugmark, Forest Stewardship Council (FSC)
Representative list of NGOs involved	Environmental: (Sierra Club, World Wildlife Fund/Worldwide Fund for Nature -WWF), Labour: (AFL-CIO, UAW), Corporate: (US Chamber of Commerce, National Association of Manufacturers)	Labour: (Trade Union Advisory Committee to the OECD, International Confederation of Free Trade Unions), Environmental: (WWF, World Resources Institute, IUCN – the World Conservation Union), Human Rights: (Amnesty International, Human Rights Watch)	National chambers of commerce, national technical standards groups (American National Standards Institute), national industry associations, International Organisation for Standardization	Labour: (The International Textile, Garment and Leather Workers' Federation, Union Network Intl.), Development: (Save the Children), Human Rights: (Amnesty International), Environmental: (National Resources Defense Council, National Wildlife Federation, WWF)

NGOs keen on forming women SHGs should have expertise in education, rural health and hygiene, tribal development, etc. A large number of case studies on women SHGs reveals that individually these women had accepted their poverty and miseries as due to divine fate or destiny and had little hope of improving their life. But the formation of SHGs has led to growing awareness, education and availability of information has led to confidence-building and the ability to handle complex issues.

There are a large number of NGOs that have undertaken the task of financial intermediation. Majority of these NGOs are registered as a trust or a society. Many NGOs felt that combining financial intermediation with their core competency activity of social intermediation is not the right path. Therefore, they have been performing non-financial functions like sociocultural and capacity building activities, facilitate training of SHGs, undertake internal audit, promote new groups, etc. NGOs, which work with deprived or disadvantaged sections, typically do so with a conception of benefits rather than rights. The functioning methodology of NGOs, most often, is project based, engaged with time-bound programmes of opportunity creation in specific spheres. Secondly, most NGOs work closely with and are dependent for funding upon state agencies, international development agencies and multilateral organisations. In group-lending programmes, the functions of screening, monitoring and enforcement of repayment, to a large extent, are transferred from the bank's agent to the borrowers, that is, the group members themselves. Compared with socially and physically distant bank agents, group members can perform all such functions more effectively and at a lower cost. The group members are able to access complex and sensitive information just like informal lenders. Transaction costs are thus reduced. The mismatch between demand and supply is minimised because the group uses the money according to its own needs. Flexibility of loan repayment is also enhanced, as the repayment schedule of the individual to the group need not match that of the group to the bank. It is not the rigidity of banks but their constraints due to high transaction costs and risks because of asymmetric information, that they cannot extend such credit to individual borrowers. The impact of SHGs has relatively been more pronounced on social aspects than on the economic aspects. One of the major contributions of microfinance is towards women's empowerment, for this credit also goes to NGOs. As women's groups exclusively dominate the SHGs, their empowerment both on the economic and social fronts is one of the greatest opportunities in the mainstream of development activities. Opportunities for earning through deposits and higher off-farm activities improve their disposable income. Consequently, family incomes substantially increased. There are tremendous social changes too. The women command more respect, get their due affection and rightful place in the family. Their involvement in family decisions has been substantially enhanced. In addition to meeting financial requirements, the SHG has become a platform for exchange of experiences and ideas beyond social participation by members, especially women. The SHGs are making the process of development participatory and democratic and are displaying their sustainability even in the absence of any subsidy. However, interventions by NGOs' in themselves are too small to make a significant difference in the national context. While there is a national policy to support priority sector lending and some schemes have begun to partner credit with training and group action, what is missing is a national institution responsible for really pushing the partnership of urban microcredit and self-help across India's cities. A very important step towards making credit the core component is the creation of an Apex Bank for Urban Development (ABUD). An apex bank's role could be to act as a nodal national-level agency for urban microcredit, learning in part from the success of NABARD's experience in rural microcredit.

The Role of NGOs as Catalysts/Facilitators in Promoting Microfinance

It is intendend that the involvement of NGOs in financial inclusion inculcate financial discipline amongst poor by mobilising their savings and making the SHGs active. Thus, banks can be pulled in automatically for enhancing accessibility of financial services to the poor. The NGOs would also be helpful to create a social pressure for regular payment of installments, which will further encourage banks to increase their lending to the SHGs. Moreover the actual management of SHGs will continue to be in the hands of members of the group especially women. They will be the major stakeholders in the entire operation of financial inclusion process, thus, it will contribute in making financial inclusion a success. It is projected that the demand for financial services by poor is bound to increase in the future and NGOs

It was expected in addition to the credit, the poor will be better off if, some credit plus services particularly marketing support for value added products are provided by the NGOs which can certainly ensure the success of inclusive growth.

Part II

Specialised Financial Institutions (SC/ST/BC/FDC) and Financial Inclusion

9 Specialised Financial Institutions for Financial Inclusion

Introduction

One of the major concerns of Indian planning has been the welfare and development of the weaker sections of society and among them especially that of the scheduled castes who constitute nearly 17 per cent of the total population. The scheduled castes are not a homogeneous group in social, educational or economic terms. It is a category, which comprises a number of communities hierarchically ranked. The scheduled castes have been at the lowest end of the Hindu (social) caste hierarchy based on birth. In the past, the social system ascribed occupations to this group which were not only low in social ordering but were also characterised by very low productivity. With ascription on the basis of birth, the system did not permit occupational mobility. Consequently, this group remained at the lowest rung of the economic hierarchy as well.

The strategy adopted for development of the scheduled castes since Sixth Five Year Plan (1980-1985) comprises:

(a) *Special Component Plan (SCP):* The Special Component Plan (SCP) is designed to channelise the flow of outlays and benefits from the general sectors in the plans of the states and the Central Ministries for development of scheduled castes, at least, in proportion to their population to the total population. Twenty-one states and three Union Territories are formulating their respective SCPs. The SCPs of the states are supplemented with Special Central Assistance (SCA) with a view to creating a multiplier effect and help filling the gaps, which the normal financial flows from the Central and State Plans are not able to provide.

(b) *Special Central Assistance (SCA):* Special Central Assistance (SCA) to Special Component Plan of the states/UTs for scheduled caste people is linked to Government of India's strategy for the socioeconomic development of these people. The centrally sponsored scheme the is most important programme of the Ministry of Social Justice and Empowerment for the alleviation of the poverty among scheduled caste people. The underlying objective behind SCA which provides hundred per cent grant to states and UTs as an additive to their Special Component Plans is that it would be used to give an added thrust to the development programmes for scheduled caste people with reference to their occupational pattern and the need for increasing the productivity of and income from their limited assets by taking up family oriented schemes for them. The SCA is used to fill the critical gaps and vital missing inputs in family oriented income-generating schemes and through non-recurring items, so as to make the schemes more meaningful and effective.

(c) *Scheduled Castes Development Corporations (SCDCs):* In order to implement economic development programmes for scheduled castes living below the poverty line and specially to mobilise institutional credit and credit at confessional rate, the Government of India decided in 1978-79 to participate in the share capital of Scheduled Castes Development Corporations (SCDCs) in the states/UTs with significant SC population. The centrally sponsored scheme for participating in the share equity of the SCDCs in ratio of 49:51 was introduced in 1979. At present, SCDCs are functioning in 26 states/ UTs, include 9 SCDCs that serve the needs of both SCs and STs. These corporations have been established with the basic motive of implementing welfare oriented programmes for downtrodden and to lift them from the poverty line not merely quantitatively but also in qualitative terms.

The main functions of SCDCs include identification of eligible SC/ST families and motivating them to undertake economic development schemes, sponsoring the schemes to financial institutions for credit support, providing financial assistance in the form of margin money at low rate of interest, providing subsidy out of the funds made available to the states under the scheme of SCA to SCP of the states with a view to reducing the repayment liability and providing necessary tie-up with other poverty alleviation programmes. For facilitating loans to the scheduled castes, the SCDCs tie up with the local banks, National Scheduled Castes Finance and Development Corporation (NSFDC) and National Safai Karamcharis Finance and Development Corporation (NSKFDC). Thus, the SCDCs are playing an important role in providing credit and missing inputs by way of margin money loans and subsidy to the target group.

The SCDCs finance employment oriented schemes covering: (i) agriculture and allied activities including minor irrigation, (ii) small scale industry, (iii) transport, and (iv) trade and services sector.

It is no doubt true that the SCDCs have been performing a crucial role in development of the scheduled castes, it is, however, necessary to assess their viability and sustainability under the present financial structure. This research study, therefore, has made a critical examination of the functioning of the SCDCs at macro level with special focus on their viability and sustainability under the present financial structure, and suggest measures for their improvement. The objectives of the study are given below.

Objectives

The specific objectives of the Part II of this book are to:

i. Discuss the viability and sustainability of the SCDCs in the context of their current financial health and mode of functioning in terms of their resources, level of utilisation of loan disbursement capacity, recoveries of the loans and interest thereon, expenditure pattern, level of operations required to break even in order to incur loss, present net worth in relation to paid capital etc.

ii. Outline the administrative and institutional arrangements of the SCDCs for development of the scheduled castes and their financial inclusion.

iii. Map out the nature of convergence that takes place in implementation of the SCDC programmes with the SCP, SCA and other poverty alleviation programmes and covering financial inclusion.

iv. Present the social, economic and technical viability of the schemes financed by the SCDCs for development of the scheduled castes, and difficulties in recovery of the loans financed by the SCDCs.

v. Assess the impact of various schemes being implemented by the SCDCs on the target group in terms of increase in income level, employment generation, creation of assets, diversification and mobility in the occupation pattern; and

vi. Augment a future roadmap for SCDCs to make them viable, sustainable by way of improving their capacity to mobilise more resources, improving their recoveries to an appropriate and achievable benchmark, rationalising of their functioning.

The SCDCs during the Ninth Five Year Plan (1997-2002) and also on the basis of Central and state share capital available with them. This is given in Table 9.1 below:

Table 9.1

Select State SCDCs

Name of the State	*No. of Beneficiaries during Ninth Plan (1997-2002)*	*State's Share Capital as on 31.3.2005 (in Crore)*	*Central Share Capital as on 31.3.2005 (in Crore)*	*Total Central and State Share Capital as on 1.3.2005 (in Crore)*
1. Andhra Pradesh	5,55,419	164.83	158.37	323.20
2. Uttar Pradesh	4,53,348	81.52	78.32	159.8
3. Tamil Nadu	4,16,826	47.17	45.32	92.4
4. West Bengal	4,06, 630	48.72	56.05	104.7
5. Rajasthan	3,35,215	6.70	6.44	13.1
6. Orissa	1,95,458	6.09	6.05	12.1
7. Karnataka	1,01,082	6.55	6.29	12.8
8. Maharashtra	73,100	55.37	53.20	108.5

Source: Prasad and Teki (2006).

As shown in Table 9.1, Andhra Pradesh state has highest beneficiaries, while Maharashtra has least number of beneficiaries, during the Ninth Plan. Andhra Pradesh by and large has been leader in all aspects of the above shown table, because of such sizable efforts the financial inclusion and quality of life of poor people in Andhra Pradesh is more satisfactory.

10 Profile of the Scheduled Castes

Introduction

Development is essentially a process of change initiated with an objective of improving the quality of life. For certain sections of society, who are considered as weaker sections, the process of change would aim at bringing them into the mainstream of socioeconomic system. Left to itself the process of change even if initiated by an external stimulus, would not be sustainable for these sections.

India is a welfare state, committed to the welfare and development of its people in general and of vulnerable sections in particular. Preamble, Directive Principles of State Policy, Fundamental Rights and specific sections, namely Articles 38, 39 and 46 in the Constitution of India stand testimony to its people. As a matter of strategy the Government of India has resorted to planned development for minimising inequality in income, status and opportunities for its people. This strategy is directed to secure distributive justice and utilisation of economic resources to subserve common good. Programmes are directed to promote educational and economic interests of weaker sections in general and those of scheduled castes (SCs), scheduled tribes (STs), backward classes and minorities, in particular to avoid injustice and exploitation. Development planning is introduced to improve the quality of life of the people.

It is against the national honour to leave a very large segment of the population, mostly belonging to the SCs, in sub-human state, exploitation, financial exclusion and poverty. The amelioration and integration of the SCs with the mainstream should, therefore, be taken as a challenge to the nation. Effective steps must be taken for improving and bringing them on par with the others. They should get their due share in the fruits of overall development and feel a sense of participation in economic, social and political activities. The goal should be to improve the quality of life and ensure them human dignity.

One of the major concerns of Indian planning has been the welfare and development of the weaker sections of society and among them especially that of the SCs who constitute nearly 17 per cent of the total population. With a view to understanding the various efforts that have been made to ensure rapid development of the SCs, it is perhaps necessary to first understand the socioeconomic characteristics of the scheduled castes.

Scheduled Castes

The SC population, according to 2001 Census, was 16.7 crore constituting 16.2 per cent of the total population. They are primarily concentrated in Uttar Pradesh (3.51 crore), West Bengal (1.84 crore), Tamil Nadu (1.18 crore), Andhra Pradesh (1.23 crore) and Bihar (1.3 crore). These five states account for 53.36 per cent of the SC population. Uttar Pradesh has the highest concentration of the SC population in terms of the absolute number; whereas Punjab occupies first position in terms of percentage of SCs to the state population.

The habitations of the scheduled castes are generally scattered in parts of villages or small villages all over the country. The SCs are not a homogeneous group in social, educational or economic terms. It is a category, which comprises a number of communities hierarchically ranked. They are economically the worst sufferers. In the year 1999-2000, the percentage of SC population below the poverty line in rural areas was 38.47 as compared to the all-India percentage of 27.09. It has been rightly said that, 'no nation can progress leaving aside a large chunk of the population struggling hard for existence under the stress of economic, educational and social disabilities'.

The economic backwardness of the SCs is due to the injustice, exploitation and oppression suffered from other castes for centuries in the past. They were excluded from access to property rights, civil rights, and education except the labour to the castes above them. Their deprivation became more severe as they also suffered from physical and social segregation from the rest of the Hindu society through the institution of untouchability. It is this institutionalised and multiple exclusion of the low caste untouchables from access to economic rights, civil rights and human development, which had severe consequence to their economic conditions. SCs had been made use of for the economic uplift and wellbeing of higher castes in society. From time immemorial they worked under chains as slaves. They were sold like commodities for hard labour and betterment of others. This continued for centuries together. As a result, these groups had been suffering from social discrimination, economic deprivation and educational backwardness.

With a view to enabling these groups to join mainstream development, various protective and developmental measures have been taken up. These measures relate to:

(i) Protective—as enshrined in constitution and enactments by legislation; (ii) Developmental by providing economic benefits through various schemes/programmes; and (iii) Positive discrimination—in education and employment facilities etc.

The term 'scheduled castes' appeared for the first time in the Government of India Act, 1935. In April 1936, the British government issued the Government of India (Scheduled Castes) Order, 1936, specifying certain castes, races and tribes as scheduled castes in the then provinces of Assam, Bengal, Bihar, Bombay, Central Provinces & Berar, Madras, Orissa, Punjab and United Provinces. Prior to that, these castes were generally known as the 'Depressed Classes'. The Depressed Classes were systematically categorised in 1931 by J.H. Hutton, the Census Commissioner of India. The list of scheduled castes issued in 1936 was a continuation of the earlier list of depressed classes. The list drawn in 1950 was a revised version of the list of SCs under the Government of India (Scheduled Castes) Order, 1936. The test applied was the social, educational and economic backwardness arising out of the historical custom of the untouchability. After the Constitution came into force, the lists of SCs were notified by the President, in accordance with the provisions of Article 341 of the Constitution.

Although 1,086 SCs have been specified in 28 states/Union Territories, there are in fact only 470 individual castes belonging to the SC category. Bulk of the SCs belong to a few numerically predominant castes. For example, the Chamar caste, largely confined to Uttar Pradesh, Bihar, Rajasthan and Haryana, constitutes 27 per cent of the SCs in India. In several states, the three largest SCs account for over 55 per cent of all SC population. For instance, in Andhra Pradesh 59 scheduled castes have been notified. But the SCs like Madiga, Mala and Adi Andhra constitute 91 per cent of the total SC population in the state. Similarly, in Uttar Pradesh, where population of the SCs constitute 23 per cent of the total population of the SCs in India, the three SCs namely, the Chamar (54.61%), Pasi (13.9%) and Dhobi (6.2%) constitute 75 per cent of the state's SC population.

The number of states, districts and blocks in the country having 20 per cent or more SC population is shown in Table 10.1.

Table 10.1

Number of States, Districts and Blocks in the Country Having 20 Per cent or More SC Population

Percentage of Scheduled Castes Population	*In Number of*		
	Blocks	*Districts*	*States*
20 - 30	1016	210	17
30 - 40	257	88	13
40 - 50	64	34	09
50 & above	36	22	09

Source: Selected Statistics on SCs, Government of India, Ministry of Home Affairs, 1984.

Increase in Literacy

The literacy statistics of the last decennial census offers significant positive trends of social transformation for both males and females belonging to SC population. A comparative statement indicating the percentage trends is given in Table 10.2.

Table 10.2

Literacy

(Percentage)

Year	Total			Scheduled Castes		
	Male	Female	Total	Male	Female	Total
1991	64.13	39.29	52.21	49.91	23.76	37.41
2001	75.00	54.00	65.00	66.64	41.90	54.69

Source: Prasad and Teki (2009).

Table 10.2 shows that the literacy rate among the SCs increased by 17.28 per cent over the last decennial whereas the total literacy rate logged at 12.79 per cent. In terms of gender analysis, the SC females recorded a magnificent 18.14 per cent increase as against comprehensive average of 14.71 per cent. This phenomenon indicates reduction in the literacy gap between the general and the SC population.

Reduction of Poverty

The percentage of SCs and total population below poverty line during 1993-94 and 1999-2000 is as under Table 10.3.

Table 10.3

Percentage of Total and Scheduled Castes Population Living below Poverty Line in 1993-94 and 1999-2000

Year	Total		Scheduled Castes	
	Rural	Urban	Rural	Urban
1993-1994	38.20	39.09	48.11	49.48
1999-2000	27.09	23.62	36.62	38.47

Source: Prasad and Teki (2009).

The above table indicates steady decline of poverty among all sections of the society including SCs. The incidence of urban poverty among the SCs has witnessed a steep decline.

Incidence of Poverty

Table 10.4 presents the poverty ratio of SCs, STs and others (non-SCs/STs for 1983-84, 1993-94 and 1999-2000 at the all-India level (the poverty estimates are based on methodology used by the Planning Commission to estimate the poor).

Table 10.4

All-India Poverty Ratio

	All-India Poverty Ratio (Rural)				*All-India Poverty Ratio (Urban)*		
	1983-84	*1993-94*	*1999-2000*		*1983-84*	*1993-94*	*1999-2000*
SCs	58.1	48.1	36.2	SCs	56.5	49.9	38.6
STs	63.8	52.2	45.9	STs	54.2	42.4	34.8
Other	37	31.3	21.6	Other	39.1	30.6	20.6
All	45.6	37.1	27.1	All	42.2	33.7	23.7
	Net Changes (Rural)				*Net Changes (Urban)*		
	1983-1993	*1993-2000*	*1983-2000*		*1983-1993*	*1993-2000*	*1983-2000*
SCs	-9.9	-11.9	-21.9	SCs	-6.6	-11.3	-17.9
STs	-11.6	-6.3	-17.9	STs	-11.8	-7.6	-19.4
Other	-5.7	-9.6	-15.3	Other	-8.5	-10	-18.5
All	-8.5	-10	-18.5	All	-8.5	-10	-18.5
	Annual Compound Rate (Rural)				*Annual Compound Rate (Urban)*		
	1983-1993	*1993-2000*	*1983-2000*		*1983-1993*	*1993-2000*	*1983-2000*
SCs	-1.9	-4.6	-2.9	SCs	-1.23	-4.2	-2.36
STs	-2	-2.1	-2	STs	-2.4	-3.2	-2.73
Other	-1.7	-5.9	-3.3	Other	-2.42	-6.4	-3.91
All	-2	-5.1	-3.2	All	-2.2	-5.7	-3.5

It is evident from Table 10.4 that the incidence of rural poverty among the SCs has declined from 58 per cent in 1983-84 to 48 per cent in 1993-94 and further went down to 36 per cent in 1999-2000. The percentage of rural poor reduced at the per annum rate of 2.9 per cent during 1983-2000—the rate of decline reduced to 1.9 per cent during 1983-1993 but improved significantly around 4.6 per cent during 1993-2000. The rate of decline thus is much higher during the 1990s. Due to the problem associated with 55th round of the NSS, this result has to be taken with lot of caution. In 1999-2000 the incidence of poverty was the highest among the agricultural labour households. The poverty level was about one-third among the remaining livelihood categories, namely self-employed in farm and non-farm households and non-farm labour in rural areas (Table 10.5).

The incidence of poor among the SC urban households has also declined from 56.5 per cent, in 1983-84 to 49.9 per cent in 1993-94 and further down to 38.6 per cent in 1999-2000, that is by about 2.36 per cent per annum during 1983/2000. The rate of decline is relatively high during the 1990s (4.2% per annum) compared with the 1980s (1.23%). The poverty level was highest among the casual labour (other labour and others), close to 60 per cent, followed by self-employed (45.28%) and regular wage and salaried (Table 10.5).

Table 10.5

Head Count Ratio for All-India Rural Population by Social Groups, Cross-Classified by Means of Livelihood: 1993-94-1999-2000

(Per cent)

Social Groups/ Household Type	*1993-94*				*1999-2000*			
	SCs	*STs*	*Others*	*All Social Groups*	*SCs*	*STs*	*Others*	*All Social Groups*
Self-employed in agriculture	35.34	43.30	22.40	26.08	30.11	39.97	17.97	21.62
Self-employed in non-agriculture	35.59	45.82	26.57	29.18	32.76	40.87	21.06	24.09
Agriculture labour	57.02	59.51	48.19	52.97	46.20	60.69	39.39	44.64
Other labour	38.34	46.25	31.99	35.82	32.82	44.22	22.59	27.79
Others	32.98	33.88	17.36	21.69	22.45	23.55	12.81	14.93
All	45.69	48.81	28.30	34.19	38.38	48.02	23.23	28.93

Source: Sundram and Tendulkar (2002).

The differences in the direction and rate of change in rural and urban poverty between SC and non-SC/ST needs to be noted. At all-India level the rural poverty has declined both for SC and others. During 1983/2000 the rural poverty among the non-SC/ST declined at slightly higher rate (3.3 %)

as compared with SC (2.9%). In the 1980s there is not much difference in the rate of decline among the two social groups. In 1990s the poverty among the SCs has declined at lower rate (4.6%) as compared with non-SC/ST group (5.9%). Thus decline in the rural poverty among the SCs is generally lower during overall period, 1983/2000, and also during the 1990s, while it is about the same during the 1980s.

The urban poverty among the SCs has also declined by less per annum rate compared with non-SC/ST during the overall period and also during the two periods. The urban poverty declined at per annum rate of 2.36 per cent for the SC as compared to 3.91 per cent for non-SC/ST during 1983/2000. Similarly urban poverty decline at the per annum rate of 1.23 per cent and 4.2 per cent during 1980s and 1990s respectively for SC as compared with 2.42 per cent and 6.4 per cent for non-SC/ST during 1980s and 1990s respectively.

Has the gap in the incidence of poverty between the SCs and others declined? In 1983-84, about 58 per cent of rural SCs were poor compared to 37 per cent for non-SC/ST. The disparity index was 00.37 (0 value of disparity index (modified by Amitabh Kundu) indicate equality while any value greater than 0 indicate disparity). Between 1983/1993, the disparity index (between SC and non-SC/ST) has declined by 6.95 per cent. During 1993/2000, however, disparity index has increased by 1 per cent. During the overall period 1983/2000, the disparity index had declined by 16.12 per cent. Thus, disparity in the rural poverty between SC and non-SC/ST has increased during the 1990s—the period which coincides with liberalisation of Indian economy. Unlike disparity in rural poverty, (which showed a decline during the overall period, 1983/2000, and during 1980s but increased during the 1990s), the disparities in the urban poverty have enhanced during overall period by about 26 per cent and also during both 1980s and 1990s.The rate of increase in the disparity was higher during the 1980s as compared to the 1990s.

To combine the trend in poverty and disparity, it is clear that in the case of rural poverty the decline in its incidence among the SCs was accompanied by decline in disparity in 1980s. During the 1990s, however, the decline in rural poverty among the SCs was associated with increase in disparity between SCs and non-SC/ST. In the case of urban poverty decline in urban poverty was associated with increase in disparity both during 1980s and 1990s and the overall period between 1983/2000.

One heartening feature of the above-stated results is that, notwithstanding their social and economic disadvantages, the SC households, the agricultural labour households and the double-disadvantaged group of agricultural labour households located among the SC population have experienced rates of reduction in all the three poverty indicators that have matched or bettered the poverty reduction experienced by the rural population on an average. The same is true for the urban SCs, the casual labour households and the casual labour households in the SC population in urban India. This fact holds the important message that the benefits of growth have indeed been accessed by the socially and economically disadvantaged groups in India.

Undernutrition and malnutrition: Besides poverty, the human development is also captured by some critical health indicators such as life expectancy, and indicators of mortality and morbidity. The life expectancy estimates (Thorat, 2004a) for 1998-99 and 1992-1993 bring out the situation of SCs *vis-à-vis* the non-SC/ST. In 1998-99, overall life expectancy at national level was 65 years, and about 62 years for SCs and 66 for non-SC/STs. In 1992-93, the life expectancy was 62, 63 and 58 years for all-India average, others and SCs respectively. Thus, in 1992-93 the life expectancy of SCs was lower compared to non-SC/ST by about five years and four years compared to the all-India average respectively. In 1998-99, the life expectancy of SCs was lower by four and three years compared with non-SC/STs and all-India average.

High mortality and morbidity (and hence the life expectancy) is closely associated with undernutrition and malnutrition. Malnutrition is generally considered a common disseminator of deprivation that reduces the chances of child survival. Taking the health status of women in 1998-99, about 56 per cent of them suffered from anaemia as compared to only 47.6 per cent among non-SCs/STs (Table 10.7). The incidence of anaemia among the SC children is also quite high as nearly 78 per cent of the SC children suffered from anaemia as compared with 72 per cent among non-SC/ST children (Table 10.7).

Table 10.6

Infant Mortality: 1998-99

Indicators	*Scheduled Caste (1998-99)*	*Scheduled Tribe (1998-99)*	*Other Backward Caste (1998-99)*	*Others (1998-99)*
Infant mortality	83.00 (88.0)	84.00 (87.00)	76.00 (82)	61.8 (69)
Child mortality	39.5	46.3	29.00	22.2
Under-five mortality	119	126	103	82

Note: Figure in the bracket indicate the infant mortality in rural area.
Source: *National Family Health Survey*, 1998-99.

Table 10.7

Morbidity: 1998-99

Indicators	*Scheduled Caste (1998-99)*	*Scheduled Tribe (1998-99)*	*Other Backward Caste (1998-99)*	*Others (1998-99)*
1. Prevalence of				
(i) ARI (in percentage)	19.6	22.4	19.1	18.7
(ii) Fever (in percentage)	29.4	31.4	28.1	30.40
(iii) Diarrhoea (in percentage)	19.8	21.1	18.3	19.10
2. Percentage of children with anaemia	78.3	79.3	72.00	72.7
3. Percentage of children vaccinated				
4. Percentage of public medical services as sources of childhood vaccination	87.2	86.3	83.0	77.3
5. Treatment of diarrhoea from public health facilities (in percentage)	64.6	52.2	63.8	66.10
6. Weight for age				
(i) % below—3SD	21.2	26.00	18.30	13.80
(ii) % below—2SD	53.5	55.9	47.3	41.1

Source: *National Family Health Survey*, 1998-99.

The nutritional status of women and children brings out the disparities between SC and non-SC/ST women and children. The indicator of undernourishment (in terms of minimum weight for age) of the children is much higher for SC children (54 per cent) than the non-SCs/STs children (47 per cent).

The indicators of nutritional status of women also bring out similar disparities between SCs and non-SCs/STs. These include height below 145 centimetre (that is less than minimum) and body mass index (BMI). The values of both indicators are generally higher for SC women—17 and 42 per cent for SC women as compared with 12 and 32 per cent for non-SC/ST women respectively.

Among the measures of mortality, the infant mortality rate (IMR) is generally considered as the most sensitive and important indicator of health status of a population. While the government of India has adopted the national goal of reducing the present level of IMR to 60 by 2000, the SCs IMR, child mortality and under-five mortality were 83, 40 and 119 respectively in 1998-99 as compared to 61.8, 22.2 and 82 for others respectively (Table 10.6).

The discussion in the preceding section indicates that there has been improvement in the level of living of SCs in rural and urban area, measured in terms of level of poverty. The percentage of poor among the SCs in rural and urban has declined in early 1980s. But the rate of decline has not been adequate enough to reduce the gap between them and other sections of Indian society and hence the level of deprivation of SCs continues to be of high order. In fact the disparities increased in the 1990s.There are a number of reasons for the persistence of disparities and higher degree of economic deprivation of the SCs. The access of SCs to the capital assets, land and non-land assets is still very limited—reflected in low proportion of self-employed cultivators and businesses and exceptionally high incidence of wage labour. Compared to non-SCs/STs, the unemployment rate among SCs is also very high. Educational development in terms of literacy and educational level is equally poor. All this adds to the high incidence of poverty and poor health situation.

In the following section we take a closer look at the changes in access of SCs to the land and non-land assets, employment, education etc.

Access to Land and Capital

Table 10.8 gives the occupational pattern of scheduled castes and others (excluding SC/ST) in rural and urban area for 1999-2000 based on the NSS employment survey. In 2000, of the total SC households about 16

Table 10.8

Distribution of Occupational Pattern by Household Type

Household Type	*1987-88*		*1993-94*		*1999-2000*	
	SC	*Other*	*SC*	*Other*	*SC*	*Other*
			Rural			
Self-employed in agriculture	18.90	43.3	19.12	42.42	16.4	41.1
Self-employed in non-agriculture	11.0	13.8	10.32	13.89	12.0	14.8
Self-employed (total)	29.8	57.1	29.49	56.31	28.4	55.9
Agricultural wage labour	51.7	23.2	50.6	22.37	51.4	19.0
Non-Agricultural wage labour	11.4	09.7	10.22	6.67	10.0	6.3
Rural wage labour (total)	63.1	31.1	60.28	29.14	61.4	25.3
Others	06.9	11.5	9.67	14.62	10.2	18.7
			Urban			
Self-employed	28.0	35.2	24.08	35.05	27.3	35.5
Regular wage/salaries	39.4	45.0	39.27	43.11	37.6	46.5
Casual labour	26.0	10.3	26.96	10.57	26.5	7.4
Others wage	08.5	09.2	9.67	11.25	8.5	10.5

Note: SC= Scheduled caste; Others = Non-SC/ST (excluding, scheduled caste and scheduled tribe).

Source: *NSS Employment/Unemployment Survey*, 1987-88, and 1993-94, Delhi: CSO.

per cent pursued cultivation as self-employed occupation (compared to 41.1 per cent for others) and another 12 per cent were engaged in some kind of non-farm self-employment activities (or businesses). Thus, about 28 per cent of households had acquired access to land and non-land assets. Due to lack of access to fixed capital assets, about 61.4 per cent of the total SC households depended on wage employment (as compared to only 25 per cent for other households).

In 1999-2000, in the urban areas only 27 per cent were engaged in petty businesses, designated as self-employed households compared to 35.5 per cent for other households. The share of casual labour on the other hand was about 26 per cent, four times higher than other households (7.4%). Difference in the proportion of regular wage earner/salaried persons between SCs and other households was however less, compared to self-employment and wage labour occupation, presumably due to positive outcome of affirmative action policy of the government.

Thus if we take proportion of self-employed households engaged in farm and non-farm sector in rural area as a measure of access to capital assets, then by 2000, about 28 per cent in rural area and 22 per cent of SC households in urban area had acquired some access to capital assets. Notwithstanding these gains the proportion of self-employed SC households was much lower as compared with other household and consequently an exceptionally high proportion of them depended on wage labour—61 per cent in rural area and about 46 per cent in urban area (regular wage/salaried). Wage labour as a traditional occupation thus continues to constitute a main occupation of the SCs.

Table 10.9 represents information on the ownership of agricultural land by the SCs in rural area for 1982 and 1992 and provides some insights into the reasons for low proportion of self-employed cultivators among the SC households in rural area. In 1992 about 13 per cent of SC households were landless and 87 per cent owned some land. Among the landowning

Table 10.9

Percentage of Landless and Near Landless Households among Scheduled Castes (% to Total Rural Households): All-India

	1982				
All-India	*Landless*	*Less than Half Acre*	*Between Half and One Acre*	*Up to One Acre*	*Landless and up to One Acre*
SC	12.62	47.97	9.53	57.50	70.12
ST	17.12	16.30	7.15	23.45	70.17
	1992				
All-India	*Landless*	*Less than Half Acre*	*Between Half and One Acre*	*Up to One Acre*	*Landless and up to One Acre*
SC	13.34	47.50	8.89	56.39	69.73
ST	11.50	22.26	7.22	29.48	40.98
	2000				
All-India	*Landless*	*Less than Half Acre*		*Land Less and up to One Acre*	
SC	10.0	65.0		75.0	
ST	7.2	39		46.2	

Source: NSS Landholding Survey, 1981 and 1991, and *Employment Survey 1999-2000* (for 1999-2000).

households, however, about 56 per cent owned less than one acre (of which 47.50 per cent owned less than half acre). Landless and near landless (that is those owning less than one acre) put together account nearly 70 per cent of the total SC households in 1992. The 2001 NSS landholding survey results are not yet published. However, the Employment/Unemployment Survey of 1999-2000 give the land ownership pattern among the SCs. Although it is not a landholding survey, nevertheless it gives some idea for more recent year. The landless and near landless (that is those owning less than one acre of land) put together constitute 75 per cent of all SC households in rural area in 2000. Thus, it is clear that a small proportion of SC landowners could operate as self-employed cultivators because of the non-viable character of marginal landholding.

The non-viable character of small and marginal landholding of the SC households and their eventual conversion into wage labour is reflected in the land ownership background of wage labour household in rural area. The break-up of wage labour households into those without and with land, and of latter (that is landowning labour household) by size of land possessed, helps to understand the reason as to why even landowning household resort to wage employment. It is obvious that not all wage labour households are landless. Some of them do own some land but the size of the land being small, their major source of income remained wage labour. In 1993-94, about 30 per cent of the SC rural labour households owned some land. Of these about three-fourth of them owned less than one acre of cultivated land. So majority of landowning wage labour households are those who owned tiny pieces of land.

Employment

Since more than 61 per cent of the SC households in rural areas and about 64 per cent in urban areas depend on wage employment (daily and regular) their earnings are determined by level of employment and wage rates. The unemployment rate based on usual principle status (UPS) and usual principle and subsidiary status (UPSS) tend to be similar for SC male and other male population. The disparities, however, clearly emerged in the case of employment rate based on current weekly (CWS) and currently daily status (CDS). These rates capture the underemployment of the employed persons. The employment rate of male worker turns out to be

50.5 per cent and 46 per cent for SC male worker under CWS and CDS compared to 51 per cent and 48 per cent for other male workers respectively. Thus, although the SC workers do not lag behind other workers with respect to open employment (based on UPS and UPSS), they do suffer from low underemployment (employment based on CWS and CDS). In urban area the SC households indeed suffered from lower employment, under all statuses, in greater degree. As compared to other workers (non-SC/ST workers), the employment rate for the SC male turns out to be lower under all the statuses. For instance the employment rate for SC workers based on UPS, UPSS, CWS and CDS are 49.8 per cent, 50.3 per cent, 48.6 per cent and 45.8 per cent respectively, which were lower compared to 51.95 per cent, 52.4 per cent, 51.55 per cent and 49.65 per cent respectively for other households (Table 10.10).

Table 10.10

Employment Rate: Male (All-India)

Level	*UPS*	*UPSS*	*CWS*	*CDS*
Rural	Male	All India	1999	
SC	52.4	53.1	50.5	46.2
ST	55.3	55.8	53.9	50.5
Other	51.65	52.6	50.8	48
Rural	Male	All India	1983	
SC	62.64	64.15	58.45	53.09
ST	67.28	68.56	64.67	61.64
Other	60.21	62.56	58.78	55.75
Urban	Male	All India	1999	
SC	49.8	50.3	48.6	45.8
ST	47.5	48	47.5	45.1
Other	51.95	52.4	51.55	49.65
Urban	Male	All India	1983	
SC	55.49	56.69	54.24	50.14
ST	56.95	61.87	55.61	52.71
Other	56.96	58.2	56.19	53.97

Source: Employment Survey, various rounds, NSS, Delhi.

This implies that although SC workers managed to get some work around the year, and appeared to be fully employed, however they are not adequately employed on weekly or daily basis, and hence suffer from higher underemployment in greater degree than the other male workers. This is also reflected in higher unemployment rate based on CWS and CDS. In the case of unemployment rates based on UPS and UPSS, the difference between the SCs and other workers is not significant. The unemployment rates based on CWS and CDS, however, tend to be generally higher for the SC workers as compared with other workers. For instance the unemployment rate according to UPS, UPSS, CDW and CDS for SCs are 1.2 per cent, 1 per cent, 2.5 per cent and 5 per cent respectively, compared to 1.25 per cent, 1 per cent, 2.05 per cent and 3.35 per cent for other workers in rural area. Similarly, the unemployment rate in urban areas among the SC workers under UPS, UPSS, CWS and CDS are 2.8 per cent, 2.7 per cent, 3.7 per cent and 5.2 per cent, compared to 2.55 per cent, 2.4 per cent, 3 per cent and 3.75 per cent for other workers respectively (Table 10.11).

Lower employment of the SC workers in rural and urban area also reflect the low quality of human resource which restrict their ability to take advantage of skilled jobs in rural and urban area. In 1991, only 37 per cent of SCs were literate as against 58 per cent for the others. The situation in respect of SC females was particularly bad. The female literacy rate improved, almost by four-fold, that is, from 6.44 per cent in 1971 to 23.76 per cent in 1991, but it still continues to be distinctly lower.

From the above data one can easily argue that feature relevant to the design of anti-poverty policies and programmes is the sizable share of the self-employed among the poor in India: 40 per cent in rural India and 44 per cent in urban India where the self-employed are easily the (numerically) dominant group among the urban poor. At this point it is worth emphasising a feature of the employment situation of the usual status (principal plus subsidiary status) workforce in self-employed households that tends to get submerged in general discussions about under-employment in the country. Male workers in these households are at work, on the average, for 344 days in a year in rural India and for 349 days in the year in urban India. Even allowing for the fact that women workers work fewer days in the year (260 days in rural India and 282 days in urban India), usual status workers (males plus females) in self-employed

Table 10.11

Unemployment Rate: Male (All-India)

Level	*UPS*	*UPSS*	*CWS*	*CDS*
Rural	Male	All-India	1999	
SC	1.2	1	2.5	5
ST	0.7	0.6	1.5	3
Other	1.25	1	2.05	3.35
Rural	Male	All-India	1983	
SC	1.14	0.76	3.22	7.16
ST	0.49	0.34	1.47	3.29
Other	1.49	1.03	2.15	4.03
Urban	Male	All-India	1999	
SC	2.8	2.7	3.7	5.2
ST	2.3	2.2	2.7	3.7
Other	2.55	2.4	2.95	3.75
Urban	Male	All-India	1983	
SC	3.71	3.05	4.36	7.2
ST	2.97	2.77	4	5.49
Other	3.53	3.13	3.95	5.28

Source: *Employment Survey*, various rounds, NSS Delhi.

households are at work for between 315 (in the case of self-employed in agricultural activities) and 321 days (for self-employed in non-agricultural) in a year in rural India, while in urban India they are at work for 337 days out of the 365 days in the year. Characterisation of this situation as one of underemployment is a serious misrepresentation of the problem: Do we or should we, expect them to be at work on all 365 days in the year? More important, such a characterisation shifts the focus away from quality of employment in general and productivity in particular towards quantity of employment in terms of number of days of employment. The central problem of poverty in the self-employed households is not that they are at work for only a few days in the year but that the returns to their labour input are too low. Therefore, the focus of policy should be more on raising the returns from the asset-base of the self-employed—chiefly land in rural India—and raising their skill profile—especially in urban India.

Economic Discrimination and Exclusion

While the 'exclusion in past from right to property and income earning capital assets possibly explain the lack of access to land and non-land assets—as a legacy of the past, they also continue to suffer from economic exclusion and discrimination in the present. Therefore chronic poverty and continuing inequality of the SCs has its roots both in historical exclusion whose impact is carried forward in the present and also in continuing economic exclusion and discrimination in present, particularly in land, capital, labour market and non-market transactions.

The nexus between inequality, poverty and caste-based market and non-market discrimination has been the most neglected area in Indian economics. Consequently we know little about the economic deprivation arising out of caste and untouchability-based economic discrimination and exclusion in Indian society. Limited micro-level studies such as those from Andhra Pradesh (Venketeswarlu, 1990) and Karnataka (Khan, 1995) provide some evidence on economic discrimination in occupation, employment, wages, and the credit market as well as in other economic spheres. The Andhra Pradesh study observed that SCs faced occupational segregation and restrictions in efforts to change their occupation. Similarly, the Karnataka study revealed that nearly 85 per cent of the SC respondents continue to be engaged in their traditional occupations, whereas only 15 per cent were able to make a switchover. The Orissa study (Tripathy, 1994) observed discrimination in land lease, credit and labour markets in rural areas. Nearly 96 per cent of untouchable respondents in one village and all untouchable respondents in the second village were discriminated against in wage payment, with 28 per cent in one village and 20 per cent in another facing discrimination in payment of rent.

A recent study by Action Aid (2000) revealed that in the labour market, exclusion and discrimination is practised both in hiring and wage payment in a significant number of sample villages. In about 36 per cent of villages (out of 550 villages) the SCs were denied wage employment in agriculture in that year. In about 25 per cent of villages, the SC workers faced discrimination in wage payment. The SC wage labourer thus received daily wages at a rate less than both the market wage rate and the wages paid to non-SC workers. What is also striking is that in 37 per cent of the villages, untouchability was practised in the physical distribution of wage payment—SCs received wages in cash or kind from a 'respectable distance' so that the dominant caste dispensers of wages could avoid physical touch with the SCs. Belief in 'purity' and 'pollution' also affects hiring of SC wage labourers in housing construction—in about one-third of villages they were excluded from employment for construction of houses. In a sizable number of villages, the SCs were forced to carry on their traditional occupation—considered to be unclean and polluting. For urban area, Banergee and Knight (1991) observed that: '"there is indeed discrimination by caste, particularly job discrimination" and that "discrimination appears to operate at least in part through traditional mechanism, with untouchables disproportionately represented in poorly-paid dead-end jobs."' Even if discrimination is no longer practiced, the effects of past discrimination could carry over to the present. This may help to explain why discrimination is greatest in operative jobs, in which contracts are more important for recruitment, and not in white-collar jobs in which recruitment involves formal methods. The economic function which the system performs for favored castes suggests that taste for discrimination is based, consciously, or unconsciously, on economic interest, so making prejudice more difficult to eradicate"'.

These are some of the important facts, which are to be borne in mind while understanding the viable and sustainable role being played by the Scheduled Castes Development Corporations (SCDCs), which are envisaged to inter-face between the poor SC entrepreneurs and the financial institutions in respect of bankable schemes of economic development of the SCs.

11 Credit Needs of Weaker Sections of Society in India

'Growth and development with social justice' has been the basic objective of the development planning in India since independence. In the beginning of the First Five-Year Plan (1951-1956), almost half of the Indian population was living below the poverty line, 80 per cent of which lived in the rural areas. The incidence of poverty in villages was widespread. This problem was further aggravated by disparities that existed among the states, between men and women and among different social groups. The magnitude of poverty and disparities that existed between various social groups necessitated a planned state intervention to provide succour and relief to millions reeling under poverty, particularly the disadvantaged and marginalised social groups, such as scheduled castes, scheduled tribes, other backward castes, women, children, the physically handicapped and the disabled.

There has been sustained effort through government intervention to deal with the problem of poverty in India. Since Independence, in the last five decades the country has made a significant stride in many areas. It is now a net exporter of food grains. There has been significant improvement in a range of human development indicators. There has been noticeable achievements in the area of poverty alleviation as well. With the sustained efforts of government interventions the proportion of population, below the poverty line (BPL) has been brought down from 54.8 per cent in 1973-74 to 35.9 per cent in 1993-94 and further to 26 per cent in 1999-2000. The rural poverty during this period has also been brought down from 56.4 per cent in 1973-74 to 37.27 per cent in 1993-94 and 27.09 per cent in 1999-2000.

The point of concern, however, is that, over a quarter of the world's poor still live in India. An estimate by the Planning Commission (2001) shows that more than 260 million people continue to live below the poverty line, which is about 26 per cent of the country's population. There is still high concentration of the poor in the rural areas. Out of the total population, 193 million poor live in the rural area which is about 75 per cent of the total poor in the country. The poor are also concentrated mostly in backward regions like dryland, rainfed, drought-prone, tribal, hill and desert areas. The concentration of the poor continues to be more among the weaker sections of society particularly among SCs, STs, and backward classes.

It is well known that the burden of indebtedness in rural India is very huge, and that despite major structural changes in credit institutions and forms of rural credit in the post-Independence period, the exploitation of the rural masses in the credit market is one of the most pervasive and persistent features of rural life in India. Rural households need credit for a variety of reasons. They need credit to meet short-term requirements of working capital and for long-term investment in agriculture and other income-bearing activities. Agricultural and non-agricultural activities in rural areas typically are seasonal, and households need credit to smoothen out seasonal fluctuations in earnings and expenditure. Rural households, particularly those vulnerable to what appear to others to be minor shocks with respect to income and expenditure, need credit as an insurance against risk. In a society that has no law of free, compulsory and universal school education, no arrangements for free and universal preventive and curative health care, a weak system for the public distribution of food and very few general social security programmes, rural households need credit for different types of consumption. These include expenditure on food, housing, health and education. In the Indian context, another important purpose of borrowing is to meet expenses on a variety of social obligations and rituals.

If these credit needs of the poor are to be met, rural households need access to credit institutions that provide them a range of financial services, provide credit at reasonable rates of interest and provide loans that are unencumbered by extra-economic provisions and obligations. Historically, there have been four major problems with respect to the supply of credit to the Indian countryside. First, the supply of formal sector credit to the countryside as a whole has been inadequate. Second, rural credit markets in India themselves have been very imperfect and fragmented. Third, as the foregoing suggests, the distribution of formal sector credit has been unequal, particularly with respect to region and class, caste and gender in the countryside. Formal sector credit needs specially to reach backward areas, poor income households, people of the oppressed castes and tribes, and women. Fourth, the major source of credit to rural households, particularly poor income working households, has been the informal sector. Informal sector loans typically are advanced at very high rates of interest. Further, the terms and conditions attached to these loans have given rise to an elaborate structure of coercion—economic and extra-economic—in the countryside.

The need to improve financial access for India's poor, the overwhelming majority of whom are concentrated in rural areas, motivated the establishment of a vast network of rural cooperative credit banks in the 1950s, followed by a drive to nationalise commercial banks, launched in 1969. This led to thousands of new bank branches in rural areas across the country. The strategy during the 1970s and 1980s gave the lead role to the nationalised (state-owned) commercial banks, who were charged with loosening the grip of traditional informal sector moneylenders through the use of targeted low-priced loans. The 1990s saw the partial deregulation of interest rates, increased competition in the banking sector, and microfinance approaches, most notably, a nationwide attempt, pioneered by non-governmental organisations (NGOs) and now supported by the state, to create links between commercial banks, NGOs, and informal local groups ('self-help groups', or SHGs). Better known as 'SHG Bank Linkage', this approach has grown dramatically over the past decade, and while its outreach is still modest in terms of the proportion of poor households served, many believe it is destined to become the country's dominant system of mass-outreach banking for the poor. However, informal sector lenders remain a strong presence in rural India, delivering finance to the poor, the vast majority of whom still do not have access to either formal or semi-formal (microfinance) sectors. Scaling up access to finance for India's rural poor, to meet their diverse financial needs (savings, credit, insurance against unexpected events, etc.) through flexible products at competitive prices, presents a formidable challenge in a country as vast and varied as India. But the opportunities too are plentiful, and government has an important role to play in creating space and a flexible architecture for innovations.

For assessing the current level and pattern of access to formal finance for India's rural households, with a focus on the poor, a survey was conducted jointly by the World Bank and the National Council of Applied Economic Research, India (NCAER)—the *Rural Finance Access Survey, 2003* (RFAS-2003). It highlights inadequacies in rural access to formal finance and the extortionary terms of informal finance, which provide a strong need and ample space for innovative microfinance approaches—that combine the safety and reliability of formal finance with the convenience and flexibility of informal finance—to serve the financial needs of India's rural poor.

According to the RFAS-2003, some 41 per cent of rural households have a deposit account and 21 per cent of rural households have access to credit from a formal source. Amongst formal institutions, commercial banks are by far the most dominant source of formal finance for rural households. They have the largest share of household deposits among rural banks, and are also the most important source of credit for those rural households who have access to the formal sector.

While achievements over the past decades should not be underestimated, poorer households in rural areas in India still have very little access to formal finance. The RFAS-2003 indicates that rural banks serve primarily the needs of the richer rural borrowers: some 66 per cent of large farmers have a deposit account; 44 per cent have access to credit. Meanwhile, the rural poor face severe difficulties in accessing savings and credit from the formal sector: 70 per cent of marginal/landless farmers do not have a bank account and 87 per cent have no access to credit from a formal source.

Access to formal credit is particularly a problem for meeting unforeseen expenditures—family sources and the local moneylender dominate. Over 90 per cent of households report meeting their unusual expenses from cash at home, while the second most important source of financing such expenses was reportedly informal loans from family, friends, or moneylenders. Newer sources, such as the recently introduced Kisan Credit Cards, are still statistically insignificant. Access to other financial services, such as insurance, also remains limited for the rural poor, although many would like to have access to insurance. Over 82 per cent of households surveyed in RFAS-2003, did not have any insurance and practically none of the poorest households surveyed had insurance.

What Explains the Lack of Access to Formal Finance by the Scheduled Castes?

The failure of India's rural banks to deliver finance to the scheduled castes may be attributed to a combination of factors affecting both banks and their clients. From the perspective of the rural banks, serving the scheduled castes is a high-risk, high-cost proposition. First, is the problem of uncertainty. Uncertainty about the repayment capacity of scheduled caste borrowers, and their irregular/volatile income streams and expenditure patterns, in the absence of credit information, serve to drive up default risk. Problems of uncertainty are exacerbated by the borrower's inability to provide collateral, and/or difficulties in contract design and enforcement and in repossession of collateral. Also, the scheduled castes are perceived as 'bad clients' because they typically want to borrow for consumption smoothening rather than investment purposes, and if they do borrow for investment, they lack information on how to make their business viable.

Second, the transaction costs of rural lending in India are high, mainly due to the small loan size, high frequency of transactions in rural finance, large geographical spread and heterogeneity of borrowers, and widespread illiteracy. For private sector banks—their lack of a rural branch network is an additional problem.

Income and expenditure patterns of the rural poor: Rural households have highly irregular and volatile income streams. Irregular wage labour and the sale of agricultural products are the two main sources of income for rural households. The poorest rural households (landless and marginal farmers) are particularly dependent on irregular wage employment: About two-thirds of marginal farming households surveyed rely on wage labour as their primary source of income (in contrast, only 9 per cent of large farming households rely on wage labour for primary income and none of these households rely on irregular wage labour.), while 29 per cent rely on selling farm produce.

Rural households also have irregular expenditure patterns. In a study conducted, revealed that over one-half of the households report the bulk of their expenditures as being either daily or irregular. The typical expenditure profile of rural households surveyed is that of small, daily or irregular expenses, incurred all through the month. Furthermore, some 99 per cent of households report having incurred at least one unusual expenditure over the past six months, with the most frequent reasons for the latest unusual expenditure reported as medical or social purposes (related to births, marriages, etc.).

For the poor, the dividing line between production and consumption needs is very thin. In the absence of access to short-term consumption loans, the productive investments are impaired. It is, therefore, important to provide the small borrowers with a credit mechanism to fall back on for meeting their emergent and consumption needs. Further, it has also been brought out by various studies that the repayment of loans by the poor does not come necessarily from the 'incremental' income from the investment alone, but also from their other sources of income. Banks should provide a separate flexible revolving credit limit to the small borrowers of production or investment loans for meeting their temporary shortfalls in family cash flow.

From the perspective of small, rural borrowers (the users), rural banks are unattractive for the following reasons. First, rural banks do not provide flexible products and services to meet the income and expenditure patterns of small rural borrowers. As noted above, small rural borrowers have irregular/volatile income streams and expenditure needs, and therefore, prefer to borrow frequently, and repay in small installments, but most banks do not offer such products. Also, while small rural borrowers seek savings and lending products, they also seek insurance (life, health, crop), which banks do not generally offer.

Second, the transaction costs of dealing with formal banks are high. In part, high transaction costs stem from distance to the nearest financial institutions. According to the RFAS-2003, the median distance to the nearest financial institution ranges from 2 km (post office branches) to 5 km (commercial banks, cooperative banks); the median time taken to travel to the nearest commercial bank, cooperative or regional rural banks (RRBs) is 30 minutes (post offices are available at closer proximity). Furthermore, procedures for opening an account or seeking a loan are cumbersome and costly (with high rejection rates) and, as indicated by the RFAS-2003, clients have to pay hefty bribes (ranging from 10 per cent-20 per cent of the loan amount) to access loans, so that the ultimate cost to borrowers is very high (despite interest 'caps'). On an average, some 27 per cent (and 48% in UP) of sample households who borrowed from an RRB report having to pay a bribe to get the loan, a little under 27 per cent of households who borrowed from a commercial bank paid a bribe, and 10 per cent of households who borrowed from a credit cooperative paid a bribe. The bribe amounts appear to vary from anywhere between 10 per cent of the loan amount (in the case of banks) to 20 per cent (in the case of cooperatives). Moreover, longer processing times for loans, together with bribes, could result in higher effective costs to borrowers and consequent credit rationing. It takes, on an average, 33 weeks for a loan to be approved by a commercial bank.

A third factor that makes formal banks unattractive for rural borrowers is that banks demand collateral, which poor rural borrowers lack. Indeed, the majority of loans extended by commercial banks, RRBs and cooperatives are collateralised, with 89 per cent of households who borrowed from RRBs, and 87 per cent of households who borrowed from commercial banks, reporting that they had to provide collateral (RFAS-2003).

Informal finance: The dependence on informal finance is greater, around 44 per cent of the households surveyed by RFAS-2003 report having borrowed informally at least once in the preceding 12 months; the interest charged on informal loans averages 48 per cent per annum. Not surprisingly, informal borrowing is very important for the poorest (marginal and commercial categories), who are the most deprived of formal finance, though it is important for virtually all household categories.

A research study reported that the main source of informal borrowing is moneylenders (some 56% of households who report having borrowed informally in the past 12 months approached moneylenders), followed by friends/relatives (21%).10 The crucial uses of informal loans are for meeting 'family emergencies' (29%) and 'social expenditures' (19%) arising from events such as births, marriages, deaths. Some 13 per cent of borrowers report using informal loans for investment-related informal loans which tend to be of a short tenor. Close to 50 per cent of the households who report having borrowed informally in the preceding 12 months took loans with a tenor of less than (or up to) six months. Other significant features that make informal loans more attractive to the poor include flexible repayment, the convenience and frequency with which such loans can be accessed, and less reliance on collateral (only 16.5 per cent of households report providing collateral against the loan). But among those who report providing collateral for informal loans, the overwhelming collateral cited is 'self labour'—evidence of interlinked credit contracts spanning credit and labour, or bonded labour. Almost all cases reporting self-labour as collateral are landless/marginal farmers, who are too poor to offer any assets as collateral, and hence most vulnerable to harsh contracts linking their labour to loans.

The major impediments to the flow of institutional credit to the disadvantaged sections are: higher transaction cost to banks and borrowers, procedures, systems and documentation formalities not being client friendly, inability of borrowers to provide tangible collateral securities, distortion of the normal banking principles on account of linking of credit with capital/interest subsidies under various poverty alleviation programmes, announcements of interest/loan waivers vitiating the recovery climate, legal difficulties in foreclosure of loans, non-availability of tenancy agreements/updated land records, inadequate risk mitigation mechanism available to small borrowers in the events of failure of their micro-enterprises and to the banks in the event of loan failures, and the mindset that banking with the poor is not profitable, etc.

12 Role of SCDCs in the Financial Inclusion

As many know, the weaker sections of the society are economically poor not because they cannot manage their money; or their business activities are not profitable—they are poor because their resource base is too small. Simply speaking they have too little capital—too little money and assets. Since the early national plans, successive governments in independent India have emphasised the link between improving access to finance and reducing poverty. One of the 'missing inputs' which is recognised as crucial to the development of scheduled castes is the easy access to financial services on reasonable terms. Flow of bank credit is low on account of the assumed non-creditworthiness of scheduled castes due to their subsistence economy, lack of entrepreneurial skill and scheme/assets management ability.

With a view to effectively tackling the operational aspects involved in the implementation of economic development programmes for the scheduled castes particularly in the mobilisation of institutional credit for income generating schemes, the Government of India recommended the establishment of Scheduled Castes Development Corporations (SCDCs) in the states having significant population of scheduled castes. It was conceived as an organisation in the field which could intervene at crucial points and act as promoter and guarantor ensuring necessary linkages and tie-ups with different agencies and helping to ensure that the flows of benefits from the family oriented schemes in the Special Component Plan (SCP) do actually reach the scheduled caste families in the magnitudes envisaged. It was also expected to meet part of the investment required for acquiring an income-generating asset as a margin money loan, encouraging financial institutions to come out on a sufficiently large scale to assist scheduled castes by making the scheme more viable to individual participants. While the SCP was meant to tackle the multifarious problems of scheduled castes such as social, educational and economic backwardness, the SCDCs were expected to work for the economic development of scheduled castes. SCPs were required to indicate clearly the targets and outlays for SCDCs separately.

In 1980 the Central government constituted a working group for the formulation of strategies and priorities for the development of scheduled castes, scheduled tribes and other weaker sections. A sub-committee on scheduled castes was established in this working group. The SCP of the Sixth Five Year Plan (1980-1985) is largely a result of the recommendation of this working group. The major recommendations of the working group regarding SCDCs were the following:

1. They should concentrate on a limited number of selected schemes, carefully planning various stages from supply of raw material to the final marketing of products.
2. Scattering of programmes/schemes is to be avoided and a cluster-cum-saturation approach to be adopted. Meaningful linkages should be established with the existing district and block level machinery. They should help scheduled castes to benefit from the state plan and the Central and state sponsored schemes.
3. Instead of taking up programmes on their own, they should play catalytic role through appropriate linkages with credit and marketing institutions as well as technical departments. Officers with the right attitude and requisite experience should be placed in charge of the corporations and provided orientation and training.
4. A provision of Rs. 100 crore was made in the centrally sponsored scheme of assistance of States for investment in the share capital to the corporations. The existing scheme should be modified to include assistance for essential staff expenditure on monitoring and evaluation, recovery etc., and for taking up promotional activities.

Before the commencement of the Sixth Plan, SCDCs were in existence in Andhra Pradesh, Gujarat, Haryana, Kerala, Punjab, Tamil Nadu and West Bengal. Some state governments such as Punjab and Haryana had set up SCDCs in the 1970s. The states of Haryana and Punjab were the first to set up SCDCs (January 1971). Seven other states set up their corporations on Government of India's direction. These were Kerala (1972), Tamil Nadu

the corporation has been set up. This is reinforced by the fact that the coverage during 2002-03, 2003-04 has once again started increasing after touching a low of 78,965 beneficiaries in 2000-01. The relatively long tenure of C. Uma Malleshwar Rao (one year, eight months and twenty days and J.C. Sharma (two years, seven months) have pulled the fiscal coverage to the slopes of recovery.

It is essential that the APSCCFC is providing continuity in leadership both at the official and community levels by ensuring reasonable tenures for the office bearers. It is suggested that the tenures of the vice chairman and managing director should be a minimum period of three years, and that security of tenure is provided to all the incumbents. As regards chairman and nominated members of the Board, it may be useful, if only persons known to be committed to the development of the SC community are nominated. The present practice of making the post available to those who missed a berth in the cabinet should be discontinued with. It is also suggested that the Government may consider nominating to the APSCCFC Managing Committee, representatives of the lead banks and NABARD to enable better coordination of flow of budgetary and credit resources in the implementation of the programme. The Government should also review the manner of selection and the period of deputation of staff members in a district societies and assign a specific role to the VC and MD of the APSCCFC in the selection and control of district staff.

West Bengal Scheduled Castes and Scheduled Tribes Finance Development Corporation (WBSCSTDFC)

The SCDC in West Bengal is a statutory corporation. The paid-up capital from the State government is Rs. 4.65 crore, unchanged from 2001 for three financial years, but has increased to Rs. 5.99 crore from 2004-05. The paid-up capital from the Union government, unchanged during this period, is Rs. 2.995 crore.

The SCDC in West Bengal works closely with the Panchayati Raj System, where beneficiaries are nominated by the *panchayats*. The income-generation schemes funded during 1999-2005 include: readymade garments, poultry, leather products, carpentry, silver ornaments, power tiller, auto-rickshaw, medical store, diesel trekker and taxis, garage servicing, *batik* print, internet cafe, piggery, battery manufacturing, fast food centre, xerox printing, steel fabrication, etc.

The corporation has 64 general managerial staff (out of which 23 are on deputation), 92 project monitoring staff, 78 non-managerial staff, and 48 personnel working in Group-D category. This includes the personnel spread across the districts. The corporation has to pay more than Rs. 3 crore as annual salary to these personnel (data available upto 2002-03: Rs. 3.325 crore).

Orissa Scheduled Castes and Scheduled Tribes Finance Cooperative Corporation Limited (OSFDC)

The SCDC in Orissa is a monopoly organisation established in 1979, and has a share capital of Rs. 1214.95 lakh (Rs. 609.41 lakh from the state and Rs. 605.54 lakh from the Centre). The paid-up capital from the state government was Rs. 14.61 crore in 2002-2004, and 15.35 crore in 2004-2005. The Central government provided a paid-up capital of 8.64 annually during 2002-2005. Each year, the corporation funds about 20,000 cases in the SC sector, processes another 2,000 applications in the scavenger sector sponsor to banks for finance.

Recent schemes funded by the corporation include animal husbandry, fishery, agricultural development and land reforms, minor irrigation, soil conservation, horticulture, small stationery shops, ambassador car, mini tractors, etc. Unlike West Bengal, *panchayats* do not play a major role in selection of beneficiaries. The schemes are advertised in newspapers in local languages.

The office has 112 staff, out of which 84 are managerial, with an operating expense of around Rs. 3 crore. Interest-income is a meagre Rs. 2 crore per annum, sometimes less. The board has been dissolved and development commissioner–cum–additional chief secretary to the Government of Orissa is the present chairman of the board. However, lack of continuity and frequent change at senior and middle level in the post of managing director, district managers and insufficient manpower at the field level becomes a threat to the organisation for better reach and recovery.

In order to have better recovery, the new managing director has taken the following steps: (i) all the district welfare officers are now renamed as district managers and delegation of more power to them, (ii) welfare registration officers are now called assistant managers, and are supposed to keep in touch with the beneficiaries every fortnight for recovery of light-cost schemes, (iii) issuance of red notices under signature of the managing director to defaulters, (iv) simplification of documents for obtaining loans, and (v) regular interaction between the officials at headquarter with the field-staff. However, these have not yielded expected results. The district welfare officials are complaining of too much work, and seem to be overburdened. This is also the case with the assistant managers because of low-key staff.

Uttar Pradesh Scheduled Castes Finance and Development Corporation Limited (UPSCFDC)

With a view to increasing the pace of economic development of scheduled castes, the UPSCFDC was set up in March 1975 under the Companies Act, 1956. The main objectives of the corporation are as follows:

- To promote, assist, organise, finance and undertake task of socio-economic and educational upliftment of the scheduled castes in Uttar Pradesh.
- To manage, establish, operate and conduct small scale industries for benefit of scheduled castes.
- To provide financial, technical, managerial and marketing assistance to scheduled castes entrepreneurs, and
- To procure loans through institutional finance and sanction of grants to scheduled castes entrepreneurs.

Since inception of Special Component Plan in 1980-81, the corporation has been entrusted with the task of enabling the scheduled caste families to raise them above the poverty line. The responsibility to carry out schemes from Special Central Assistance for overall development of scheduled caste people living below poverty line in the state was entrusted to this corporation by the state government. In view of providing better service to eligible beneficiaries, the state government had set up district offices of the corporation under the close supervision of district magistrate.

The organisational structure of the corporation is weak. Though there are 70 districts in Uttar Pradesh, the sanctioned post exists only for 58 districts. There is no post at the block level, and opportunities for promotion do not exist. The retirement age for the corporation employees is 58 whereas for the other employees of the state government is 60.

The Karnataka Scheduled Castes and Scheduled Tribes Development Corporation Limited (KSCTDC)

The Karnataka Scheduled Castes and Scheduled Tribes Development Corporation (KSCTDC) was registered in the year of 1975, dated 10th March. It started its business operations from the year of inception itself. In the 30th Annual General Meeting of the KSCTDC held on 16 August 2005, it was decided that the name of the company be changed from Karnataka Scheduled Castes and Scheduled Tribes Development Corporation to Dr. B.R. Ambedkar Development Corporation Limited (BRADCL). Honourable Minister for Social Welfare Department is the chairman of the board of directors. The board has nine members.

Organisational Structure

The KSCTDC has its own organisational setup from state to the *taluka* level. The *taluka* level functionary is the *taluka* development officer (field officer), who is the grassroot level worker. A self-contained organisational setup exists at district level. A policy-level decision has been taken for appointing a divisional level administrative officer. The organisational structure of the KSCTDC has been exhibited in Figure 12.1.

The exhibit reveals that there are four general managers under the direct supervision of the managing director, who is the chief executive. The general managers are for personnel, administration, development information and finance.

Figure 12.1

Organisational Structure of the KSCTDC

Organisational Chart of KSCTDC Head Office

Board of Directors

Chairman

Managing Director

GM (PDA)*	CGM	CGM (IT)	GM (Finance)
Senior office manager, office superintendent, first division assistants, stenographer, second division assistants, senior typist, driver, *dalayathi*	Deputy general manager (development), drilling engineers, senior office manager, superintendents, first division assistants, stenographers, second division assistants, senior typist, driver, *dalayathi*	Deputy general manager, management (appraisal), superintendent, first division assistants, stenographers, second division assistants, typist, driver, *dalayathi*	Deputy general (audit) superintendent (accounts), superintendent internal, auditors, accounts assistants, first division assistants, stenographer, second division assistants, typist, driver, *dalayathi*

Computer Section	Engineering Wing
Senior computer programmer, data entry assistants	Executive engineer, assistants executive engineer, assistant engineer, first division assistants, second division assistants, typists, driver, *dalayathi*

Source: * GM (PDA) – General Manager (Personnel Administration Development).

The district officers are headed by the district managers. Organisation chart at the district level is given in Figure 12.2.

Management

The KSCTDC is managed by a board of nine members. The board is constituted by the state government. The board has the representative of Government of India, Government of Karnataka, elected representatives such as MLAs and social workers. The composition of nine members is: a) chairman who is nominated by the state government (generally, Ministry of Social Welfare), b) representative of Government of India, Ministry of Social Justice and Empowerment—two, c) representatives of Social Welfare Department, Government of Karnataka—two, d) representative of Department of Finance, Government of Karnataka—two, e) representative of social workers—two, f) the managing director of the corporation—one, who functions as a convener. The board is the supreme policymaking body of the corporation. The board meets as and when required.

There are no other sub-committees of the board to manage specific activities. All the activities are managed and monitored by the board.

Figure 12.2

Organisational Chart of District Officers of KSCTDC

District Manager

↓

Senior Office Managing Recovery Officer

↓

Taluka Development Officer

↓

Assistants

↓

Junior Assistants/Typists

↓

Drivers

↓

Dalayathis

Rajasthan Scheduled Castes & Scheduled Tribes Finance & Development Cooperative Corporation (RSCSTFDCC)

This Corporation has been established on 28th March 1980 and registered under the Cooperative Societies Act, 1965 to mobilise resources for development and employment generation of scheduled caste families. In the year 1993, scheduled tribe population was also included as target group. Employment opportunities are also provided to handicapped people of the state. Special attention is given to scavengers and *safai karamcharis* of the state.

The state government has nominated this corporation as a State Channelising Agency of all the four apex national corporations namely:

1. National Scheduled Castes Finance & Development Corporation (NSCFDC).
2. National Scheduled Tribes Finance & Development Corporation (NSTFDC).
3. National Safai Karamchari Finance & Development Corporation (NSKFDC).
4. National Handicapped Finance & Development Corporation (NHFDC).

The Rajasthan state has also constituted two corporations for benefiting minority and OBC categories which are titled as under:

1. Rajasthan Minority Finance & Development Cooperative Corporation.
2. Rajasthan State Backward Classes Finance & Development Corporation.

The director, Social Welfare Department is managing director of these above two state corporations.

Tamil Nadu Adi Dravidar Housing and Development Corporation (THADCO)

Tamil Nadu Adi-Dravidar Housing and Development Corporation (THADCO) is a public sector undertaking of the Government of Tamil Nadu under the Department of Adi-Dravidar and Tribal Welfare. Founded in 1974, initially for construction of houses for scheduled castes and scheduled tribes, THADCO is now the chief development agency of the Tamil Nadu government for implementing economic development schemes for the welfare of scheduled castes and scheduled tribes.

THADCO has a total staff strength of 534 employees, which includes 100 engineers. Development schemes are implemented through the district manager's office located in all the 30 district headquarters and construction works are undertaken by the executive engineer's office located in seven places. At the district level, the THADCO's office is headed by the district manager.

The total strength of the THADCO's manpower is 502. Of this 122 are managerial staff, and 380 personnel in the non-managerial. There are 39 personnel in the staff who are on deputation. The board composition has two government nominees, and 10 government directors.

The Mahatma Phule Backward Class Development Corporation Ltd. (MPBCDC), Mumbai

The Mahatma Phule Backward Class Development Corporation Ltd. (MPBCDC), Mumbai was set up on the 10th of July 1978 by the Government of Maharashtra to act as a catalyst in enhancing the economic development of the scheduled castes, non-Buddhists, scheduled tribes, Vimukta Jati and nomadic tribal communities. The main focus of activities was to pursue a non-purposeful and deliberate promotional agenda, liasioning with the various banking institutions to promote a variety of self-employment opportunities for the socially backward individuals who live below the poverty line. In the year 1984, the section of Vimukta Jatis and nomadic tribe was entrusted to the Vasantrao Naik Vimukta Jatis and Nomadic Tribes Development Corporation Ltd. The scheduled caste community segment of Matang, Madgi and Mang was transferred to Lokshahir Annabhau Sathe Development Corporation which was established in the year 1985-86. The MPBCDC has thus been entrusted exclusively with the responsibility for the development of scheduled caste and Buddhist communities.

Figure 12.3

Mahatma Phule Backward Class Development Corporation Ltd., Mumbai

Number of Departments/Divisions

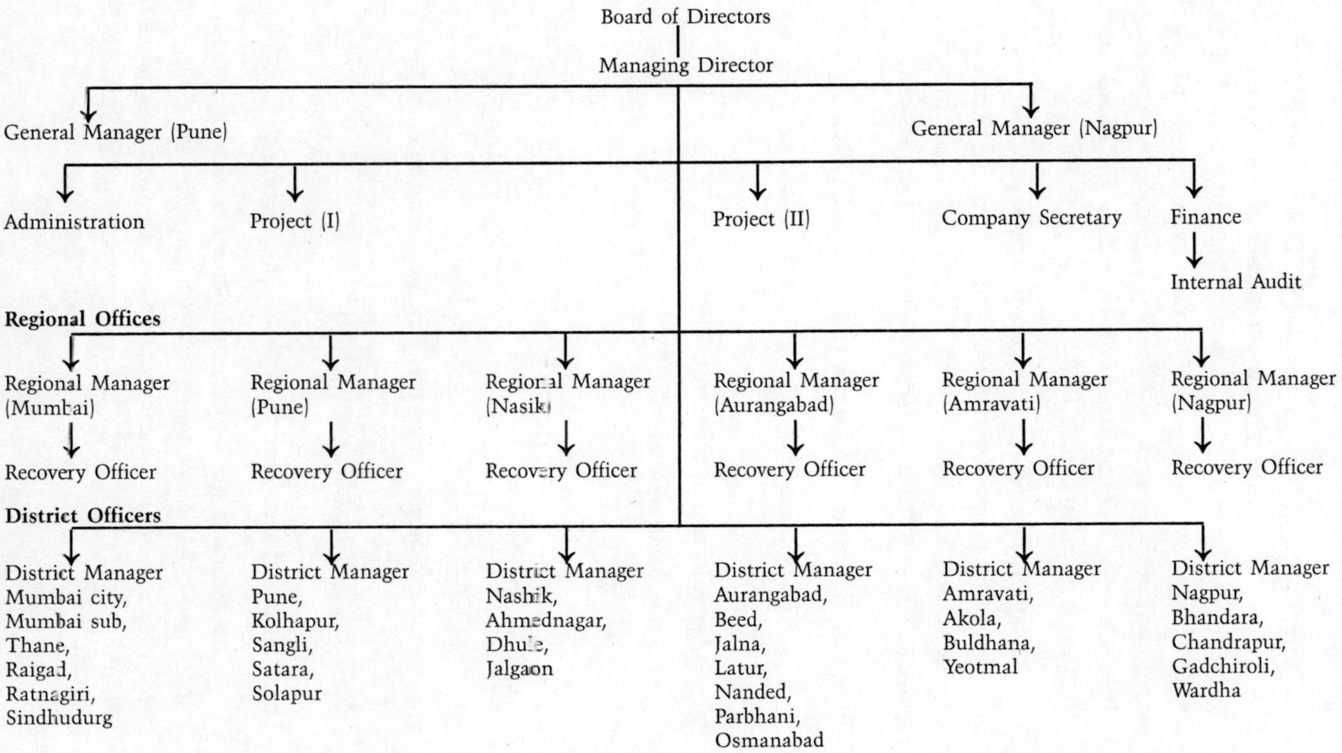

Management

The management of the MPBCDC is spearheaded by a board comprising 15 members with a representative from the Social Welfare Department. The term of the board extends to a period of three years. The board is mainly empowered to take policy decisions related to the implementation of various schemes applicable to the scheduled castes. There are no sub-committees constituted by the board. Its organisational structure is given in Figure 12.3.

The total manpower strength of the corporation is 360 of which 67 are managerial positions, and 242 non-managerial. The corporation spends approximately Rs. 496.10 lakh towards payment of annual wages and salaries. The percentage of wages to operating expenses is 77.80 per cent.

Types of Schemes Implemented by the SCDCs

The SCDCs mainly take up employment oriented schemes in the following areas:

- Agriculture and allied including minor irrigation;
- Small scale industry;
- Transport; and
- Trade and services sector.

Eligibility Criteria

A person belonging to scheduled castes living below the poverty line is eligible for assistance under this scheme from the state SCDC.

Main Features of Loan

Loan cum Subsidy and Margin Money Scheme

This loan has mainly three components, subsidy, margin money loan (MML) and bank loan. A subsidy with a maximum ceiling of Rs. 10,000/- per beneficiary is provided by the Special Central Assistance to the Special Component Plan. SCDCs provide margin money loan (MML) from the funds available from share capital and the remaining amount is provided through loan from the local bank which is tied up by the SCDCs. While the subsidy amount is not recovered, MML is provided at 4 per cent rate of interest and the bank loan at prescribed rate of interest. This loan is provided to SC persons living below the poverty line.

The purpose of margin money loan is three-fold:

It is intended to reduce the burden of loan on commercial/cooperative banks; by undertaking to share this burden the state government will demonstrate its involvement with the schemes; it will make the scheme viable for scheduled castes families by reducing their burden (by charging low interest and spreading out the repayment period. Margin money is not a grant but a loan; in cases where banks do not demand margin money, the corporations may provide it on their own initiative, in order to draw out banks to take up a sufficiently large programme for scheduled castes. Provision of margin money even in differential rate of interest (DRI) cases is expected to be particularly helpful in areas where commercial bank branches have not so far taken up any substantial activities and where even DRI cases continue to be kept pending.

Pattern of Assistance

The schemes for assistance to SCDCs was introduced in the year 1978-79 as a centrally sponsored scheme in the states/UTs having sizable scheduled caste population to strengthen the share capital base of the SCDCs. At present, 26 SCDCs are being assisted in states/UTs which are mobilising finances for economic development of the scheduled castes. The Central share capital is sanctioned to SCDCs. Government of India and state governments participate in the ratio of 49:51 towards the share capital of SCDC. The cost norms of the projects/schemes have been left to the State Governments and SCDCs. The Central share of equity capital is sent directly to the state SCDCs. Wherever necessary, the Ministry of Social Justice and Empowerment, Government of India, might route the funds through the National Scheduled Castes Finance and Development Corporations (NSCFDC). The budget allocation for 2004-05 is Rs. 49 crore excluding budget allocation of Rs. 1 crore for northeastern states. The Tenth Five Year Plan (2002-2007) allocation is Rs. 150 crore.

The pattern of funding is as follows:

Share capital: Proportionate share by state government and Government of India in the ratio of 51:49, respectively.

Special Central Assistance for Filling the Infrastructural/Viability Gaps

Matching assistance: For promotional activities and surveys and studies—one per cent of cumulative share capital contribution of the Government of India; and setting up monitoring, evaluation, recovery and technical wings—three per cent of cumulative share capital contribution of the Government of India; managerial support; and grant from state government.

Pattern of Release of Funds to SCDCs

The existing pattern of release of funds to SCDCs has been reviewed by the Central government and it has now been decided that instead of automatic release in the ratio 49:51. Central share equity shall be released subject to: (i) recovery position of loans disbursed by SCDCs to beneficiaries, (ii) utilisation of share equity capital released by Central government to SCDCs, (iii) prior release of state share to SCDCs, and (iv) ability of the SCDC to raise additional resources from financial institutions including banks.

NSFDC Loan

The National Scheduled Castes and Scheduled Tribes Finance and Development Corporation (NSFDC) was incorporated by the Government of India on 8th February 1989 as a Government Company under Section 25 of the Companies Act, 1956. The Corporation was set up for providing institutional finance for self-employment activities of SCs and STs at a concessional rate of interest. In addition, the NSFDC was also providing grants for organising skill oriented training programmes for educated unemployed SC/ST youth, through reputed training institutions.

With the formation of a separate Ministry of Tribal Affairs to look after the welfare of scheduled tribes, the corporation was bifurcated on 10th April, 2001 into the National Scheduled Castes Finance and Development

Corporation (NSCFDC) to assist the scheduled castes and the National Scheduled Tribes Finance and Development Corporation (NSTFDC) to assist the scheduled tribes. The NSCFDC is the apex institution for financing, facilitating and mobilising funds from other sources and promoting of economic development activities of scheduled castes.

This corporation receives budgetary support in the form of equity share capital through the Ministry of Social Justice and Empowerment, Government of India, for meeting their operational requirements. Internal resources generated by way of recoveries of the loans and seed capital assistance extended, interest earned on assistance provided to SC beneficiaries and interest by way of short-term deposit of surplus funds, etc., are redeployed in providing assistance to the eligible SC beneficiaries.

NSFDC provides term loan for projects costing upto Rs. 30 lakh. It may provide term loan upto 900/0 of the cost of project subject to the condition that the state level channelising agencies (SCAs) contribute their share of assistance i.e., MML and subsidy (wherever applicable). There are several other schemes of NSFDC under which loans are extended to SC persons living below double the poverty line. The funds for the sanctioned projects/schemes are released by NSFDC on specific request from the SCAs and generally subject to certain conditions which include state government guarantee/bank guarantee. SCAs have been advised to keep a balanced approach in sectoral allocation of the loans which include 40 per cent to agriculture and allied sector, 50 per cent to services sector and 10 per cent to industrial sector.

Objectives of the Corporation

Financing income-generating schemes for the SCs through the SCAs and other recognised institutions nominated by the respective state/UT governments. Providing grants for skill development programmes channelised through SCAs.

Providing Advisory Services to the Target Group and the SCAs

Upgrading skills of officers of the state level channelising agencies, through periodic training programmes. Providing grants to the SCAs for setting up electronic data processing (EDP) cells for computerising the database relating to the schemes.

Being an apex corporation, the NSCFDC operates through its channelising agencies (mostly state/UT corporations: 34 in number) which have branches/offices at district/block levels. The NSCFDC has branches only at the zonal level covering southern zone (Bangalore), eastern zone (Kolkata and Patna), northeastern zone (Guwahati), north zone (Chandigarh), western zone (Mumbai) and central zone (Lucknow).

Schemes under the Corporation

The NSCFDC has formulated schemes for providing financial assistance/credit facilities to ameliorate the conditions of persons belonging to the scheduled castes. Scheduled caste families living below double the poverty line (i.e., Rs. 31,952 p.a. in rural areas and Rs. 42,412 p.a. in urban areas) are assisted through projects costing up to Rs.30 lakh. To cover maximum number of beneficiaries, within the overall allocation, 90 per cent of the fund is allocated for projects/units costing up to Rs.5 lakh. The NSCFDC provides: (i) term loan, (ii) seed capital loan, (iii) bridge loan, (iv) working capital loan, (v) microfinance, and (vi) grant for skill and entrepreneurial programmes.

The funds mobilised in each year by the corporations are notionally allocated to the channelising agencies of the NSCFDC in the states/UTs in proportion to the SC population represented by the respective state/UT. Each channelising agency is intimated the amount of allocation for sanctions in the beginning of the financial year. Channelising agencies have been advised that flow of funds in the states/UTs may be caused in such a manner whereby in each district/region, proper balance is maintained keeping in view the scheduled castes population of that district/region *vis-à-vis* the state and UT scheduled castes population.

Within the overall allocation, funds are further allocated as detailed below:

a. For projects/units costing upto Rs.5 lakh 90 per cent.

b. For projects/units costing above Rs.5 lakh 10 per cent.

However, the channelising agencies are at liberty to avail hundred per cent of their notional allocation for small value projects. The channelising agencies have been advised to ensure the flow of funds as follows:

a) Educated unemployed/underemployed beneficiaries (60 per cent).

b) Women beneficiaries (20 per cent).

c) Other beneficiaries (20 per cent).

Channelising agencies have also been advised to keep a balanced approach on sectoral allocation while forwarding schemes to the NSCFDC for consideration. Broad norms of sectoral allocation are as under:

Sector	*Percentage of Notional Allocation*
Agriculture & allied sector	40%
Services sector (including transport)	50%
Industrial sector	10%

The NSCFDC maintain coordination/liaison and flow of funds for economic development of SCs whose annual family income is below double the poverty line limit by channelising their funds through state level channelising agencies which are required to identify and formulate the schemes and examine and recommend them to the corporations for consideration.

Term Loans

The NSCFDC provide term loan at interest rates ranging from 7 to 9 per cent per annum chargeable to beneficiaries. However, the SCAs are required to pay only 4 to 6 per cent per annum and spread of 3 per cent is available to them for meeting their various costs. Term loan is provided to the extent of up to 90 per cent of the total project cost and the balance is tied up in the form of margin money portion from the SCAs and promoter contribution from beneficiaries. The SCAs implement the schemes from time to time and make repayments to the corporations. Therefore, the corporations are not providing any refinance to them. The beneficiary is required to pay a minimal portion of the project cost as promoter's contribution as his/her participation in the project.

Security for Loans

The NSCFDC obtains state government guarantee/bank guarantee/ government assurance/order for the loans released to the state channelising agencies. Through the channelising agencies, upto 85 per cent of the recurring expenditure in the form of grant is provided by the corporations for imparting skill and entrepreneurial development training to the target groups.

Letter of Guarantee

After issuance of the final selection, the district office of the SCA shall arrange for the execution of loan documents in the formats prescribed by the Head office of the SCA along with letter of guarantee. 'Letter of Guarantee' is to be executed at the time of extending loan to the beneficiaries under NSFDC-credit linked schemes.

Eligibility of guarantors is as follows:

	Project Cost for Scheme		*Eligibility of Guarantor*
1.	Scheme upto 1.5 lakh	i)	All categories of government/semi-government officials.
		ii)	Persons holding property double the project cost. Alternatively keeping of mortgage the landed property of beneficiary in favour of the corporation whose value shall not be less than the value of project undertaken by the beneficiary.
2.	Project cost from Rs.1.5 lakh to Rs.4 lakh	i)	All categories of government/semi-government officials except Group-D. Alternatively at least two groups. Group 'D' category officials. or
		ii)	Persons holding property double the project cost. Alternatively keeping of mortgage the landed property of beneficiary in favour of the corporation whose value shall not be less than the value of project undertaken by the beneficiary.
3.	Project cost above Rs.4 lakh	i)	Government/semi-government officials of Group 'B' and above. Alternatively at least two Group 'C' or three Group 'D' officials of government/semi-government. or
		ii)	Persons holding property double the project cost. Alternatively keeping of mortgage the landed property of beneficiary in favour of the corporation whose value shall not be less than the value of project undertaken by the beneficiary.

Guarantor is not required in case of beneficiaries who are willing to take loan keeping their landed property as mortgage in favour of the corporation.

The Delhi Scheduled Castes Finance and Development Corporation Ltd. (DSFDC) for safeguarding the government funds, insists that the beneficiary shall have to either mortgage property/assets equivalent to the loan amount and interest thereon. The applicant shall have to produce one government employee's surety drawing take home salary of Rs. 4,000/- per month Applicant shall have to deposit post-dated cheques for the entire loan amount including interest towards repayment of loan in advance on the basis of equated monthly installments before disbursement of the loan amount. He shall also be required to deposit all essential documents like caste certificate, a copy of ration card, income certificate, proof of date of birth, SSI, registration certificate (for those, who wish to go for industrial activity), lease deed/latest rent receipt etc.

Fund Utilisation

Funds drawn from NSCFDC are to be utilised within 90 days. NSCFDC funds released by the SCAs to the beneficiaries or advanced towards procurement of assets under the project shall alone be considered as fund utilised. However, fund transferred by SCAs to its branch/district offices are not considered as fund utilised.

Funds not utilised within 90 days from the date of release by NSCFDC will attract interest of 10 per cent (inclusive of normal interest). Funds returned to NSCFDC unutilised by SCAs even within 90 days shall attract interest of 10 per cent.

Progress Report is to be submitted to NSCFDC in the prescribed format within 210 days from the date of release of fund failing which interest at 10 per cent shall be charged.

Awards to the NSCFDC for Outstanding Performance

The NSCDFDC has received the following wards/merit certificates for its outstanding performance:

- MoU award for outstanding performance (2001-02) from the President of India on 5th April 2003.

- Merit certificate for Excellence in achievement of MOU Target (2002-03) by Honourable Prime Minister on 4th September 2004.
- NSCFDC's Annual Accounts (2003-04) adjudged best among 'not for profit' organisations by Institute of Charted Accountants of India, and
- 'ICAI Award for Excellence in Financial Reporting' conferred by H.E., the Governor of Jammu and Kashmir.

The NSCFDC was set up to improve the economic lot of the scheduled castes by working as catalytic agents besides extending both 'forward' and 'backward' linkages of credit and marketing facilities to the micro-level agencies towards improving the economic lot of these groups. While, NSCFDC was expected to become self-reliant over a period of 2-3 years of their establishment, it is becoming more and more dependent upon the Government support. There is a need to bring forth necessary reforms to make it an effective financial instrument in empowering the scheduled castes.

NSKFDC Loan

National Safai Karamcharis Finance and Development Corporation (NSKFDC) was incorporated on 24th January 1997 under Section 25 of the Companies Act, 1956, as an apex institution for all round socioeconomic upliftment of the *safai karamcharis* and their dependents throughout India and to extend concessional financial assistance to the *safai karamcharis* beneficiaries for establishment of income generating viable projects. NSKFDC provides loans to the *safai karamcharis* and their dependents through state channelising agencies

Target Group

The target groups of the corporation are 'scavengers' which means persons wholly or partially employed for manual handling of human excreta and their dependents and '*safai karamcharis*' which means persons engaged in or employed for any sanitation work and their dependents.

No income limit is fixed for availing financial assistance. However, other things being equal, the corporation accords priority to the economic development and rehabilitation of:

i) Scavengers, and amongst them those scavengers whose income is below double the poverty line;

ii) Women from among the target group; and

iii) Disabled persons among the target group.

SCDCs are also the SCAs for NSKFDC. A person engaged in sanitation work, cleaning dry latrines, open drains, cess pools, manholes drains, septic tanks, garbage etc., and his dependents are provided loan through SCDCs at a concessional rate of interest which is at par with the interest rates prescribed by NSCFDC for their projects. No income limit is fixed for availing financial assistance. Loans and subsidy under the National Scheme of Liberation and Rehabilitation of Scavengers is also provided by the SCDCs. Under this scheme the financing includes subsidy of up to Rs. 10,000/-, rv1ML of 15 per cent and the remaining funding through banks. NSKFDC has also started financing the projects under this scheme, through SCDCs.

Training

SCDCs provide training to SC youth in traditional and non-traditional trades. These programmes are for both the urban and rural youths. During the training, the trainees are provided stipend and the cost of training is also borne by the corporations. After training the beneficiaries are assisted through one or the other lending scheme of the SCDCs.

Performance Review of SCDCs

The scheme of assistance to share capital of the corporations has been operating since 1978-79. Initially SCDCs were providing subsidy and margin money loan and were tying up with the local banks for arranging loans to the SC beneficiaries living below the poverty line. With the emergence of the apex corporations *viz.*, NSFDC and NSKFDC the responsibility of implementing the schemes of these corporations also fell on SCDCs.

Share Capital Scenario

The financial resources of the corporations in terms of authorised share capital also vary depending on the size of the states as well as the size of their budgets. A statement indicating the authorised share capital and paid share capital till 30th September 2004, with the share of the Central government and state governments enclosed in Annexure Table A-12.1. It may be seen from therein that inspite of continuation of the scheme from a very long time, the paid up capital remains to be significantly less than the authorised share capital. The paid up share capital of states like Andhra Pradesh, Bihar, Chhattisgarh, Haryana, Punjab, Uttarakhand and West is far less than their authorised share capital. Both the Centre and state governments are required to provide assistance to enable the corporations to function at their optimum level of authorised share capital. Out of the paid-up capital, the share of the states and Central government should be in the ratio of 51:49. It is seen that during 2004-05, Central government was yet to pay a total equity share of Rs.35.58 crore to 16 states by October 2004. There are five states namely, Assam, Bihar, Madhya Pradesh, Orissa and Punjab and also union territories like Daman & Diu and Dadra & Nagar Haveli which are yet to pay their proportional share.

Progress in Coverage of Beneficiaries

A statement showing the coverage of beneficiaries during the Ninth Five Year Plan (1997-2000) and the two years (2002-2004) of Tenth Five Year Plan is enclosed in Annexure Table A-12.2. The statement indicates that during the Ninth Plan there was a decline in the coverage. As Against 6.15 lakh beneficiaries covered during 1997-98, the coverage during the last year of the Ninth Plan i.e., during 2001-2002 was only 5.40 lakh. However, during the Tenth Plan, the situation seems to be improving. During 2002-03, the scheme covered 6.28 lakh beneficiaries and during 2003-04, the number of beneficiaries was expected to be 7.64 lakh. Thus, the performance of SCDCs is improving in the Tenth Plan.

Loan Recovery

The most crucial problem that the SCDCs are facing is their poor recovery rates from the beneficiaries. This has emerged as mirror of the functioning of the SCDCs. The level of recovery is a significant fact in the erosion of the net worth of the SCDCs and their capacity to recycle the funds which would ultimately affect the growth of these corporations. Several states have reported stringent measures to improve the recovery by way of involving district administration, invoking of collateral security and various other administrative measures, but it appears that these measures are not effective in mobilising the recovery to a significant level, although some improvement in this regard is seen. A statement showing the rates of recovery achieved by various SCDCs is given in Annexure Table A-12.3.

Performance Review of the SCDCs under Study

The research study on viability and sustainability of the SCDCs in eight states compiled data on important financial parameters to examine the financial viability of the SCDCs. The data collected pertained to:

Margin money loan advanced and recovered, and policy regarding bad debts; loan amount received from the NSFDC and NSKFDC, and returned including penal interest, if any; Central and equity capital fund parked in the banks for earning interest. Table 12.2 presents an analysis of the empirical data on the above financial parameters to develop a clear perspective on the financial viability of the SCDCs studied under this research study.

Table 12.2

Status of Recovery of Margin Money Loan and Policy on Doubtful and Bad Debts since Inception of the SCDCs

(Rs. in Lakh)

S.No.	*State*	*Total Margin Money Disbursed*	*Interest Accrued on Margin Money*	*Recovery Made on Margin Money Disbursed*	*Difference between Margin Money Disbursed and Recovered*	*Provision for Settlement of Bad and Doubtful Debts*
1.	Andhra Pradesh	34495.08	1691.30	2581.51	31913.57	A sum not exceeding 15% of the net profit should be carried to bad debt reserve and for unforeseen losses
2.	Karnataka	13392.65	3142.24	2635.75	10756.9	Proposal sent to government to waive off the bad and doubtful debts
3.	Maharashtra	2853	-	-		-
4.	Orissa	1663	Not provided	368	1295	No specific policy
5.	Rajasthan	Not available	Not available	Not available	Not available	No specific policy
6.	Tamil Nadu					
7.	Uttar Pradesh	18449.78	5236.84	4463.75	13986.03	1% of the net profit
8	West Bengal			Not provided		

Source: Records of NSFDC, New Delhi/NSFDC Annual Reports.

It may be seen from above statement that highest amount of recoverable margin money loan is in the state of Andhra Pradesh followed by Uttar Pradesh, Karnataka and Orissa. This figure shows both recovery performances in terms of principal as well as recovery of the interest accrued on that principal.

We tried out best to compile data on the status of margin money loan scenario in West Bengal Scheduled Castes Development Corporation, but could not get adequate data till the time of writing of the IPE Report.[1] Due to non-availability of data on margin money loan advanced, recovered, extent of bad debts and policy towards the outstanding bad debt, we are not in a position to give our analysis on this aspect. But we did receive data on the status of the NSFDC loan, and we are giving below a critical analysis on the same.

Table 12.3 and 12.4 gives an account of the loan amount received from the NSFDC and the NSKFDC, and amount actually recovered from the beneficiaries, and returned to the NSFDC and NSKFDC. It may be seen from the Table 12.3 that the difference between the loan amount given and recovered is highest in the state of Andhra Pradesh (81%), followed by Uttar Pradesh (76.2%), Rajasthan (76%), West Bengal (73.1%), Orissa (68%) and Karnataka (68%). Again if we compare the figures related to difference between the loan amount actually recovered and returned to the NSFDC, then we find that this gap is highest in the state of Uttar Pradesh (49.3%), followed by Andhra Pradesh (40.8%), West Bengal (29.35), Rajasthan (19.6%).

The total margin money loan disbursed to the scheduled caste beneficiaries in Orissa since inception i.e., 1979-80 to 2005-06, is Rs. 16.63 crore. Out of which the cumulative collection up to the year 2005-06 was Rs. 3.68 crore (22.12%) and the outstanding balance in this regard is Rs 12.95 crore (77.88%). Thus, the total bad and doubtful margin money loan declared by the corporation is Rs. 12.95 crore.

Orissa government has no specific policy to write off the bad and doubtful debt of the beneficiaries. The collection position of OSFDC under

1. *Evaluation Study Report: Viability and Sustainability of the Scheduled Castes Development Corporations*. Hyderabad: IPE. Sponsored by the Ministry of Social Justice and Empowerment, Government of India.

margin money loan programme was very miserable for which OSFDC has stopped advancing of margin money loan to the beneficiaries since 1999-2000. According to the tie-up arrangements made with the financing agencies, the margin money loan of the corporation is to be recovered by the participating banks along with their own loan. After recovery, the banks are required to remit the recovered margin money loan to the corporation. The banks are not remitting the margin money loan to corporation timely.

The government has also not provided any such assistance for collection of bad and doubtful loans from SC and ST groups and no share capital under SC sector is being released by government from 1997-98 onwards.

Table 12.3

NSFDC Financial Assistance Received, Disbursed, Recovered and Repaid

		Loan Received from NSFDC, Disbursal and Recovery Made (Rs. in Lakh)				
S. No.	*State*	*Received*	*Disbursed*	*Actual Amount Recovered from Beneficiaries*	*Difference between Loan Amount and Recovery Made*	*Amount of Loan Returned to NSFDC without Recovery from Beneficiaries*
1.	Andhra Pradesh	20747.23	20747.23	3787.44 (18.25)	16959.79 (81.75)	8463.37 (40.8)
2.	Karnataka	7014.40	6777.29	3076.39 (45.4)	3700.90 (54.6)	237.11 (3.5)
3.	Maharashtra					
4.	Orissa	2881.00	2881.00	923.19 (32)	1957.81 (68)	193.61 (6.7)
5.	Rajasthan	3614.00	3019.00	727.40 (24)	2292.60 (76)	593.27 (19.6)
6.	Tamil Nadu	1522.05	1408.08	1060.20 (75.3)	348.88 (24.7)	Nil
7.	Uttar Pradesh	9840.09	8200.34	1956.97 (23.8)	6243.37 (76.2)	4045.94 (49.3)
8.	West Bengal	45.02	43.42	11.68 (26.9)	31.74 (73.1)	12.74 (29.3)

Note: Figures in parenthesis indicate percentage to the total amount disbursed.
Source: Records of NSFDC, New Delhi.

NSFDC in West Bengal

The total amount of loan received by the SCDC in West Bengal from the NSFDC during 1999-2005 was Rs. 45.02 crore, while the amount of loan disbursed to beneficiaries was Rs. 43.42 crore. However, the actual amount of NSFDC loan amount recovered from the beneficiaries is only Rs.11.68 crore. This shows the enormous gap between the money disbursed and the money recovered, about 73 per cent. Amount of loan returned to NSFDC without having actually recovered it from the beneficiaries during this period was Rs. 12.74 crore.

Although the total number of projects under NSFDC, NSKFDC and SCP have been considerable (3,272, 5, and 85,736 in 2004-05 respectively), and total number of beneficiaries during 1999-2005 have been 17,98,111—it seems there has been a colossal problem in recovery of loans. This poses a serious problem in the viability and sustainability of the schemes. In the next section, the problems related to this issue are discussed in details.

The recovery percentage of NSFDC loans is given in Figure 12.4.

Figure 12.4

Recovery Percentage of NSFDC Loans

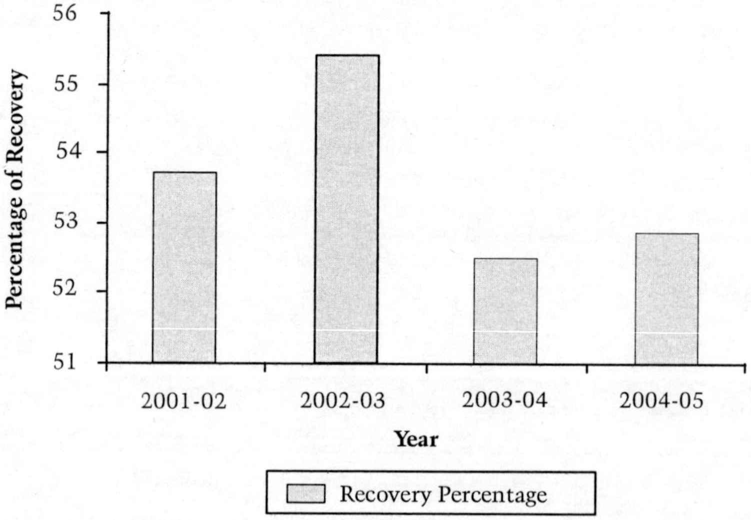

Source: Same as Table 12.2.

Under the schemes of national corporations, fund is taken on loan from the apex corporation and is given as loan to the beneficiaries below double the poverty line. Since this fund is meant for the economically weaker section for their income generation, the SCDC does not insist on collateral security as done by other financial institutions like banks. Loan is provided only against hypothecation of assets created from the loan and an official guarantor, which is more of a ritual. Guarantors are government employees, but since their pay is not attached, the guarantor becomes a paper security only. Therefore, the recovery depends mainly on persuasion and placement of post-dated cheques. Infrastructure of the corporation at the district level is poor; there are not enough field officers. Their routine work also seems to overburden them with sponsoring of cases, inspection, etc.

Although about 47 per cent of the SCDC loan to the beneficiaries remains unrecovered, it has to pay 100 per cent of the loan taken from the NSFDC, since this loan is covered under a state government guarantee. In this process, a major portion of the SCDC's own fund is gradually being depleted. Unless a major step is taken now, the corporation will become sick, and might eventually have to wind up.

Also, the SCDC gets loan from the NSFDC/NSKFDC at 3 per cent and 5 per cent interest under regular schemes and provides loan to the beneficiaries at 5 per cent and 8 per cent, thus keeping a margin of only 3 per cent to cover all its administrative expenses for sponsoring, supervision, recovery, etc. This margin of 3 per cent is considered low to cover such expenses. The overall expenses during 2001-02 and 2002-03 (until when data is available) were Rs. 6.62 and Rs. 6.22 crore respectively.

Not only the margin of interest is low for the SCDC, but also the interest is charged by NSFDC/NSKFDC from the date of disbursement of the fund to the SCDC. On the other hand, the SCDC charges interest from the beneficiary from the date of its disbursement of fund to the beneficiary, which normally takes three to four months' time. Therefore, the SCDC has to bear this interest burden of three to four months from its own exchequer.

In addition, it is often argued by the SCDC officials that the present process of obtaining loans from the NSFDC or NSKFDC is tedious and a lengthy one. Sanction is to be obtained in the form of Letter of Intent (LoI) for one particular scheme and then fund is to be requested giving particulars of the beneficiary. For one scheme, it is custom to produce one LoI. It may be appreciated that requirement of fund vary from one beneficiary to another depending upon the location of the business, requirement of the beneficiary, etc. For instance, fund required for establishing a grocery in a city might not be the same for the same scheme in a remote area. Hence, an amount of flexibility needs to be incorporated with the SCDC, as is the usual case with other financial institutions like banks.

It seems the SCDC has to incur a good expenditure of persuasion, recovery and advertisement to make the schemes of NSFDC popular. Since the SCDC is working at a very low margin, it becomes difficult for this body to undertake optimum expenditure in this field. This often results in the poorest not having enough information on schemes, which are steered by the local 'big men' for their own benefits, often through political relations.

Another major problem suggested by field officers in Cooch Behar and Nadia districts was about training. Many SC people approaching for loan neither have the idea of benefits of certain schemes, not any required training in the field. The officials suggested rigorous training in schemes related to agricultural sector (like operation of power tillers).

NSFDC in Orissa

During 1999-2005, a total of Rs. 28,81,00,000 was received by the SCDC in Orissa from NSFDC. This total amount was disbursed as loan, out of which Rs. 9,23,19,000 was recovered only. This produced a deficit of Rs. 19,57,81,000. About 10 per cent of this money, an amount of Rs. 1,93,61,000 was returned to NSFDC from the corporation's own funds. Recovery percentage in 2004-05 for NSFDC projects was 46.25 per cent, and 26.24 per cent only. The difference in lent money and the recovered money was spent from the corporation's own funds. In the two districts used as sample, loan recovery rate was 33.22 per cent in Dhenkanal and only 7.33 per cent in Kendrapara. All this has led to problems of non-repayment of loans from NSFDC. The grand total of Rs. 74,68,30,734—the balance amount not paid, on which OSFDC has to pay an interest of Rs. 17,16,660.

During the period of 1999-2005, bankable schemes parked in the deposit account and banks were Rs. 5,79,91,000. Banks are primarily using the subsidy money of the not releasing any amount towards loan. As a result, the beneficiaries in most cases are receiving Rs. 10,000 or less only. Also, the banks are claiming deposit of advance subsidy to OSFDC for financing the SC beneficiaries under bankable income generating scheme (IGS).

Table 12.4 gives an account of the performance of the NSKFDC schemes in eight states.

Table 12.4

NSKFDC Financial Assistance Disbursed and Recovered by the SCDC

S. No.	State	NSKFDC Funds Disbursal and Recovery Made (Rs. in Lakh)		
		Disbursed	Actual Amount Recovered from Beneficiaries	Difference between Loan Amount and Recovery Made
1.	Andhra Pradesh	12097.95	393.95	1748.59
2.	Karnataka	5105.68	449.93	4655.75
3.	Maharashtra	N/A	N/A	N/A
4.	Orissa	N/A	N/A	N/A
5.	Rajasthan	884.59	141.01	N/A
6.	Tamil Nadu	N/A	N/A	N/A
7.	Uttar Pradesh	3848.27	289.62	3558.65
8.	West Bengal	N/A	N/A	N/A

Note: Figures in parenthesis indicate percentage to the total amount disbursed.
Source: Records of NSFDC, New Delhi.

It is evident from the data made available by some of the states under study that the difference between loan amount disbursed and recovered was found to be the highest in Karnataka, followed by Uttar Pradesh and Andhra Pradesh. As in the case of the NSFDC, the SCDCs have to meet the same terms and conditions for availing loan fund and for timely repayment of loan; failing which they have to pay penalty.

The research[2] study also found that the SCDCs park a good amount of money in the banks in the form of fixed deposits and short-term deposits in order to earn interest to meet their administrative and other costs. In fact, the money parked with banks for a longer time should be used in

2. *Evaluation Study Report: Viability and Sustainability of the Scheduled Castes Development Corporations*. Hyderabad: IPE. Sponsored by the Ministry of Social Justice and Empowerment, Government of India.

disbursement of margin money loan to the scheduled caste borrowers. Similarly, banks keep the SCDCs' margin money and subsidy amount for long time which is given by the SCDC while forwarding to the scheduled caste beneficiaries. Margin money is the contribution given by the beneficiaries while taking loans from SCDCs.

Where the banks have not agreed to give loan to scheduled caste applicants, the margin money and subsidy component forwarded by the SCDC remain locked in the banks for considerable time without attracting interest thereon. Only after long persuasion, the banks agree to refund the margin money and subsidy amount to the SCDCs. For example, the Karnataka SC/ST Development Corporation Limited recovered Rs. 14,96,326, which was lying with the bank as SCDC's contribution towards subsidy and margin money loan. Similarly, the THADCO recovered Rs. 922513153.60 during the year 2004-05. This figure was Rs. 870470273.60 during the year 2003-04. The statement given (Table 12.5) below throws some light in this aspect. It is quite necessary that the banks should return the margin money and subsidy amount to the SCDCs when the applicants have not been considered for giving bank loan.

Table 12.5

SCDC's Contribution towards Subsidy and Margin Money Loan

		Financial Data Particulars on (Rs. in Lakh)				
S. No.	*State*	*Budgeted Scheme Funds Parked with Banks*	*Scheme Funds Parked in Short-Term Deposits with Banks*	*Scheme Funds Lying Idle in Bank Account*	*Amount Remained Unspent as of March 2005*	*Undisbursed Subsidy & Margin Money Loan Refunded by Banks to the SCDCs*
1.	Andhra Pradesh	Nil	Nil	Nil	Nil	Nil
2.	Karnataka	17196.05	7544.06	Nil	7174.42	14.96
3.	Maharashtra					
4.	Orissa	579.91	550.00	29.91	800.55	Not available
5.	Rajasthan	Nil	Nil	Nil	Nil	Nil
6.	Tamil Nadu	37752.43	25130.61	23193.19	3813.45	7126.08
7.	Uttar Pradesh	-	-	-	-	2767.37
8.	West Bengal	NA	NA	NA	NA	NA

Source: Same as Table 12.4.

As regards the average unit cost of the bank-linked and the NSFDC loan-linked projects, it was reported by the Uttar Pradesh Scheduled Castes Finance and Development Corporation Limited that the average unit cost of the bank-linked projects for the year 2003-04 was Rs. 22,555 and Rs. 22,250 for the year 2004-05. In the case of the NSFDC loan-linked projects, it was Rs. 24,912 for the year 2003-04 and Rs. 30,051 for the year 2004-05. This means that there is only nominal variation in the range of the average unit cost of the bank-linked and NSFDC loan-linked scheme. One wonders whether given the current price index, this level of average unit cost of the projects is adequate to enable the borrowers to cross the poverty line. There is a need to make substantial increase in the average unit cost of the projects. In case of the Uttar Pradesh Scheduled Castes Finance and Development Corporation, it was found that the bank-linked scheme constituted 82.48 per cent and 78.99 per cent for the year 2003-04 and 2004-05, respectively.

Proportion of the Bank-Linked and NSFDC/NSKFDC Schemes

The data collected from the SCDCs revealed that majority of the schemes implemented by these are linked with banks, and schemes funded by the NSFDC and the NSKFDC together constitute less than 20 per cent. For example, in Uttar Pradesh the SCDCs had implemented 83.48 per cent and 78.99 per cent of the bank-linked schemes in the year 2004-05 and 2005-06 respectively. For the NSFDC schemes, this figure was 9.77 per cent and 7 per cent. In case of the NSFDC schemes, this figure was 1.30 per cent and 3.12 per cent.

In the case of bank-linked schemes, the role of the SCDCs is confined to releasing of the subsidy amount and margin money loan, and forwarding of applications to the banks. The entire process of receiving applications from the eligible beneficiaries is carried out by the regular *mandal*/block level administration, and Panchayati Raj administrative machinery at the village level. One wonders whether we should have the office of the SCDC at the state and district level just to add margin money loan and subsidy amount in the applications for scheduled castes for credit support. Why this role can not be also carried out by the existing District Rural Development Agency (DRDA) which also takes care of the scheduled caste beneficiaries under the rural development programmes like Swarnajayanti Gram Swarozgar Yojana (SGSY), etc. We may consider giving some additional staff to the DRDA for carrying out the SCDC related work related to giving subsidy and margin money to the scheduled caste borrowers.

The activities of the SCDC related to NSFDC work, as channelising agency, is limited to less than 10 per cent in the overall activity chart of the SCDCs. But for this small aspect of the work, the SCDCs find themselves in a very difficult position as they have to work under very difficult and stringent financial norms for lending their money and recovery schedule, and also paying penal interest, and commission to the state government towards standing guarantee. The SCDCs are required to repay the NSFDC loan even without recovering the same from beneficiaries. All these nitty-gritty details of the NSFDC work is making the SCDCs unviable and unsustainable. It is therefore necessary to review the relationship between the NSFDC and SCDCs, and make it more sustainable and viable. This can be done only when the NSFDC treats the SCDCs as its partner and appreciates the constraints under which the SCDCs have to operate. In the absence of this partnership based on mutual appreciation of roles and constraints, the SCDCs relationship with the NSFDC as the channelising agency cannot be sustained. If SCDCs fail to recover the NSFDC loan amount from the borrowers, the NSFDC should bask under the glory of having recovered the loan (80 per cent and above) from the state channelising agency (SCA) with interest under the cover of state guarantee. In this bargain, the ultimate loser is the SCDCs.

Convergence with DRDA and Other Schemes

The state and the district scenario in almost all the states is marked by multiplicity of organisations devoted to SC, ST, OBC and minority welfare apart from other rural development agencies charged with implementation of self-employment and income generation schemes. The target groups and pattern of assistance of these organisations vary even though in many cases the agencies operate in the same sector of economy or locality. There is scope for convergence of schemes now implemented by the district level agencies of Departments of Social Welfare and Rural Development. While the collector of the district is expected to provide the necessary coordination between agencies, the sheer multiplicity of schemes, agencies and persons involved makes it difficult for the collector to ensure at all times a required degree of coordination. There is a need for coordination at the state level also. One possible avenue for ensuring the coordination of flow of funds from budgetary and credit sources are the credit plans which are finalised at the district and state levels. Attention to these aspects in the months of May and June, immediately following the approval of the State Budget by the Legislature may enable the district administration and banks to coordinate their action and achieve better results in the field.

Further, it was found that the district level offices of the SCDCs are not collaborating with the sectoral departments dealing with the special component plan (SCP) schemes. For example, the district manager of the SCDCs does not know what scheme is being implemented by the agriculture, irrigation, animal husbandry, social conservation departments for the scheduled castes in his district. As a result, the district managers of the SCDCs fail to bring any convergence between their schemes and the schemes of the sectoral departments for the scheduled castes. It is therefore necessary that the district manager of the SCDCs be made the nodal officer for bringing about convergence between the SCDC schemes and the schemes of different income generating and infrastructural schemes of different sectors under SCP. For example, if a member of scheduled caste has taken credit from the SCDC for purchasing pump set for irrigating his agricultural fields, then the district manager must try to bring in convergence of that beneficiary with the schemes of the agriculture, social conservation etc., so that the beneficiary also gets the agricultural inputs from the agriculture department, and improvement in the land owned by him from the social conservation department under the SCP schemes. This would ensure that the beneficiary of the SCDC scheme also get benefits from other schemes under SCP which would increase the chances of making bigger returns from his credit based investments.

Annexure Table A-12.1

Statement Showing Authorised Share Capital & Paid-up Capital of State Scheduled Caste Development Corporation as on 31.10.2004

S. No.	State Name	Authorised Share Capital	State Share	Central Share	Paid-up Capital	Short (-) + Excess (+)
1.	Assam	10	462.93	536.79	999.72	92.01
2.	Madhya Pradesh	25	886.59	938.29	1824.88	86.47
3.	Punjab	60	1732.24	1746.68	3478.92	82.37
4.	Bihar	50	1107.63	1113.27	2220.9	49.08
5.	Daman & Diu and Dadra & Nagar Haveli	10	193.01	227.23	420.24	41.79
6.	Orissa	25	609.41	605.55	1214.96	20.04
7.	Pondicherry	5	142.24	136.66	278.9	0.00
8.	Delhi	30	1277.19	1227.15	2504.34	0.05
9.	Tamil Nadu	100	4717.5	4532.5	9250.0	0.00
10.	Gujarat	25	1265.0	1215.39	2480.39	0.00
11.	Rajasthan	15	670.74	644.43	1315.17	-0.01
12.	Tripura	20	329.27	306.75	636.02	-9.61
13.	Karnataka	150	6143.11	5508.28	11651.39	-393.92
14.	Chandigarh	10	556.5	534.67	1091.17	-0.01
15.	Uttar Pradesh	150	7651.84	7351.76	15003.6	-0.01
16.	Kerala	50	2389.94	2035.41	4425.35	-260.81
17.	Jammu & Kashmir	20	724.0	556.4	1280.4	-139.21
18.	Haryana	40	1434.47	1368.58	2803.05	-9.64
19.	Goa	5	164.67	103.76	268.43	-54.45
20.	Sikkim	10	389.0	132.18	521.18	-241.57
21.	Himachal Pradesh	30	1327.62	1070.9	2398.52	-204.66
22.	Uttarakhand	15	202.0	98.0	300.0	-96.08
23.	Andhra Pradesh	450	16843.46	14862.86	31346.32	-974.19
24.	West Bengal	200	6101.85	5588.78	11690.63	-273.78
25.	Maharashtra	100	5537.116	4900.0	10437.11	-419.97
26.	Chhattisgarh	50	1336.54	803.55	2140.09	-480.58
	Total	**1570**	**63835.86**	**58145.82**	**121981.68**	**-3558.48**

Annexure Table A-12.2

Statement Showing Number of Beneficiaries Assisted during Ninth Five Year Plan, 2002-03 and 2003-04 (Expected) by Scheduled Caste Development Corporations

S.No.	Name of SCDC	Number of Scheduled Castes Beneficiaries Assisted							
		1997-98	1998-99	1999-2000	2000-2001	2001-2002	Total Ninth Plan	2002-03	2003-04 (Expected)
1.	Andhra Pradesh	99313	165675	113911	78965	97555	555419	131554	115000
2.	Assam	2972	4978	4814	5278	12189	30231	11377	20651
3.	Bihar	1044	1971	1194	1156	1880	7245	NR	NR
4.	Chandigarh	653	732	729	665	698	3477	319	650
5.	Chhattisgarh	1585	1447	1212	1062	2391	7697	226	1097
6.	Daman & Diu and Dadra & Nagar Haveli	21	6	5	7	2	41	34	75
7.	Delhi	3469	3602	4391	391	904	12757	13043	17310
8.	Goa	27	39	29	37	15	147	12	20
9.	Gujarat	10582	9714	8783	8402	7201	44682	7587	14300
10.	Haryana	12580	13988	3935	11183	10583	52269	10343	10000
11.	Himachal Pradesh	3712	3502	3819	3590	4066	14627	3164	3500
12.	Jammu & Kashmir	782	758	529	277	591	2937	195	1016
13.	Karnataka	28805	23558	16417	16423	15879	101082	15493	26825
14.	Kerala	2208	2564	2361	2075	781	9989	1789	3943
15.	Madhya Pradesh	16090	15817	11686	10443	14321	68357	14941	15000
16.	Maharashtra	17940	10351	15517	13249	16043	73100	11289	12000
17.	Orissa	66718	44222	30746	29854	23918	195458	24870	37367
18.	Pondicherry	965	1230	1012	1229	1176	5612	1297	1395
19.	Punjab	11786	9906	7963	3118	1574	34347	11700	26300
20.	Rajasthan	72211	70098	68030	62444	62432	335215	253	440
21.	Sikkim	32	2545	2013	1082	3755	9427	78	150
22.	Tamil Nadu	124504	111912	101166	30569	48675	79244	143822	195879
23.	Tripura	35	42	34	160	171	442	794	1000
24.	Uttar Pradesh	86952	95789	80973	96264	93370	453348	113766	125000
25.	Uttarakhand	-	-	-	4381	4661	9042	5278	172
26.	West Bengal	50768	52422	57793	124864	120783	406630	105493	135000
	Total	**615754**	**646868**	**539062**	**502787**	**540953**	**2845424**	**628717**	**764090**

Annexure Table A-12.3

Rate of Recovery Reported by Scheduled Caste Development Corporations

(in percentage)

S.No.	*Name of SCDCs*	*1997-98*	*1998-99*	*1999-2000*	*2001-01*	*2001-02*	*2002-03*	*2003-04*
1.	Andhra Pradesh	45	47	50	24	35.47	33.3	26.49
2.	Assam	10	10	N.A	N.A	N.A	N.A	N.A
3.	Bihar	39.18	4.35	5.54	3.79	16.01	17.43	18.39
4.	Chandigarh	77.28	72.53	72.75	57.54	62.85	54.26	53
5.	Chhattisgarh	*New Corporation*					2.85	32.06
6.	Daman & Diu and Dadra & Nagar Haveli	N.A	N.A	N.A	N.A	N.A	N.A	N.A
7.	Delhi	N.A	N.A	N.A	N.A	N.A	N.A	N.A
8.	Goa	72.29	64	N.A	N.A	N.A	N.A	N.A
9.	Gujarat	35.48	32.59	55.34	60.83	63.09	65.52	N.A
10.	Haryana	77.01	71.14	63.63	64.19	N.A	58.91	71.66
11.	Himachal Pradesh	73	64	59	57	44	33	40
12.	Jammu & Kashmir	62.03	N.A	N.A	N.A	58	45	64
13.	Karnataka	24	16	12.36	21.92	21	N.A	7033
14.	Kerala	68.61	67.74	67.89	68.09	68.2	N.A	N.A
15.	Madhya Pradesh	N.A	N.A	N.A	12.6	N.A	N.A	N.A
16.	Maharashtra	25	8	8	N.A	N.A	34	N.A
17.	Orissa	N.A	N.A	0.19	1.89	1.87	N.A	N.A
18.	Pondicherry	32.41	36.64	29.29	27.46	18.98	14.89	51.57
19.	Punjab	N.A	N.A	N.A	73.38	75.76	74.89	74.83
20.	Rajasthan	41.59	45.31	52.85	N.A	N.A	N.A	N.A
21.	Sikkim	N.A	N.A	N.A	57	N.A	N.A	N.A
22.	Tamil Nadu	43.7	26	37.2	20.17	N.A	N.A	N.A
23.	Tripura	18	25	27	N.A	N.A	N.A	N.A
24.	Uttar Pradesh	48	24.17	23.96	26.39	9.46	9.65	N.A
25.	Uttarakhand	*New Corporation*					N.A	N.A
26.	West Bengal	2.75	N.A	N.A	N.A	N.A	N.A	N.A

13 Viability and Sustainability Issues in the Scheduled Castes Development Corporations

Introduction

Performance review of the Scheduled Castes Development Corporations (SCDCs) is available in the reports of various Working Groups on Development of Scheduled Castes Reports, Commissioner for Scheduled Castes and Scheduled Tribes, National Commission for Scheduled Castes and Scheduled Tribes, Audit Reports of the Comptroller and Auditor General of India (CAG). These reports provide a good deal of information and insights on various problems that have been faced by the SCDCs in the recent past, and offer inputs for further review about their performance at present. It also provides an opportunity to understand as to what extent the problems reported earlier persist and what are the new issues related to their viability and sustainability that need to be addressed. In what follows, we present important findings related to the performance of the SCDCs from various documented reports.

I. Report of the Commissioner for Scheduled Castes and Scheduled Tribes (April 1979–March 1980) made the following observations regarding working of the SCDCs.

> Neither the State Governments nor the Government of India have undertaken to meet the managerial cost towards running of the Corporations with the result that some of the Corporations are making payment of salaries to staff out of the interest earned by them from the fixed deposits lying with the banks while others are meeting the charges from out of their share capital. Both result in depletion, blocking of the capital meant for betterment of the Scheduled Castes. The Central Government should share managerial cost with the State Governments on the same basis as

they are participating in the equity contribution that is 49:51 bases for a period of 5 years so as to make the Corporations stable and viable units.

II. 28th Report of the Commissioner for Scheduled Castes and Scheduled Tribes (1986-87) noticed the following constraints in working of the SCDCs.

a. The SCDCs in Andhra Pradesh, Haryana, Kerala, Maharashtra, Orissa, Rajasthan, Tamil Nadu and the SCA released to the State Governments concerned. Most of these corporations were using this amount to give subsidy to individual beneficiaries. However, in Andhra Pradesh and Tamil Nadu and to some extent in Orissa it was used for providing infrastructure for group schemes in the form of common work-sheds and machinery. In Andhra Pradesh 90 per cent of the SCA was reported to have been utilised for infrastructure building.

b. The SCDCs in Assam, Kerala, Gujarat, Punjab, Rajasthan and Tamil Nadu were reported to be unable to use the major portion of their share capital for programmes of assistance to the Scheduled Castes. Some corporations like those in Gujarat and Rajasthan were earning huge amounts of interest from the share capital funds kept in fixed deposits. The corporations in Assam, Karnataka, Maharashtra, Rajasthan and Delhi were reported to be using a large portion of their share capital for meeting their administrative expenses. According to the guidelines these funds should have been used to provide assistance for bank tie-up schemes to scheduled caste families.

c. The position regarding the recovery of margin money loans was reported to be quite unsatisfactory in Andhra Pradesh (7%), Assam (2%) and Uttar Pradesh (8.5%). The corporations having good recovery position were Himachal Pradesh (36.5%), Orissa (54.8%) and West Bengal (35.7%). Some corporations are reported to have received little cooperation from banks in effecting recovery of margin money loans. In Andhra Pradesh and Maharashtra the corporations had to recover their margin money loans themselves and in Bihar and West Bengal the banks agreed to recover margin money loans after their own components had been recovered. There was no problem of recovering margin money loans in the corporations in Gujarat, Kerala and Madhya Pradesh since they provided margin money deposits and not loans to the banks. In the case of other corporations the banks were reported to have agreed to recover margin money loans almost simultaneously with their loans. According to the commercial banks a considerable number of beneficiaries identified and sponsored by the corporations were found on verification either to defaulters or were not interested in taking up the subsidy schemes which resulted in delay in the sanction of project.

d. According to the corporations, the banks, particularly at the field level, were not very enthusiastic to lend to the scheduled castes probably with the fear of non-recovery of dues or due to the belief that poor entrepreneurs were not viable. They were also of the view that the banks often violated the Reserve Bank of India directive not to insist on security and guarantee for loans not exceeding Rs.5,000.

Since the margin money loan programme had not succeeded in generating institutional finance of the magnitude required due to conceptual and operational problems inherent in the scheme, the Ministry of Home Affairs constituted a Standing Committee in 1984 for suggesting an alternative scheme which would be less cumbersome and easier to operate. The Committee recommended a new programme entitled 'New Pattern of Assistance to Scheduled Caste Families through SCDCs' for adoption by all the SCDCs.

The margin money loan programme was to be discontinued. On the other hand, the corporations were to provide to the financing institutions seed money deposits equivalent to 25 per cent of the project cost of the schemes. However, deposits were not to be linked to each individual account but only to the total disbursals during a given period. Thus, the corporations were to become partners in development lending along with financing institutions providing them lien and risk cover to a limited extent.

Clubbing of subsidies from different sources was to be stopped. Persons availing of subsidy from the Integrated Rural Development Programme (IRDP) or other agencies were to be excluded from the programme.

III. Report of the Working Group on the Development of Scheduled Castes during the Seventh Five Year Plan, 1985-90.

It made the following observations:

a. Most of the corporations entered into agreements with banks for participation in the development of scheduled castes and have been implementing margin money loan programme. However, the achievements now in most states have been less than expected. The Scheduled Castes Development Corporations have been able to provide assistance to about 24 lakh beneficiaries till now contributing Rs. 79.50 crore as margin money. This contribution has mobilised Rs. 351.75 crore of institutional finance and Rs. 351.75 crore of institutional finance and Rs. 133.40 crore of subsidy.

b. The average assistance thus provided to a beneficiary family has amounted to only Rs. 2,352. As against this the share capital of all the Scheduled Castes Development Corporations together as on March 31, 1984 was Rs. 111.24 crore. Nearly 71 per cent of the total share capital has been utilised for operating the margin money loan programme.

c. The relatively limited success by Scheduled Castes Development Corporations to mobilise institutional credit compared to the magnitude required may be ascribed to various factors. It should be admitted that most of the corporations were only at the formative stage during the major part of the Sixth Five Year Plan (1980-1985). The concept of margin money as a catalyst for institutional finance and its operational strategy were not too clearly understood by all concerned. However, the major problem centred around reaching clear-cut agreements with financial institutions on the *modus operandi* and procedures of lending as well as recovery of both margin money and bank loan.

   The operational problems centred around recommending borrowers from outside the operational area of banks, sending application in large numbers at the fag end of the financial year, delays in release of margin money/subsidy, interference by the intermediaries, etc. The banks also wanted that applications should be sponsored from compact SC clusters and suitably phased in the financial year and should be from within the catchment area of bank branches.

d. A major difficulty faced by banks was the near non-existence of follow-up, supervision and monitoring of beneficiaries on the part of the government agencies/corporation staff, which resulted in poor recoveries. This they felt was further complicated by the difficulty of accounting for small amounts of recovery of margin money to be posted in numerous accounts and the need of transmitting the same to the corporations, where the banks were required to recover the margin money loans of the corporations.

e. The Scheduled Castes Development Corporations on the other hand allege that the banks, particularly at the field level, are not very enthusiastic to lend to scheduled castes probably out of fear of non-recovery of dues *or* due to the belief that the poor entrepreneurs are not viable. Besides they complain that often there is a violation of RBI directives on the part of bank managers such as insistence on security and guarantee even for loan not exceeding Rs.5,000/-, insistence on non-encumbrance certificates, provision of inadequate amount of loan for schemes requiring larger amount, over charging of interest etc. They also allege that very often the cases sponsored by corporation are kept pending for long durations without ascertaining reasons and this is often attributed to shortage of technical and administrative staff at branches especially in rural areas.

The Working Group recommended that the margin money loan programme needs to be revamped if it is to perform effectively as catalyst and guarantor for institutional credit. Presently, the meagre staff of the corporations is caught up in the formalities for release of margin money/subsidy to the banks in the accounts of numerous small borrowers. In order to minimise the operational impact and financial effectiveness, the Working Group recommended:

1. Margin money loan programme may be converted into a seed money deposit programme.
2. The corporations should identify clusters of villagers with concentration of scheduled castes population and which are served preferably by a single bank branch target for each financial year for each cluster and, bank branch should be fixed within the operational area of the branch. A project report

should be prepared at the beginning and a proportion of the project cost depending on the financial viability analysis be deposited, for terms found appropriate, with that bank branch. The interest on the deposits could be shared between the corporation and the beneficiaries in the ratio of 40:60 in accordance with the amount of the margin money loan of each beneficiary. However, the benefit of interest may not be available to the beneficiaries who default repayment of three consecutive installments of bank loan till the time they repay the bank. The bank branch should finance the entire cost of each beneficiary scheme minus subsidy, if any.

3. Before preparing the project report the corporation's field staff should identify beneficiaries in clusters under each bank branch through a socioeconomic survey.
4. The seed money could be deposited with the participating bank branch at the beginning of each financial year and suitably augmented in pace with the progress achieved subsequently.
5. The staffing pattern of the district level of the corporations should be suitably strengthened.
6. The personnel policy of the corporation from top to bottom may need to be reoriented in such a manner that professional competence and commitment are given prime consideration and continuity of personnel is ensured. If such personnel cannot be found among the present government bureaucratic system, open recruitment from universities, voluntary agencies, social workers, etc., may be explored.

IV. The Report of Working Group on Development and Welfare of the Scheduled Castes during the Eighth Five Year Plan (1990-95).

1. Most of the corporations entered into agreement with banks for implementing margin money loan programme. Under this programme, the SCDCs provide margin money to beneficiaries normally @25 per cent of the unit cost from out of their share capital at low rate of interest i.e., 4 per cent. In the Sixth Plan, the state corporations disbursed Rs.106.59 crore as margin money, which generated bank loan of Rs.370.84 crore for about 28.69 lakh

families. The subsidy of Rs.100.50 crore were also given to these beneficiaries. The total assistance given to about 29 lakh families during the Sixth Plan thus was of the order of Rs.578 crore and average assistance per family was around Rs.2,000.

2. Of late certain states namely Kerala, Madhya Pradesh, Gujarat, Tamil Nadu, Puducherry have modified the margin money loan programmes to suit their local conditions. These states are implementing what is known as 'Margin Money Deposit Scheme'. Under this scheme a portion (20 to 25%) of the cost of the scheme is placed with banks as term deposit against which bank finance is given to beneficiaries. The interest accrued out of this deposit is to be shared between the beneficiaries and the corporation.
3. Though the achievement of SCDCs in terms of physical coverage and financial assistance mobilised for the target groups would appear to be quite impressive, the efforts, when viewed with reference to the size of SC population and per capita outlay, have been quite meagre. The average quantum of assistance per beneficiary has been so low that the incremental incomes generated through the schemes have not been enough to lift the families above the poverty line in most of the cases.
4. There is no need for any margin money or down payment up to certain levels of assistance i.e., up to Rs.10,000 in the case of farm sector and Rs.25,000 in the case of non-farm sector. Certain composite schemes allow for higher levels of straight loan without any margin money from or on behalf of the loanees. But still certain banks insists on margin money loan even on smaller loans within the limits. This results in unnecessary accounting, delay in recovery, etc.
5. Originally margin money loan programme did not envisage any subsidy component for individual family oriented schemes. The large dose of subsidy available under IRDP and other programmes like JALDHARA have made the margin money loan programmes less attractive to beneficiaries. This has forced most of the state corporations to introduce subsidy component in their self-employment schemes. Several distortions have taken place after

introduction of the subsidy. Certain states are giving fixed amount of subsidy irrespective of the cost of the schemes while some have introduced a very high component of subsidy even ranging between 50 per cent and 75 per cent in some of their schemes.

6. In view of the ceiling of Rs.12,000 for non-recurring cost of schemes, many state corporations are finding it difficult to take up viable economic development projects. This, coupled with the relatively low absorptive capacity of the beneficiaries of the target groups is the principal factor for inadequate level of average assistance offered to the target groups.
7. Most of the SCDCs are not equipped with qualified functionaries for formulation of economically viable projects. There is lack of backward and forward linkages.
8. The skeleton staff available at the field level is inadequate for close monitoring of the economic development schemes and identifying the missing critical inputs required for successful implementation of the projects.
9. There is frequent change of personnel in the key positions including the managing directors and general managers. This seriously affects the efficient functioning of the corporations.
10. Generally most of the SCDCs suffer from handicaps of inadequate or suitable staff support.
11. Whatever limited staff is available with some corporations, they are mostly engaged in accounting and reconciliation of work in relation to the margin money loans as a result of which adequate attention is not being paid to development work including projects formulation, supervision, and monitoring and evaluation.
12. The share capital contribution of the state as well as Central government is meagre when compared to the size and magnitude of the problem. During the Seventh Plan, the Planning Commission could allocate only Rs.60.75 crore towards share capital contribution of 21 state corporations which include the matching assistance required for the promotional role and setting up technical, monitoring and recovery units. This was even less than the original amount of Rs.69.75 crore agreed to by the Planning Commission for

release during the Seventh Plan period. As a result of inadequate release of funds, the backlog amount to be released to state corporations as matching share capital has mounted to more than Rs.20 crore.

13. Certain state governments had not provided adequate fund for their share capital contribution which has resulted in lopsided distribution of share capital assistance among the state corporations. Again, some of these state governments had not released the stipulated amount in time.
14. Most of the state corporations have failed to formulate proper annual action plans and link their plan to the credit plan of the banks. This resulted in failure to mobilise the requisite institutional credit. For the same reason, many corporations have not been able to utilise their share capital which have been accumulating over the years.
15. The recovery position in respect of most corporations has been very poor resulting in erosion of their share capital and prevention of recycling of the funds.
16. Most of the corporations are not providing their contribution in respect of matching assistance for promotional activities, technical, monitoring and recovery wing. This has given rise to the practice of diversion of share capital for meeting their administrative expenses.

Recommendations

Having regard to the above, the following measures to strengthen the functioning of SCDCs so as to ensure that schemes undertaken by these corporations generate adequate incremental income for the target groups.

1. The margin money loan programmes needs to be suitably modified with the following end in view:
   (a) Greater emphasis should be given in the formulation of economically viable schemes having proper backward and forward linkages and favourable incremental capital output ratio.
   (b) The accounting and other procedural functions of the corporation should be minimised and more staff should be

engaged in closer monitoring of the schemes so that problems in the implementation of any scheme are sorted out quickly and the critical inputs wherever necessary made available.

(c) Annual action plan of the corporation should be prepared well in advance so that the banks have enough time to examine the viability of the schemes, linking the annual action plan of the corporation to the credit plan of various banks.

2. The existing arrangement of margin money loans needs to be suitably modified, avoiding provision of margin money where it is not required as per Reserve Bank of India guidelines. The modification should also aim at rationalisation and simplification of the accounting system and other procedural matters relating to margin money loan so that adequate staff is available for other developmental work.
3. The SCDCs should equip themselves with all relevant information regarding the target group, namely: academic background, traditional skills, aptitudes, whether already covered under any development schemes, the quantum of assistance given and their performance in implementing such schemes, etc. Similarly, information could be collected about availability of linkages, basic infrastructure etc., in SC habitats. Attempts should be made to formulate schemes on the basis of the information gathered about the beneficiaries.
4. Entrepreneur development training programmes in relevant fields like leather works, food processing, horticulture, handloom, powerloom, assembly of low technology electronics, electrical goods like radios, two-in-ones, TVs, mixers, heaters, electric fans etc., could be developed for SC youth with the help of technical institutes, government organisations like Khadi and Village Industries Commission (KVIC), Small Industries Development Organisation (SIDO), etc., who are working in the field of development of small scale and village/cottage industries.
5. The SCDCs should work out a commercial tie-up with the State Industries/Electronics Development Corporation as well as leading companies in the private corporate sector involving them in such entrepreneurial development training programme so as to equip the

beneficiaries with the appropriate technical know-how and quality control. Such tie-ups should provide for job opportunities and ancillary arrangement for the trained SC youth for manufacture of goods on behalf of State Industries/Electronics Development Corporation or private sector who will market these goods under their brand names or use the items supplied.

6. The goods manufactured by the SC entrepreneurs should be exempted from sales tax/octroi/excise duty in order to make their products competitive in the market.
7. The newly formed National SC/ST Finance and Development Corporation (NSFDC) could work out, at the national level, a suitable training-cum-production plan in consultation with the State Industrial/Electronics Development Corporations and leading brand name owners of low technology assembly oriented electronic goods.
8. The existing level of average assistance per beneficiary is much too low for having any significant impact on the income level of the target groups. The inability of the SCDCs to take up schemes with higher investments which ensure optimal return is the principal factor behind most of the beneficiaries remaining below poverty line even after a decade's efforts of SCDCs and even other organisations. It was felt that the existing unit of Rs.12,000 should be raised to at least, Rs.35,000 to 50,000, which should be the project cost of the schemes that could be taken up by the SCDCs without prior approval of the Government of India. There should be scope for flexibility to allow even higher levels of financing for schemes particularly in secondary and tertiary sectors. The SCDCs should make use of this enhanced ceiling to raise the average level of assistance significantly and ensure higher return from schemes.
9. Special central assistance (SCA) should be used for developing infrastructure and filling the critical gaps in the existing infrastructure. The practice of giving individual subsidy could be dispensed with where schemes given to individual beneficiaries are viable. However, where subsidy support cannot be dispensed with it should be with reference to the actual viability gaps in the schemes.
10. The SCDCs should make an effort to redeem the agricultural land belonging to SC members mortgaged to private moneylenders. A

package programme should be drawn up for those distressed SC farmers which should include loan on soft term for redemption of purchase of land, provision of irrigation facilities, adoption of suitable remunerative cropping patterns, arrangement for supply of seed, etc., and thus rehabilitating those distressed farmers.

11. SCDCs have to give more stress on the scheme of purchase of cultivable agricultural land for allotment to the landless SC agricultural labour as is being done in the state of Kerala. The SCDCs could purchase the lands put in auction by financial institutions and development banks, commercial banks, cooperative banks, etc., also.
12. The financial institutes are normally reluctant to grant loans to farmers unless their names figure in land revenue records. In many cases the land records are not updated. The SCDCs should take up with the state governments the cases of SC farmers and arrange for updating of the land records. For share croppers the SCDCs should arrange loan for short-term purposes through cooperatives, etc.
13. Specific programme for the development of traditional occupations of SCs like leather work, weaving, fisheries, animal husbandry, etc., should be taken up by providing modern technology in this area.
14. The National Corporation could arrange to support the groups who are marginally above the poverty line but struggling hard to gain economic self-sustenance. Special survey to identify these groups has to be done by the SCDCs and special care needs to be taken to ensure that they do not slide back below poverty line. This group comprises relatively better trained, experienced, professional and enterprising members of the community and they could provide a good medium for higher investment through the National Corporation.
15. In the earlier recommendations, lot of emphasis has been given for identification of suitable SC beneficiaries, collection of relevant information about them, conducting feasibility studies and formation of viable schemes, conducting special surveys and effective and closer monitoring of the schemes already grounded. Higher provisions are required to be made to meet these costs. It is,

therefore, suggested that their matching assistance for technical-cum-monitoring evaluation and recovery units may be raised from the existing level of 3 per cent to, at least, 5 per cent of the cumulative share capital for setting up and operating a well equipped project planning, supervision and monitoring and evaluation set up. Similarly the matching assistance for feasibility studies and promotional activities may also be increased from the present level of 1 per cent to 3 per cent.

16. The corporations should review, reorganise and strengthen staff structure to the extent necessary to secure managerial assistance from state and Central agencies. They should avoid taking share capital or SCA towards normal staff costs.
17. The corporation should arrange to take up schemes on the diversified lines.
18. The corporation should attempt to evolve a system of flow of technology from research institutes to them with regular arrangements for quality of goods—Council of Scientific and Industrial Research (CSIR) allied institutions are helpful in this regard.
19. CEOs should be selected on the basis of suitability in terms of qualifications and experience.
20. CEOs should have a minimum tenure of at least three years. The change of incumbency before completion of tenure should be only under exceptional circumstances.
21. Staff should be encouraged to acquire professional qualifications and should be posted at appropriate places.
22. There should be a clear career plan in place for the staff in various grades and need-based skill upgradation should form part of the career planning.

V. CAG Audit Report for the West Bengal Scheduled Castes and Scheduled Tribes Development and Finance Corporation (WBSCSTDFC) for the period from 1996-97 to 2000-01.

- Though various schemes were implemented in the state to ameliorate the condition of the SC and ST people, the performance under such schemes were far from satisfactory and the basic objectives of the schemes remained unfulfilled.

- This was attributable mainly to the lack of proper supervision and near total dependence of Government on WBSCSTDFC and the banks for implementation of the schemes. While large amount of Rs. 253.38 crore remained parked in the deposit account with banks, there was little follow-up and intervention by the Government to ensure that the schemes were implemented effectively and benefits accrued to the SC/ST people in a timely and effective manner.
- The programme was hampered by delayed release of fund by Government and further delay in release of funds to the implementing agencies. On the whole, the programme suffered from lack of attention and monitoring by Government, though funds were not a constraint.
- Against Rs. 355.01 crore available in deposit account of WBSCSTDFC during 1996-2001 (including Rs. 57.21 crore as opening balance at the start of 1996-97), Assistant Secretary, Department of Backward Classes Welfare (BCW) released Rs. 285.75 crore to implementing agencies leaving a balance of Rs. 69.26 crore at the end of March 2001, of which Rs. 14.45 crore related to the years 1989 to 1995. Further, out of the fund received from the Government WBSCSTDFC parked, without concurrence of the Government, Rs. 127.65 crore meant for implementing the schemes for the benefit of the weaker sections in short-term deposits as of 31 March 2001.
- Contrary to the GoI directives (October 1998), SCA funds of Rs. 130.14 crore received from GoI were not transferred to the account of WBSCSTDFC promptly by the BCW Department. The delay in transfer ranged between 3 to 12 months from the date of their sanctions during 1996-2000.
- Further, due to late receipt of suitable directives from BCW Department, the release of funds (Rs. 159.25 crore) to the executing agencies from the deposit account was also delayed by WBSCSTDFC for 3 to 23 months for implementation of the schemes during 1996-

2000 (Appendix 19). The delay on both the counts adversely affected the timely completion of the schemes. Such delays were not monitored by the Government and no responsibility was fixed for such inordinate delays.

- To obtain funds for SCA grants from GoI, the state government had to forward utilisation certificates (UCs) to the GoI. Scrutiny revealed that UC for SCA funds amounting to Rs. 191.17 crore were forwarded during 1996-2000 to GoI though funds were either not allotted to the implementing agencies or UCs were awaited from them. Thus, incorrect utilisation certificates indicating inflated figures of actual expenditure were submitted by the Government.
- Though Rs. 285.75 crore was released for implementation of the scheme, Rs. 127.65 crore had been kept in short-term deposit. Utilisation Certificates for Rs. 191.17 crore were forwarded to Government of India during 1996-2000, though not obtained from the executing agencies.
- Out of total 96,880 loan applications sent to the concerned banks by WBSCSTDFC in five districts for sanctioning of loans under Special Component Plan (SCP) and Tribal Sub Plan (TSP), 84,280 applications were approved while 12,600 applications remained with the banks at the end of 1999-2000. These applications were neither accepted nor the same were returned to the respective Panchayat Samitis for further vetting and resubmission.
- During 1996-2000 Rs. 2.98 crore (subsidy: Rs. 2.18 crore and margin money: Rs. 0.80 crore) were refunded to WBSCSTDFC by the implementing banks of the five test-checked districts. These amounts are lying undisbursed with them since 1995-96. No records indicating the number of cases involved in these amounts were made available to CAG by WBSCSTDFC.
- As per Government guidelines, 20 per cent of the project cost were to be borne as margin money by the executing agencies from its own resources. However, WBSCSTDFC decided (September 1996) to restrict payment of margin money for the schemes with project cost of Rs. 4,000 or less. As a result, shortfall of margin money loan of Rs. 13.04 crore in five districts were met through bank loan for

which the beneficiaries (number could not be ascertained) had to bear extra interest burden of Rs. 1.04 crore per annum due to higher rate of bank interest (12%) compared to interest on margin money loan (4%).

- Project cost was to be disbursed within 90 days of sanction by all banks. Scrutiny of records revealed that there were inordinate delays ranging from 6 months to 60 months in disbursing project costs in 41,409 cases involving Rs. 33 crore. In four districts project costs in 20,250 cases valued at Rs. 17.40 crore sanctioned between 1996-2000, were not disbursed by the concerned banks till March 2001, Bardhaman and Medinipur being the districts where higher number of non-disbursed projects were noticed. Reasons for such delay in disbursement of project cost as observed in audit were due to the controllable factors *viz.*, late selection and sponsoring of cases; selection disregarding essential linkages vital for the scheme; delay in holding of joint inspection and by holding back fresh disbursement by the banks to *panchayats* when loan recoveries were not prompt and regular. Undisbursed subsidy and margin money loan amounting to Rs. 2.98 crore refunded by the banks without implementing the schemes.
- Banks were to play a vital role by effective participation and monitoring at all levels for successful implementation of schemes. Besides, the WBSCSTDFC was also to see that money disbursed among the weaker sections through banks was gainfully utilised. Test check of records maintained by the 74 participating bank branches of five selected districts relating to implementation of Family Oriented schemes revealed the following irregularities/ deficiencies.
  - (i) In 33 bank branches, 2,400 beneficiaries refunded bank loan component of Rs. 1.24 crore in lump sum either on the same date or within 20 months from the date of disbursement of project cost of Rs. 2.57 crore against the repayment schedule of 40 to 60 monthly installments.
  - (ii) In 23 bank branches, a portion of 1,011 projects involving Rs. 1.03 crore were kept in term deposit/fixed deposit accounts by

the beneficiaries without utilising the fund and repaid the bank loan amount (Rs. 0.45 crore) fully or partly on maturity. The above facts indicated that the participating banks effectively arranged for repayment of loans without implementing the projects so as to show improvement in recovery position of outstanding bank loans. Thus, government subsidy of Rs. 1.79 crore failed to generate any useful economic activity.

(iii) Total project cost comprising subsidy, margin money loan and bank loan are required to be paid to the beneficiaries for successful implementation of the project but it was observed that in 414 cases, Rs. 30.47 lakh were disbursed by 20 bank branches against project cost of Rs. 44.93 lakh resulting in short disbursement of the project cost by Rs. 14.46 lakh. Moreover, excess adjustment of subsidy and margin money of Rs. 4.59 lakh were made due to non-disbursement of the full amount of bank loan component.

(iv) In 25 cases, out of project cost of Rs. 2.31 lakh, subsidy and margin money of Rs. 1.23 lakh were released by five banks branches without disbursement of the bank loan.

(v) In two banks, against project cost of Rs. 6.36 lakh, banks disbursed Rs. 3.02 lakh and started receipt of repayment of loans in installment from the beneficiaries before disbursement of full amount of the project cost. Twenty-four hundred beneficiaries refunded bank loan of Rs. 1.24 crore in lump sum without implementing the projects under financing of the project—Rs. 14.46 lakh.

(vi) In spite of holding undisbursed subsidy of Rs. 3.28 lakh and margin money of Rs. 0.45 lakh since 1994-95, one bank in Medinipur district failed to release the project cost involving Rs. 5.74 lakh including bank loan in 159 cases sanctioned during 1996-97. Thus the beneficiaries were either not encouraged or keen to initiate their projects with the amount disbursed, and instead deposited the amount in savings or term deposit account from which the bank loans were paid on maturity. As a result, no projects were taken up in these cases and the income generation schemes were not implemented though funds were available for that purpose.

(vii) Projects were to be chosen keeping in view the profile of beneficiary families, considering their needs, aptitude and available local resources. Backward and forward linkages *viz.*, supply of necessary inputs, training, rendering extension services, marketing support, etc., were also to be provided in coordination with other departments/organisations for sustenance of the projects. However, test-check showed that unviable projects were selected.

(viii) The average cost of projects undertaken in five districts during 1996-97 to 1997-98 ranged between Rs. 4,560 and Rs. 10,426 which affected the chances of a proper project to generate income as well as utilisation of fund. The WBSCSTDFC's instruction (June 1999) to the district managers to sponsor SCP and TSP cases at an optimum project cost of Rs. 18,000 for family oriented schemes, fixed by DRDA based on the 1998-99 price index so that the project could generate additional income to enable the beneficiaries to cross the poverty line, was ignored with the average cost of projects implemented during 1999-2000 and 2000-01 being Rs. 9,169 and Rs. 11,445 respectively.

(ix) Audit scrutiny of the projects undertaken during 1999-2001 revealed that 54,729 projects valued at Rs. 54.42 crore were not economically viable as the project cost was less than Rs. 18,000 in each case and thus unsuitable to generate additional income for the beneficiaries to cross the poverty line.

(x) Timely repayment of margin money loans was important for recycling of funds. The participating banks were primarily responsible for disbursing funds placed by WBSCSTDFC to the beneficiaries and for recovery of the margin money loans along with interest thereon at the rate of 4 per cent per annum. Besides, for regular inspections/visits to be made by the bank and the corporation, the bank branches would send a list of the loanees and amount due one month before the installment due to the DM, WBSCSTDFC. The district managers, in coordination with the district magistrate and the *panchayat samitis* were to make repayment drives till the installments were recovered. Scrutiny of 8 District Rural Development Agencies revealed that, against Rs. 33.14 crore over due margin money loan, only Rs. 8.34 crore (ranging between 19-30 per cent) could be recovered till 31st March 2000. Ineffective monitoring and follow up action by District Administration and failure of the participating banks in effecting recovery led to such poor recovery of margin money loans.

VI. The Comptroller and Auditor General's Audit Report of the civil accounts of the Government of Andhra Pradesh for the year end 31st March 2001, has referred to Andhra Pradesh Scheduled Castes Cooperative Finance Corporation Limited (APSCCFC), and commented on specific schemes and made an overall assessment. This was done after a review of the operations of the apex corporation and six district societies (Adilabad, Chittoor, Guntur, Krishna, Kuroool and Warangal).

Commenting on the performance of the corporation, the CAG Report observed that:

(i) Reports on physical progress were not reliable as there was no correlation between financial and physical targets and achievements and cited instances of programme for animal husbandry and artisans which showed contrasting picture. In animal husbandry, fiscal achievements were shown to be higher at 142 per cent while fund utilisation was only 45 per cent. In the programme for artisans the financial performance was reported higher by 174 per cent and while there was a shortfall of 53 per cent in physical performance.

(ii) No household survey was conducted to identify BPL families, as envisaged in the guideline for special central assistance. The CAG has observed that, 'Funds have been released to the societies by the Corporation based on its annual action plan which were not backed with survey based figures of BPL families' and that 'the release of funds without identifying BPL families did not ensure that the benefit were actually accrued to the targeted groups.'

(iii) The corporation has accorded low priority for approved schemes as seen from the shortfalls for the scheme in bonded labour, flayers, tenants, scavengers, land purchase while higher achievements was shown under Chief Minister's Empowerment of Youth (CMEY) programmes.

(iv) There is need to improve the quality of control exercised by the corporation over the implementation of schemes by the district societies, as the APSCCFC has limited its role to the mere release of funds and conduct of bi-monthly meetings to review the progress report submitted by the district societies and does not conduct their regular inspections on them.

(v) While the corporation's management is vested with board of directors comprising five elected members from the affiliated society and 10 members nominated by the Government, the corporation has been functioning without elected representatives since its very inception and without nominated members for a considerable period.

In its overall assessment the CAG Report observed 'the Corporation set up with the objective of promoting the development of SC population was managed inefficiently and incompetently, leading to its poor financial health. It had been functioning without the elected representatives and even without the nominated members since May 1999 and no Annual General Body meeting was held after 1994. The financial management by the Corporation, itself a financial institution was totally unprofessional and led to huge losses. The management of receivables in the Corporation as well as at the District Societies was insignificant. As of March 1999, loans aggregating to Rs.688.16 crore were pending recovery. Besides, Rs.36.36 crores, was due to be paid to State/GoI. No survey was done to identify eligible SC households and beneficiaries. Shortfalls in physical achievements ranged up to 63 per cent. Schemes for benefit of SCs were mostly mismanaged. Work of Societies was not monitored by the Corporation effectively. Expenditure of Rs. 13.77 crores was wasted on supply of milch animals, construction of poultry complexes, purchase of unsuitable lands, supply of mini transport vehicles under self employment scheme and horticulture programmes. Schemes funds including SCA were diverted on a large scale for CMEY programme. Number of beneficiaries who crossed the poverty line with assistance from the Corporation was not available. In short, implementation of the economic development programmes for the SC population by the Corporation has been suffering from all around mismanagement and incompetence'.

VII. Conference of Executive Directors of AP Scheduled Castes Finance Corporation & Lead District Managers, Hyderabad on 10 February 2005.

In this conference, the following important issues were raised/reported about functioning of the SCDCs in Andhra Pradesh.

1. Most of the bankers are insisting for surety, land property etc., even for loan amounting to Rs.25,000/-.
2. Some of the bankers are grounding the schemes in the succeeding financial year without issuing utilisation certificates of previous year.
3. The bankers are not sending utilisation certificate after grounding all the schemes.
4. SC corporation officers should go along with the *mandal* development officers (MDOs) to see the grounding of schemes, as 60 per cent of the schemes are not genuine.
5. Bankers are asking for security for more than Rs.50,000/- as loans and for lower amount loans they are asking for co-applicants. Bankers are giving clear-cut instructions for security and other things.
6. Every year only 20-30 per cent schemes are grounded in the same year and most of the funds are in bank only.
7. While SCDCs come out with subsidy, margin money subject to their own selection process, banks came up with loan component, which requires security in varying forms. It is at this stage where all schemes get stuck up and grounding of schemes sanctioned by government agencies gets delayed leading thereby to failure or underutilisation of the project concepts.
8. Banks are extending loans only after beneficiary depositing amounts equivalent to loans in the banks thereby causing delay in release of margin money and subsidy amount. During 2004 05 in Adilabad

district, out of 1,296 targets, only 476 cases were sanctioned out of which grounded are only 186 (14.35%).

9. Banks are not coming forward to finance scheduled castes and they finance only people above poverty line.
10. Banks are considering only small units (up to 20,000). Banks make educated to go around several times to get loans above Rs.50,000/.
11. Sanctioned schemes under ISB (industry, service and business) sector are not grounded. Bank is sanctioning only units with smaller sizes, *viz.*, up to Rs. 20,000/-. Banks even adjust corporation loans against individual loans. Bankers offer consent to individuals only to get margin money and subsidy and adjust the past account of defaulters and forget the present scheme.
12. Bankers are liberal in sanctioning schemes. But at documentation stage this is struck up. Bankers need pressure by sanctioning authorities to ground schemes. During 2001-02 to 2003-04 groundings in Nellore district never exceeded 58 per cent though sanctions were made for 98 per cent of targeted cases.
13. Bankers are stamping loans to scheduled castes as unrecoverable.
14. Service area bank manager gives consent during cluster meetings itself. But groundings do not happen. During 2004-05, out of 980 units sanctioned, only 60 units have been grounded (6.12%) in Nalgonda district.
15. Banks take lot of time to ground schemes after they receive margin money and subsidy.
16. A perusal of the feedback of executive directors makes it abundantly clear that major fault, in the beneficiary not being able to ground the scheme, lies with the banks. Though it may be difficult to pin-point any one reason, but hesitation on the part of bankers to give loan without any safety mechanism appears to be the major cause.

VIII. Study carried out on working of the Punjab Scheduled Castes Land Development & Finance Corporation between 1995-96 and 1999-2000 revealed that the administrative cost of the corporation rose to Rs.1.25 per rupee of directly disbursed loans and 49 paise per rupee of loan recovered in 1999-2000. It is much higher than that of commercial banks.

IX. Audit Report on the Karnataka SC/ST Development Corporation as on March 31, 2005.

- The company has incurred losses of Rs. 399.57 lakh at the end of the financial year 2004-05 after considering the qualifications, which are quantifiable, in this report and the accumulated losses are less than 50 per cent of its net worth as on March 31, 2005. During the financial year 2004-05 the company has incurred cash losses of Rs. 357.37 lakh, and in the preceding year the company had incurred cash losses of Rs. 551.73 lakh.

X. The Comptroller and Auditor General of India in its report for the 1997-98 to 2001-02 for the NSFDC made the following observations.

Role of the Company

- The NSFDC was set up to play a catalytic role for development of innovative economic programmes and financing schemes for targeted groups without duplicating the efforts of existing state level agencies. While the NSFDC had to identify the critical gaps in the programmes of various agencies, prepare schemes/projects to bridge these gaps and obtain necessary finance for implementation of the same, it was also supposed to work with the nationalised banks and NABARD in improving the flow of financial assistance to the beneficiaries. It is, however, observed that the NSFDC has merely been financing the schemes submitted by the SCAs and no efforts were made to avoid/check duplicity of schemes run by the SCAs. Besides, they had not taken any concrete effort to increase the flow of financial assistance by liasioning with banks and financial institutions. It was also observed that the same schemes were implemented by the SCAs under NSFDC financing and under special central assistance/margin money scheme.
- Disbursements of funds to the SCAs and non-government organisations (NGOs) by the NSFDC have been low as compared to the funds available. The funds available from internal resources were more than the amount of loans disbursed.
- Despite non-utilisation of the funds available, the GoI almost regularly released equity capital to the companies. As a result, the

Companies earned interest by keeping the undisbursed money in banks, due to which other income was more than the operational income in NSFDC.

Deficiencies in the Disbursement of the Loans

- For drawal of the loan, NSFDC required the SCAs to complete prerequisite formalities, *viz.*, selection of beneficiaries, documentation with the beneficiaries and tie-up of their share so that the funds were utilised immediately. It is observed that funds were disbursed to the SCAs without ensuring compliance of the pre-disbursement conditions as well as utilisation of the earlier funds. As a result, huge funds have been lying unutilised with the SCAs.
- Release of the funds to the SCAs without ensuring utilisation of earlier funds was mainly with a view to project better performance in terms of quantitative targets of disbursement of loans and repayments. Since the NSFDC did not effectively monitor the utilisation of funds by the SCAs and no system existed for effective monitoring of the progress of the business of the borrower, there were cases of non-utilisation as well as diversions and parking of funds for other purposes by the SCAs.
- NSFDC did not ensure compliance of the pre-disbursement conditions and released (1998-99) funds amounting to Rs.15.28 crore to a SCA of Bihar for implementation of 14 schemes, even though the amount of Rs.2.06 crore released in 1996-97 had been lying unutilised. Further, while the funds were required to be utilised within three months, the SCA could utilise Rs.71 lakh only till June 2002 and refunded (December 2001 to March 2002) Rs.7.29 crore. The amount of Rs.9.34 crore has been lying unutilised with the SCA for more than three years (March 2002).
- Though neither project report nor list of selected beneficiaries was submitted by the SCA of Tamil Nadu, NSFDC disbursed (March 1996) Rs.6.17 crore to the SCA for five schemes in transport sector on the plea that similar schemes of other SCAs had been sanctioned. As the SCA was not well prepared for disbursement of funds to the beneficiaries, it kept the entire amount in the fixed deposit and refunded the same in February 1997 stating that the scheme could

not be implemented due to considerable price escalation for all type of vehicles.

- SCA of Assam was released Rs.41 lakh in February 1993 for a jewellery shop scheme, against which it could utilise Rs.13.50 lakh. The balance amount of Rs.27.50 lakh was diverted (February 1999) to another scheme after a period of six years.

Shortfall in Government Guarantees

- In contravention to their lending policies, the companies disbursed funds to the SCAs without obtaining adequate guarantees of the state governments. NSFDC loans amounting to Rs. 43.90 crore were not covered by the government guarantees as on 31 March 2002.

Microfinancing

- As per the guidelines of the GoI (October 1998), the scheme of microfinancing was started by the NSFDC to reach the maximum number of target groups for low investment oriented income generating economic activities through self-help groups. The NSFDC had disbursed funds amounting to Rs. 35.67crore to the SCAs/NGOs under the microfinancing scheme till 31 March 2002.

Following deficiencies were observed in disbursing loans under the microfinancing scheme:

1. No bank guarantee was obtained from the NGOs before advancing loans.
2. The monitoring of the performance of the NGOs was not satisfactory.
3. Decision to sanction loan in most of the cases was based on the scrutiny of documents submitted by the NGOs, without visiting the office of the NGOs for verifications of their genuineness.

Recovery of Loans

Repayment of Principal

Term loans sanctioned/released to the SCAs are to be repaid in quarterly installments within a maximum period of 10 years in the case of

NSFDC. Following table shows percentage of recovery of principal amount of loan from the SCAs:

Table 13.1

Recovery of Principal Amount of Loan

Company	*Percentage of Recovery*				
	1997-98	*1998-99*	*1999-2000*	*2000-01*	*2001-02*
NSFDC	87	89	86	81	89

It is observed that: on certain occasions repayment of overdue amounts were adjusted by NSFDC against the disbursements. In one such case, against the proposed disbursement of Rs.4.95 crore, the SCA of Bihar was allowed to get Rs.1.50 crore adjusted against the outstanding amount of Rs.1.53 crore. In another case, NSFDC obtained a request from the SCA of Madhya Pradesh for further release of funds amounting to Rs.1.45 crore and adjusted Rs.1.44 crore against the outstanding/unutilised amount of the loans released for the earlier schemes.

Refund of Unutilised Funds

Refund of Funds without Utilisation

The NSFDC had not ensured identification of the beneficiaries and availability of matching contributions from the SCAs/beneficiaries before providing financial assistance to the SCAs. This led to refunding of funds by the SCAs without disbursing to the beneficiaries. The SCAs of Madhya Pradesh, Tamil Nadu, Bihar and Punjab refunded the amount of Rs.12.14 crore to the NSFDC after delays of 311 days to 1,517 days, without disbursing the funds to the ultimate beneficiaries.

Recovery of Interest

Loss of Interest due to Non-Compliance of Government Guidelines

According to the guidelines of the Government (October 1998), the NSFDC was required to charge interest at rates of 4 and 7 per cent per annum from the SCAs. The companies were, however, not following the guidelines, which resulted in loss of interest to an extent of Rs.7.63 crore as discussed below:

- NSFDC framed its revised lending policy without taking into consideration the Government guidelines. Accordingly, it charged interest w.e.f. 1 April 1999 at a rate of 4/6 per cent against the prescribed 7 per cent on term loans above Rs.2 lakh. As a result, NSFDC had foregone revenue of Rs.6.16 crore on account of interest till 31 March 2002 on the term loan of Rs.185.57 crore disbursed during 1999-2000 and 2001-02, besides a recurring annual loss of revenue to an extent of Rs.4.88 crore.

Non-Recovery of Higher Rate of Interest

According to terms and conditions of the loans, the SCAs were required to utilise the funds within the stipulated period, failing which they were liable to pay higher rates of interest (HRI) of 10/12 per cent. Out of total penal interest of Rs. 53.59 crore leviable on the SCAs as on 31 March 2002, Rs. 53.59 crore were recoverable from the SCAs.

Non-Recovery of Liquidated Damages

The NSFDC has been charging penal interest at rates ranging from 3 to 12 per cent on defaulted repayments against 12 per cent as prescribed by the ministry. It is observed that demands for liquidated damages (LD) were not being raised by NSFDC on regular basis. Against the demands for an amount of Rs.2.06 crore raised by NSFDC up to 30 June 2000, only a sum of Rs.3.3 lakh was received and no further demand was raised thereafter.

Conclusions

There were several deficiencies at all stages of implementation of the schemes such as release of funds without fulfillment of stipulated conditions and without ensuring utilisation of the funds released earlier. Disbursement of funds to the SCAs/NGOs have been low as compared to the available funds. Since the companies did not effectively monitor the utilisation of funds by the SCAs and no system existed for effective monitoring of the progress of the business of the borrowers, there were cases of non-utilisation as well as diversions and parking of funds for other purposes by the SCAs. In this way, the objectives for which the funds were disbursed to the SCAs have not been achieved by the NSFDC.

X. A research study on Scheduled Castes Development Corporations in India, conducted by Prof. R.K. Mishra in the *Economic and Political Weekly*, August 17, 1996 brought out the following policy issues related to effective functioning of the SCDCs.

a) These corporations in most of the states have a chairman at the helm, followed by a vice-chairman-cum-managing director/managing director, and an executive director in some cases. The hierarchy at that level ends with the general manager-credit and general manager-administration. At the middle level, there is almost an absence of senior managers. The general managers in most of the cases are assisted by executives holding the designation of managers. The managers below them do not have junior executives. They are supported by office assistants, and in some cases by assistant managers. Almost in all the cases, qualified accounting and finance personnel do not exist and the generalists handle this function. There are no executives handling corporate policy and public relations. These corporations do not coordinate well with the similar corporations known as the backward class (BC) corporations, corporations for handicapped, women development corporations, corporations for minorities, etc. They do not have effective coordination even with the district administration. This lack of coordination results in higher costs, delays and dissatisfaction to the beneficiaries. The managerial lot represents, by and large, a bunch of non-motivated personnel which has thwarted innovations, a continuous interaction with the beneficiaries and redesigning of the SC corporations.

Financial Performance

A review of the financial performance of these corporations can be undertaken as regards the growth and nature of paid-up capital, loans, fixed assets, total turnover business done, operating expenses and profit' after taxes.

a) *Paid-up capital:* The paid-up capital in the various SC corporations is marked with the general trend of increase at the rate of 10 per cent per annum. Almost all the paid up capital has come from the government. The SC corporations closely following this average are found in Andhra Pradesh, Haryana, Karnataka and Rajasthan. In some states, the paid-up capital of the SC corporations has risen much faster than the average growth of 10 per cent. These states include Himachal Pradesh, Kerala, Maharashtra, Tamil Nadu, Uttar Pradesh and the union territory of Chandigarh. One of the reasons why the SC corporations in some states have had a higher rate of growth in their paid-up capital relates to the philosophy of the ruling party in power. There is no doubt that states like Kerala, Maharashtra, Tamil Nadu and Uttar Pradesh have taken a definite position and interest in ameliorating the economic conditions of the SCs. A closely related factor leading to the growth in the share capital has been the societal concern in these states about the well-being of the SC masses. The case of Chandigarh SC corporation is somewhat different as the definition of poverty in Punjab differs when compared to many other states in the country. Further, the per capita income of Punjab/the union territory of Chandigarh is also much higher than the average per capita income of the country. There is another interesting trend found in the growth of share capital of the SC corporations. A study of the Tamil Nadu Adi-Dravidar Corporation reveals that share capital has shot up sharply in such years in which elections have taken place. This is supported by the fact that the rate of growth of share capital followed a diverse pattern in the year immediately following the election. A question crops up as to why these corporations should not diversify their equity base.

b) *Loans:* This was an unexploited resource. Excepting Andhra Pradesh, Haryana and the union territory of Chandigarh, the loan element in the capital structure was insignificant in the case of other states such as Assam, Kerala, Karnataka and Rajasthan. In the case of Andhra Pradesh, the loan component had a tendency to increase. The debt-equity ratio was 1:2 in the case of the Andhra Pradesh SC Cooperative Finance Corporation. This ratio was 3:1 in the case of the Haryana SC Corporation, 4:1 in the case of the Chandigarh SC Financial and Development Corporation. In the case of the Uttar

Pradesh SC Finance and Development Corporation, this ratio was 10:1 in 1991-92. The absence of the loan component, or its insignificant presence, points out the scope for the adding up to the capital investment. One of the reasons of no or low loan component was the heavy predominance of social objectives justifying the nature of the activities of these corporations. However, this should not have undermined the commercial nature of their working as absence of profits even in the case of enterprises having preponderance of social objectives over the commercial objectives poses a far greater danger to such corporations since the presence of such a phenomenon does not allow them to freely expand their scope of operation.

c) *Fixed assets:* Most corporations were characterised by absence of any significant stock of fixed assets which shows that they acted more as trading or financial organisations. The ratio of turnover to fixed assets was 100:1 in the case of Andhra Pradesh, 100:25 in the case of Assam, 100:1 in the case of Haryana, 100:1 in the case of Karnataka, 100:3 in the case of Kerala (State Development Corporation for SCs and STs), 100:1 in the case of Kerala (State Development Corporation for Christian Converts from SCs and BCs), and 100:3 in the case of Maharashtra. The position of the union territory of Chandigarh, Tamil Nadu and Uttar Pradesh was equally pitiable. Rajasthan was an exception as it had a ratio floating around 100:7. The presence of a negligible level of fixed assets shows that these corporations did not undertake any non-financial activities in a significant way, and remained more or less an extended arm of the state government for disbursing funds to the SCs.

d) *Total turnover:* An increasing turnover reflects growth in the overall financial activity. The capital invested in the SC corporations was seldom used well. In Kerala the total turnover was just 6 per cent of the capital investment; in Rajasthan it was 20 per cent, and in Tamil Nadu, it was a mere 1 per cent. Haryana had its turnover in the range of 20 per cent of the total sales. These figures point out clearly a lack of thinking about using the investment effectively. As pointed out earlier, these corporations have objectives but lack strategy, and hence there is no question of realisation of the fact that a greater utilisation of resources can benefit both the society and their managements.

e) *Operating expenses:* The operating expenses should always be less than sales. However, a study of the functioning of these corporations reveals that this dictum was true only in the case of Rajasthan, Kerala, the union territory of Chandigarh and Uttar Pradesh. The SC corporations in Assam and Haryana (excepting 1985-86) had always incurred operating expenses more than their revenue realisation. The case of Karnataka, Rajasthan and Tamil Nadu were no different, although they had a mixed performance. Since in most of the cases, operating expenses were more than the turnover, the profit after tax return on investment and return on equity, were subsequently negative in the case of all the corporations taken as a whole, and in the case of most of the individual SC corporations.

Management Problems

f) These corporations face a number of management problems. Their top management is weak, politicised and enjoys short tenures. The middle management is not professional and a weak link in the chain. In most cases, rung of middle management executives is absent. The junior management is not recruited from the market and is mostly composed of employees promoted from below, i.e., the clerical cadre. They are not exposed to training and management development programmes.

g) The performance of these enterprises is measured in terms of targets. This sort of approach has allowed the creation of bogus records and unfair practices. Statistics are cooked up to satisfy the requirements imposed by the policymakers and administrators. There is a lack of clear authority and responsibility regarding one's role. The financial targets have taken precedence over critical functions such as entrepreneurial development and monitoring and evaluation. Further, the SC corporations have turned out to be top heavy and have developed a bias in favour of their corporate offices. Their functioning of financial activities has been extremely weak. In many a case, a disjointed, unprofessional group handles finance personnel, projects and administrative functions. Another problem is the presence of personnel on deputation in these corporations. They do not have a cadre of their own and the SC corporations have become a berth to provide jobs and deputation facilities to the government employees who are least interested in getting involved in the day-to-day activities of the corporations. The annual accounts and reports of these corporations have remained in arrears and the quality of reporting disclosure has been poor. In one corporation, the balance sheet data were for the year 1983-84, whereas the text related to the activities of the corporation for the year 1972-73. An intensive analysis of the data further revealed that the two sides of the balance sheet were forcibly matched. This escaped the attention not only of the internal auditor but also of the commercial auditor and the audit staff of the auditor general of that state. Even the Registrar of Companies/Company Law Board did not rectify this mistake on their own.

Conclusion

h) The functioning of the SC corporations and the data on their financial performance show that though they have been addressing themselves to an important socioeconomic problem, the success attained by them has been marginal. They have not done anything tangible, except to work as an extended arm of the respective state governments to disburse financial assistance. Though they have a wide array of activities to perform, they keep themselves limited to disbursement of finance. For instance, most of the SC corporations have concentrated on schemes relating to the sanctioning of margin money, and providing cash assistance to artisans. Some innovative schemes like training for self-employment in motor driving, setting up ancillaries, starting business houses, commencing financial services etc., have not been touched at all. The targets set by them should be reflected not only in financial terms but also in physical terms. In their review meetings they must examine the extent of professionalisation added to their work content on a year-to-year basis.

i) Their management structure has been weak. They depend entirely on the equity support from the government and never try to diversify the equity base. The loan component in the capital structure is insignificant, which meant an absence of risk by the managements of these corporations. The use of the capital stock was abysmally low. The operating expenses in most of the cases exceeded their revenue generation levels. Perhaps all this happens due to a weak managerial structure, rampant corruption and heavy politicisation of these corporations.

j) All corporations need to go in for restructuring which will require these corporations to think afresh about their sources of finance, capital restructuring, portfolio of activities, pricing and costing policies, management information system and the problem of balancing between the social and economic objectives. If this is not done, these corporations would become cripple and cease to serve any economic purpose.

Summing-Up

After having scanned through a number of reports and studies on working of the SCDCs in India, now we can summarise the core issues related to their viability and sustainability. Thus,

1. Neither the state governments nor the Government of India have undertaken to meet the managerial cost towards running of the corporations with the result that some of the corporations are making payment of salaries to staff out of the interest earned by them from the fixed deposits lying with the banks while others are meeting the charges out of their share capital. Both result in depletion and blocking of the capital meant for betterment of the scheduled castes.
2. The SCA released to the SCDCs is often used to give subsidy to individual beneficiaries.
3. Some corporations are earning huge amounts of interest from the share capital funds kept in fixed deposits, and others using a large portion of their share capital for meeting their administrative expenses.
4. The average quantum of assistance per beneficiary is so low that the incremental incomes generated through the schemes is not enough

to lift the families above the poverty line. The inability of the SCDCs to take up schemes with higher investments which ensure optimal return is the principal factor behind most of the beneficiaries remaining below poverty line.

5. The programme was hampered by delayed release of fund by government and further delay in release of funds to the implementing agencies.
6. Near non-existence of follow-up, supervision and monitoring of beneficiaries on the part of the government agencies/corporation staff resulted in poor recoveries.
7. The recovery position in respect of most corporations is very poor resulting in erosion of their share capital and prevention of recycling of the funds.
8. Most of the bankers are insisting for surety, land property etc., even for loan amounting to Rs.25,000/-.
9. Some of the bankers are grounding the schemes in the succeeding financial year without issuing utilisation certificates of previous year.
10. The bankers are not sending utilisation certificate after grounding all the schemes.
11. Banks are extending loans only after beneficiary depositing amounts equivalent to loans in the banks thereby causing delay in grounding release of margin money and subsidy amount.
12. Bankers are liberal in sanctioning schemes. But at documentation stage this is struck up.
13. Bankers are stamping loans to scheduled castes as unrecoverable.
14. Banks take a lot of time to ground schemes after they receive margin money and subsidy.
15. The administrative cost of the corporations is much higher than that of commercial banks.
16. Most of the SCDCs are not equipped with qualified functionaries for formulation of economically viable projects.

17. The NSFDC has merely been financing the schemes submitted by the SCAs and no efforts were made to avoid/check duplicity of schemes run by the SCAs.
18. Same schemes were implemented by the SCDCs under NSFDC financing and under special central assistance/margin money scheme.
19. Funds were disbursed to the SCDCs by the NSFDC without ensuring compliance of the pre-disbursement conditions as well as utilisation of the earlier funds. As a result, huge funds have been lying unutilised with the SCAs.
20. Release of the funds to the SCDCs by the NSFDC without ensuring utilisation of earlier funds is done mainly with a view to project better performance in terms of quantitative targets of disbursement of loans and repayments. Since the NSFDC does not effectively monitor the utilisation of funds by the SCDCs and no system exist for effective monitoring of the progress of the business of the borrower, there are cases of non-utilisation as well as diversions and parking of funds for other purposes by the SCDCs.
21. Repayment of overdue amounts to the SCDCs are adjusted by NSFDC against the disbursements.
22. NSFDC does not always ensure identification of the beneficiaries and availability of matching contributions from the SCAs/beneficiaries before providing financial assistance to the SCAs. This leads to refund of funds by the SCAs without disbursing to the beneficiaries.
23. Despite non-utilisation of the funds available, the GoI almost regularly released equity capital to the companies. As a result, the Companies earned interest by keeping the undisbursed money in Banks, due to which other income was more than the operational income in NSFDC.
24. The capital invested in the SC corporations was seldom used well.
25. In most of the cases, operating expenses of the SCDCs are more than the turnover.
26. The skeleton staff available at the field level is inadequate for close monitoring of the economic development schemes and identifying

the missing critical inputs required for successful implementation of the projects. At the middle level, there is almost an absence of senior managers. The middle management is not professional and a weak link in the chain. In most cases, rung of middle management executives is absent. The junior management is not recruited from the market and is mostly composed of employees promoted from below, i.e., the clerical cadre. They are not exposed to training and management development programmes.

27. There is frequent change of personnel in the key positions including the managing directors and general managers. This seriously affects the efficient functioning of the corporations.
28. Whatever limited staff is available with some corporations, they are mostly engaged in accounting and reconciliation of work in relation to the margin money loans as a result of which adequate attention is not being paid to development work including projects formulation, supervision, and monitoring and evaluation.
29. Their management structure has been weak. They depend entirely on the equity support from the government and never try to diversify the equity base. The loan component in the capital structure is insignificant, which meant an absence of risk-taking by the managements of these corporations. The use of the capital stock was abysmally low. The operating expenses in most of the cases exceeded their revenue generation levels.

In the next chapter, we will examine as to what are the policy choices and roadmap for the SCDCs.

14 Policy Choices and Roadmap for the Scheduled Castes Development Corporations

The Scheduled Castes Development Corporations (SCDCs) have many issues which need to be looked into with a view to examining as to how their functioning can be made viable and sustainable. The sustainability issues can be examined and discussed from the perspectives of the various roles, which the SCDCs have been performing, and the roles that need a fresh look.

Redefining the Role of the Scheduled Castes Development Corporations

The research study on the SCDCs of eight states (discussed earlier in Chapter 12) revealed that the major activities of these SCDCs are:

- provide margin money loan;
- provide subsidy from the special central assistance (SCA);
- use of NSFDC/NSKFDC loan component to supplement with margin Money loan and subsidy and beneficiary contribution;
- identify the eligible scheduled castes beneficiaries for financing income generating schemes through the block level and local government machinery;
- forward the bankable projects to the banks along with margin money loan and subsidy component for grounding the schemes with loan component; and
- recover the margin money loan and NSFDC loan, etc.

It was found during the field study that most of the SCDCs were performing these functions in a routine way over the last 20 years. The only new component added in their functioning is the NSFDC and

NSKFDC loans. These functions were justified to a great extent when there were no alternative mechanisms to deliver credit to the rural poor and disadvantaged sections of society like scheduled castes and scheduled tribes. In view of the poor performance of the SCDCs in providing credit to the scheduled castes, which is reflected from the poor recovery performance of the SCDCs discussed in the earlier chapter, one has to think seriously whether we really need to continue in this fashion or bring about necessary changes in the operational structure of the SCDCs so as to make them more viable and sustainable in the light of the recent advancements made in the area of alternative approaches to financing the weaker sections.

The major impediments to the flow of institutional credit to the disadvantaged sections are as follows:

- higher transaction cost to banks and borrowers,
- procedures, systems and documentation formalities not being client-friendly,
- inability of borrowers to provide tangible collateral securities,
- distortion of the normal banking principles on account of linking of credit with capital/interest subsidies under various poverty alleviation programmes,
- announcements of interest/loan waivers vitiating the recovery climate,
- legal difficulties in foreclosure of loans,
- non-availability of tenancy agreements/updated land records,
- inadequate risk mitigation mechanism available to small borrowers in the event of failure of their microenterprises and to the banks in the event of loan failures, and
- the mindset that banking with the poor is not profitable.

A New Approach: Level Playing Ground for Different Institutions

In India the formal financial institutions have not been able to reach the poor households, and particularly scheduled castes, in the unorganised sector. Structural rigidities and overheads lead to high cost of making small loans. Organisational philosophy has not been oriented towards recognising the scheduled castes as credit worthy. The problem has been compounded by low level of influence of the scheduled castes, either about their credit-worthiness or their demand for savings services. Microfinance programmes have often been implemented by large banks at government's behest. Low levels of recovery have been further eroded due to loan waiver programmes leading to institutional disenchantment with lending to small borrowers.

There has been increasing awareness and realisation that financial services to the poor and disadvantaged, particularly the Dalits and women, hold the key to their mainstreaming with the development of the country. While the formal banking sector may not be in a position to provide such services in a cost-effective way, financial intermediation by various agencies in the non-formal sector has gained urgency and importance.

Inadequacies in rural access to formal finance and the seemingly extortionary terms of informal finance for the poor provide a strong need and ample space for innovative approaches to serve the financial needs of India's rural poor in general and the weaker sections like scheduled castes and scheduled tribes in particular. Over the last decade, efforts have been made by government financial institutions and NGOs, often in partnership, to develop new financial delivery approaches. These new financial delivery approaches have been designed to combine the safety and reliability of formal finance with the convenience and flexibility that are typically associated with informal finance.

There is no gainsaying that the provision of financial services to the scheduled castes will generally remain beyond the outreach of the SCDCs and formal banking institutions if they use only the traditional delivery mechanisms and products. In other words, not only newer delivery mechanisms, but also newer savings, credit and other financial products and services may have to be developed which meet the needs of the scheduled castes. While many NGOs have been responsive in this direction, given the size of the scheduled castes population and its scatter, it is also not possible for the NGO sector alone to bridge the gap, both from the point of view of number of NGOs as also financial resources that would be required. The need of the hour is probably a concerted approach with symbiotic action both by the SCDCs, formal banking system and the voluntary sector, which complement each other's initiatives. This would necessitate a level playing ground for various agencies and institutions engaged in development through microfinance.

The following three approaches for providing microfinance services to the scheduled castes through the SCDCs, therefore, seem possible:

1. The conventional weaker section lendings of the banks to individuals, groups and cooperatives, for which instructions are already laid down by the RBI.
2. The SHG-bank linkage programme, where banks lend to groups with or without the support from NGOs and other self-help promoting institutions (SHPIs).
3. The lendings of the banks and specialised financial institutions to various financial intermediaries in the non-formal sector for further on-lending to ground level groups or individuals.

This scenario, therefore, calls for a clear definition of microfinance and microfinance institutions (MFI) so that all the involved stakeholders understand and play their distinct roles. Microfinance is defined as 'provision of thrift, credit and other financial services and products of very small amounts to the poor in rural, semi-urban or urban areas for enabling them to raise their income levels and improve living standards' (*www.nabard.com*). MFIs are those which facilitate this provision.

Microfinance approach is based on certain proven truths, which are not always recognised. These are:

- That the poor are bankable; successful initiatives in microfinance demonstrate that there need not be a tradeoff between reaching the poor and profitability—microfinance constitutes a statement that the borrowers are not 'weaker sections' in need of charity, but can be treated as responsible people on business terms for mutual profit.
- That almost all poor households need to save, have the inherent capacity to save small amounts regularly and are willing to save provided they are motivated and facilitated to do so.
- That easy access to credit is more important than cheap subsidised credit which involves lengthy bureaucratic procedures—(some institutions in India are already lending to groups or SHGs at higher rates—this may prevent the groups from enjoying a sufficient margin and rapidly accumulating their own funds, but members

continue to borrow at these high rates, even those who can borrow individually from banks).

- 'Peer pressure' in groups helps in improving recoveries.

Principles of Microfinance

1. The poor need a variety of financial services, not just loans. Just like everyone else, poor people need a wide range of financial services that are convenient, flexible and reasonably priced. Depending on their circumstances, poor people need not only credit but also savings, cash transfers and insurance.
2. Microfinance is a powerful instrument against poverty. Access to sustainable financial services enables the poor to increase incomes, build assets, and reduce their vulnerability to external shocks. Microfinance allows poor households to move from everyday survival to planning for the future, investing in better nutrition, improved living conditions, and children's health and education.
3. Microfinance means building financial systems that serve the poor. Poor people constitute the vast majority of the population in most developing countries. Yet, an overwhelming number of the poor continue to lack access to basic financial services. In many countries, microfinance continues to be seen as a marginal sector and primarily a development concern for donors, governments, and socially responsible investors. In order to achieve its full potential of reaching a large number of the poor, microfinance should become an integral part of the financial sector.
4. Financial sustainability is necessary to reach significant numbers of poor people. Most poor people are not able to access financial services because of the lack of strong retail financial intermediaries. Building financially sustainable institutions is not an end in itself. It is the only way to reach significant scale and impact far beyond what donor agencies can fund. Sustainability is the ability of a microfinance provider to cover all of its costs. It allows the continued operation of the microfinance provider and the ongoing provision of financial services to the poor. Achieving financial sustainability means reducing transaction costs, offering better

products and services that meet client needs, and finding new ways to reach the unbanked poor.

5. Microfinance is about building permanent local financial institutions. Building financial systems for the poor means building sound domestic financial intermediaries that can provide financial services to poor people on a permanent basis. Such institutions should be able to mobilise and recycle domestic savings, extend credit, and provide a range of services. Dependence on funding from donors and governments—including government-financed development banks—will gradually diminish as local financial institutions and private capital markets mature.
6. Interest rate ceilings can damage poor people's access to financial services. It costs much more to make many small loans than a few large loans. Unless microlenders can charge interest rates that are well above average bank loan rates, they cannot cover their costs, and their growth and sustainability will be limited by the scarce and uncertain supply of subsidised funding. When governments regulate interest rates, they usually set them at levels too low to permit sustainable microcredit. At the same time, microlenders should not pass on operational inefficiencies to clients in the form of prices (interest rates and other fees) that are far higher than they need to be.
7. The government's role is as an enabler, not as a direct provider of financial services. National governments play an important role in setting a supportive policy environment that stimulates the development of financial services while protecting poor people's savings. The key things that a government can do for microfinance are to maintain macroeconomic stability, avoid interest-rate caps, and refrain from distorting the market with unsustainable subsidised, high-delinquency loan programmes. Governments can also support financial services for the poor by improving the business environment for entrepreneurs, clamping down on corruption, and improving access to markets and infrastructure.
8. The lack of institutional and human capacity is the key constraint. Microfinance is a specialised field that combines banking with social

goals, and capacity needs to be built at all levels, from financial institutions through the regulatory and supervisory bodies and information systems, to government development entities and donor agencies. Most investments in the sector, both public and private, should focus on this capacity building.

Players in Microfinance and their Linkages

The different MFIs operating in India can be classified as mainstream MFIs and alternate MFIs.

Mainstream MFIs

They include National Bank for Agricultural and Rural Development (NABARD), Small Industries Development Bank of India (SIDBI), Housing Development Finance Corporation (HDFC), commercial banks, regional rural banks (RRBs), the credit cooperative societies, etc.

Alternate MFIs

These are the institutions, which have come up to fill the gap between the demand and supply for microfinance. The institutions playing a major role in microfinance are the NGOs. As NGOs have entered into the commercial world of lending money, many are transforming themselves into regulated institutions—working under the law governing the world of commerce. The flow of funds to the microfinance clients can take several routes as depicted in Figure 14.1, where poor get financial services through NGOs, NGO promoted MFIs, SHGs or directly from banks. The cooperatives also play a significant role in the rural credit sector and have a great outreach. The alternate MFIs include the following:

- NGOs, which are mainly engaged in promoting SHG and their federations at a cluster level and linking SHGs with banks, under the NABARD scheme;
- NGOs directly lending to the borrowers, who are either organised into SHGs. These NGOs borrow bulk funds from SIDBI and various donors;
- MFIs, which are specifically organised as cooperatives such as the SEWA Bank and various Mutually Aided Cooperative Thrift and Credit Societies (MACTS) in Andhra Pradesh; and

- MFIs, which are organised as non-banking finance companies (NBFCs), such as BASIX, CASHPOR Financial and Technical Services (CFTS) Mirzapur and SHARE Microfin Ltd.

Taking due note of the emergence of the NGO sector in the country and their endeavours to provide microcredit and support to micro-entrepreneurs, several other institutions, agencies, ministries and government departments of the Central and state governments have started associating NGOs for reaching out credit and other welfare services to the rural and urban poor, particularly women. Rashtriya Mahila Kosh (RMK), SIDBI, Housing and Urban Development Corporation (HUDCO), National Housing Bank (NHB), SIDBI, HDFC and Ministries of Agriculture and Human Resources Development (Department of Women and Child Development) and Rural Development Department are prominent among them.

NABARD is the pioneer in leading the microfinance movement in India. NABARD works with a focussed agenda of encouraging the formation of SHGs and linking them to the banks. A few years ago, NABARD relaxed its norms to allow banks to lend to intermediary MFIs who would ultimately lend to SHGs. Apart from NABARD there are several initiatives. Most of these are microfinance activities promoted by NGOs or NGO-MFIs. The organisations undertaking these activities are incorporated under various legislations—trusts, public societies, cooperatives and for-profit and non-profit companies. Most of these entities are unregulated. Some of them are partially regulated to the extent that they have sought grants from foreign sources and have to file annual returns with the Home Ministry. The Reserve Bank of India regulates NBFCs operating in the field of microfinance—which are a few in numbers.

The new paradigm is based on the premise that the poor are bankable. Although they have no collateral to offer for the credit extended to them, if formed into cohesive, homogeneous groups, peer pressure and group dynamics act as perfect and even better substitutes. Therefore, lending to poor through the SHG mechanism is a profitable and viable proposition. Sensing this, several banks and MFIs have jumped on the microfinance wagon. The government, not to be left behind, has also found that SHGs

Figure 14.1

NABARD Encouraging Bank Linkage with SHGs

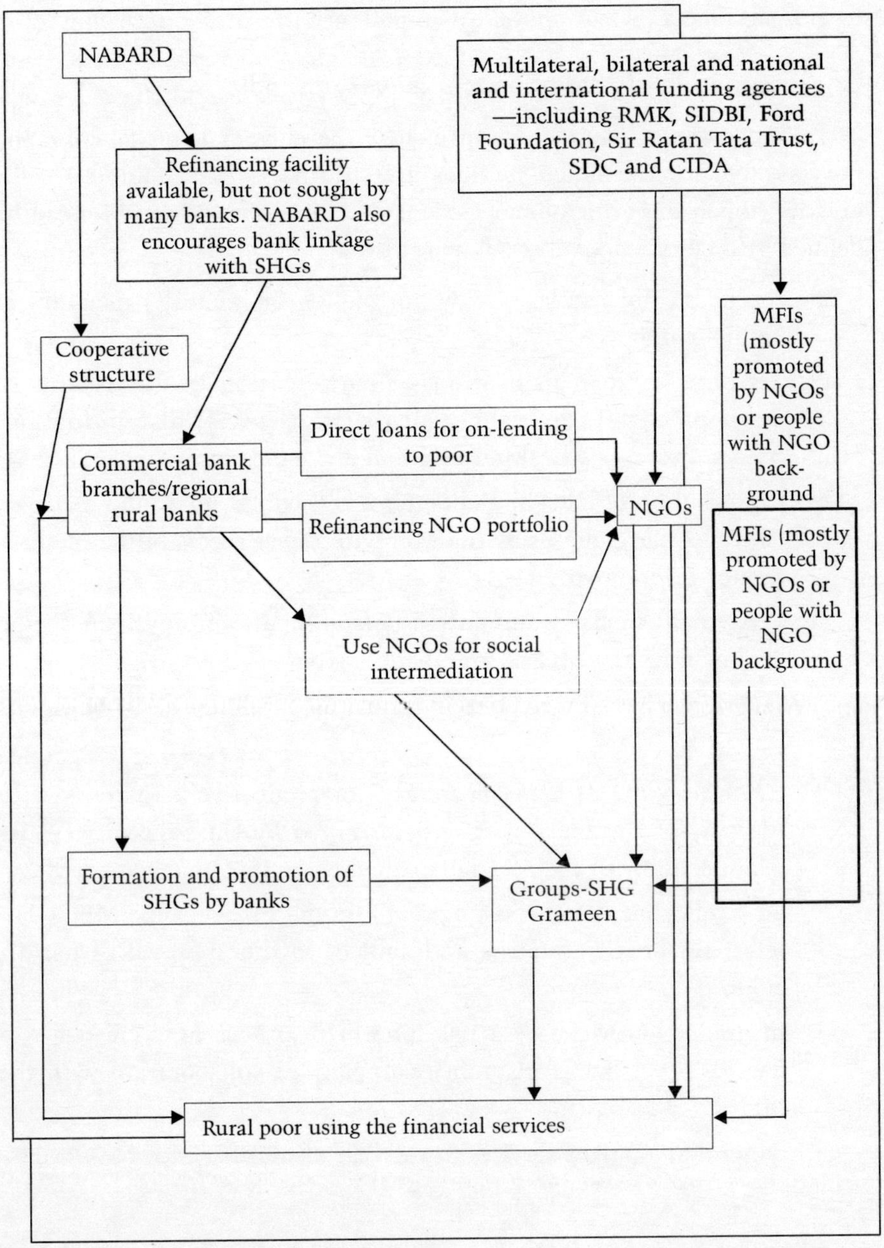

are a powerful vehicle for social empowerment, particularly for women. The Government's thrust for encouraging group formation and inclusion of this form of lending under its flagship programme, Swarnajayanti Gram Swarozgar Yojana (SGSY) shows the importance this area is receiving.

Characteristics of Microfinance delivery in India

The common characteristics across the current approaches to the provision of microfinance services are summarised in Table 14.1. In practice, the average microfinance client's relationship with an MFI can be defined by a fairly standard set of obligations.

a) Attendance of regular weekly (fortnightly or monthly) meetings of her/his group.

b) Training in 'loan utilisation' or participation in discussions of developmentally relevant issues such as social discrimination, gender awareness, health, sanitation and education.

c) Contribution of fixed amounts, termed 'savings', to a fund managed either by her group or by the MFI with direct access of the member limited or even barred.

d) Repayment of fixed amounts as installments on any loan she/he obtains from the MFI or from her/his group.

What she/he actually receives in return for fulfilling these obligations are:

- Fixed amounts of loan apparently 'for productive activities'—with the size of the loan usually determined by the longevity of her relationship with the MFI rather than by her/his financial needs.
- Emergency loans for 'consumption'—in the case of some MFIs—but relatively small amounts and subject to the approval of her/his group.
- Insurance—provided by a risk fund or insurance fund created by a few MFIs, or by an insurance company in collaboration with the MFI.
- Other development services in the case of multi-service NGO/MFIs.

Delivery Models of Microfinance

Individual Banking based Model

This is a formal banking model where individual clients are provided financial services. The group formation costs are not incurred. Group peer pressure is absent and therefore programme management and client appraisal poses specific challenges. While the individual banking model is suited for lending to enterprises the group approach is best suited to lending to pre-microenterprises and microenterprises.

Individual banking based models entail the provision by MFIs of financial services to individual clients. The model is increasingly popular for microfinance particularly through cooperatives. In the case of cooperatives, all borrowers are members of the organisation either directly, or indirectly by being members of primary cooperatives or associations that are members of the apex society. Creditworthiness and loan security are a function of cooperative membership within which member savings and peer pressure are assumed to be a key factor. Though the magnitude and timing of savings and loans are largely unrelated, a special effort is made to mobilise savings from members. There are now a large number of 'new generation' cooperative credit societies in India devoted specifically to providing financial services to the poor. Most of these are in Andhra Pradesh that was the first to enact a law permitting mutually aided—as opposed to traditional government-assisted—cooperative societies.

Loaning to borrowers outside cooperative fold is practised by the commercial banks. In such cases, effectiveness of credit delivery is enhanced through introduction of credit cards like Kisan Credit Card (KCC), Swarojgar Credit Card (SCC), Cash Credit Loan (LCC) etc. Alongside the borrowers are provided insurance cover both life and non-life.

Wholesale Banking Models

This model seeks to assist many NGOs working on non-financial development issues like health, literacy, eco-restorations etc., but have now taken to microfinance as an add-on programme. The model has the features of promptness, non-bureaucratic lending procedures and unique

Table 14.1

Characteristics of Microfinance Delivery in India

Financial Service	*Characteristics*	*Description*
	Loan amount	Determined by the longevity of the client's association with the MFI. Not often directly related to the credit needs of the borrower.
	Loan term	Usually 12 months, occasionally less, sometimes greater.
	Repayment installments	Monthly or weekly—usually fixed, equal amounts.
Credit	Interest charges	Range: 24-36 per cent, usually levied as a flat charge, partly to simplify calculations for both the MFI and the client. Some MFIs charge lower rates but suffer from poor sustainability as a result.
	Collaterals	No physical collateral but often linked to some compulsory savings component that acts as financial collateral. Reinforced by joint liability (Grameen) with other clients or peer pressure arising from membership of a community group revolving its own as well as borrowed funds (SHGs, cooperatives). Some MFIs also create reserve funds to cover the risk of default.
	Amount deposited	Grameen: Compulsory—usually a fixed proportion of the repayment installment. SHG: Compulsory—fixed amounts per (weekly or monthly) meeting to be deposited as part of the group fund; occasionally also voluntary some MFIs now offer long-term fixed deposits.
Savings	Withdrawals	Compulsory savings cannot be withdrawn except when the client leaves the group.
		Voluntary savings often require some notice of withdrawal.
	Interest paid	Most programmes pay 4-6 per cent interest (not consistent).
	Life	Some MFIs are starting to offer life insurance covering client loan repayments plus a small payment to the family in case of the death of the client. A reserve fund is created for the purpose or insurance is bought from the organised sector on behalf of the client.
Insurance	Animal	Usually linked with a formal insurance company which obtains bulk business from the MFI while the latter provides the service of premium collection; assists in the verification of claims.

package of providing both loans and capacity building support to its partners.

Intermediate Model

Banking services are provided to clients either directly or through SHGs. Shri Mahila Cooperative SEWA Sahakari bank, Sanghamithra Rural Financial Services, Basix Group are some of the MFIs successfully adopting this model in different parts of the country.

Joint Liability Group (JLG)

This is yet another supplementary credit delivery model intended to facilitate smoother flow of quality credit with the establishment of joint liability group (JLG) covering a group of borrowers. JLG is an assembly of 5–10 member clients as a group. The JLG members offer an undertaking to the bank or financial institution that enables them to jointly receive such amounts as deemed eligible by the institution for pursuing any individual or joint activities, found suitable by the group. The main purpose of JLG is to facilitate mutual loan guaranteeing and execution of joint liability agreement making them severally and jointly liable for payment of interest and repayment of loan obtained from banks. The members of JLG normally live in the same neighbourhood or village and are from the identical socioeconomic background and environment. They may be mostly engaged in the same production activities and are expected to know and trust each other well. In essence, the model also serves to provide hassle-free credit for the client and ensure quality and risk-free portfolio for the lender.

Through joint liability lending MFIs can lessen the three major problems facing formal credit institutions in lending to the poor. These problems are: (a) to ascertain what kind of a risk the potential borrower is (the problem of adverse selection), (b) to make sure she/he will utilise the loan once made, properly, so that she/he will be able to repay it (the problem of moral hazard), and (c) to find methods to force the borrower to repay the loan if she/he is reluctant to do so (the enforcement problem). By utilising the informational advantages of members belonging to the same community and their potential to exert pressure on borrowers, borrowing groups under a joint liability contract are in a better position than formal banking institutions to address these problems (Ghatak and Guinnane,

1999). Hence, the functions of screening, monitoring and enforcement of repayment are to a large extent transferred from the financial institution to the group members (Zeller and Sharma, 1998). This reduces transaction costs and renders banking with poor loan applicants less costly than traditional banking practices for financial intermediaries.

Self-Help Groups

This is by far the most important credit delivery model for reaching the unbanked rural and urban populace. From our childhood days, we hear sayings like 'Self help is the best help', 'Unity is strength' and 'United we stand, divided we fall'. We have also heard the story of the bird caught in the net. They could not have escaped if they had tried individually. But when they flew together in a 'group', they escaped. This is the crux of microfinance. The SHG tries to introduce this to the poor people. The SHG shows us how unity is strength. They show us how self-help could be the best help. Thus, it is useful if one can encourage and help the poor people to form SHGs. The next most important question what would arise is to identify the means of making this concept of SHG to work. There are some simple rules that are required for SHGs to function. They include the following:

- Common agreement on when to meet.
- Decision on time and place of meetings.
- Agreed penalties for non-attendance.
- Agreement on amount of saving.
- Giving small loans to each other, and
- Taking loan from banks, repayment habits etc.

Training of the members is an important need for proper functioning of SHGs. Training needs to be provided in the areas of basic mathematics, writing of books, scheduling of meetings, social aspects like women empowerment and basics of lending money, borrowing and repaying The basic characteristics and functions of SHG are as follows:

- The ideal size of an SHG is 10 to 20 members. The groups need not be registered.

- From one family, one member only. This will enable more families to become a member of SHG.
- The group consists of either only men or of only women, as mixed groups are generally not preferred.
- Women's group are generally found to perform better.
- Members have the same social and financial background, as this would enable better and free interaction among the members.
- The group meets regularly and there is adequate attendance to enable meaningful discussions and ensuring a large participation.

SHG–Bank Linkage Model

The SHG model focussed on participation, capacity building and empowerment of members and clients. This is a process oriented model where high emphasis is given on savings and credit activities through capacity building of the members who are organised into SHGs. SHG being a small group of 10 to 20 persons from homogeneous socioeconomic strata, usually from the neighbourhood, is highly participative and democratic in functioning. Client base is built up over a period of time in a participatory manner.

Creation of sustainable community-based institutions is the core component of this model. SHG–bank linkage programme adopted by NABARD with partner agencies has emerged as a socially significant as well as commercially viable credit delivery model.

The creditworthiness of the group is determined by the absorption capacity of the group measured in terms of the savings accumulated by the groups after about six months of formation. The loan extended varies between 1 to 4 times the corpus of the group, though a higher amount can also be given in case of very good groups.

Under the SHG-bank linkage programme, three different models of lending have emerged. In the first model, the bank takes the initiative to form the groups, nurture them, open their savings accounts and provide them credit. In the second model, while the groups are formed and nurtured by government, NGOs or community-based organisations, the credit facilities are provided by the bank. In the third model, the NGOs that formed and nurtured the groups also act as financial intermediaries. Under this model, banks lend to these intermediaries for onward financing to the groups or their members. In certain areas where a very large number of groups have been financed by banks, intermediate agencies like federations of SHGs have come up as links between banks and the groups. The banks finance these federations, which, in turn, finance their member groups. So far, the second model has remained the most popular with over 70 per cent of the total SHGs financed falling under this category.

Considering the success of this model of lending, the term microfinance—meaning extending credit or other financial services of very small amounts to the poor—has become the buzzword of rural finance. It has also given a new respect and prominence to MFIs which are now becoming increasingly important in dispensing financial services to the poor. These MFIs exist in various forms, the most popular being NGO-MFIs registered in the form of societies or trusts, non-profit companies under Section 25 of the Companies Act, 1956, mutually aided cooperative societies and non-banking financial companies (NBFCs).

The MFIs have broadly adopted three methodologies for providing credit to the poor. The first one relies on the SHG approach as adopted by banks. Some MFIs also operate microfinance programmes by organising federations of SHGs to whom they lend for onward lending to the SHGs. Under the second approach, MFIs have attempted to replicate the model adopted by Grameen Bank (of Bangladesh). Under it, groups of 3 to 8 persons are formed and the MFI lends to the individuals on guarantee from group members. Saving is a compulsory component of the loan repayment schedule but does not determine the magnitude or timing of the loan. This approach usually prescribes weekly meetings in which the MFI staff members play a key role. Under the third approach, in which loans are given to individuals, all borrowers are members of the organisation either directly or indirectly, by being members of primary cooperatives or associations which are members of the apex society.

Studies have revealed that lending through the group approach has led to lower transaction costs for the banks. In a study of 19 SHGs, 5 bank branches and 2 NGOs in Karnataka and Tamil Nadu, conducted in 1995, it was found that the transaction costs were minimum when banks used

SHGs as financial intermediaries to lend to borrowers with NGOs acting as non-financial intermediaries. Under such a scenario, the reduction in transaction costs was 40 per cent as compared to the situation in which banks lent directly to the borrowers. Another study by Indian Bank in 1995 covering its 45 branches and 101 SHGs examined the transaction costs of branches under different models of lending. It concluded that there was a saving in transaction costs to the banks, especially in follow-up and recovery, when they lent to individuals through SHGs and NGOs or to SHGs for on-lending to individuals with NGOs acting as non-financial intermediaries. The costs were lowest in the latter case (Bhatia and Bhatia, 2006).

A study of the Maharashtra Rural Credit Project conducted by Bankers Institute of Rural Development in 1996 found that due to SHG intermediation, the transaction cost of advances of rural branches of commercial banks could be brought down considerably. Another study conducted in 2000, covering 22 SHGs spread over four states, brought out that transaction costs of lending through SHG may be slightly more than normal lending for the first loan. But in case of subsequent loans, it was observed that the reduction in transaction costs was nearly 48.5 per cent. In cases where lending was through NGO the reduction was as much as 90 per cent. The reduction in costs to the borrower was also substantial. (Srinivasan and Satish, 2000). An indicative study of seven case studies of banks/ their branches (commercial, RRB and cooperative) conducted during 2001-02 found the SHG portfolio to be profitable despite lower rates of interest charged by banks. Further, the SHG portfolio not only significantly exceeded the profitability of the respective bank, branch or cooperative society but also outperformed the other banking products such as cash credit and agricultural term lending accounts (Seibel and Dave, 2002).

An impact study of 560 SHG member households from 223 SHGs spread over 11 states was conducted in 1999 by NABARD. The study found that there had been perceptible changes in the living standards of the SHG members in terms of ownership of assets, increase in saving and borrowing capacity, income generating activities and income levels. While 58 per cent of the households reported increase in assets, the average value of assets increased by 72 per cent. Besides the economic impact, involvement in the group significantly contributed in improving the self-confidence of the members. The feeling of self-worth and communication with others improved after association with the SHGs. The members were relatively more assertive in confronting social evils and problem situations. As a result, there was a fall in the incidence of family violence (Puhazhendi and Satyasai, 2001; NABARD, 2002).

In another study conducted by NABARD in Orissa, Jharkhand and Chhattisgarh in 2001-02, details were collected from 115 members of 60 SHGs to compare their socioeconomic conditions in the pre- and post-SHG situations. The study brought out that besides about 45 per cent of members reporting increase in assets in the post-SHG situation, availing loans from moneylenders and other informal sources was significantly reduced. There was also remarkable improvement in social empowerment of members in terms of self-confidence, involvement in decision-making and better communication (Puhazhendi and Badataya, 2002). A study conducted in 2002, among 190 members of 12 SHGs, spread over the four southern states of Andhra Pradesh, Karnataka, Kerala and Tamil Nadu, ascertained the social/empowerment status of women members for SHGs less than one year and over three years old. The study revealed that more members in the older groups reported a positive influence on their share in family income than those in the younger groups. Similarly, more members of older groups reported a positive influence on confidence level in dealing with people, increased awareness about health and hygiene and improvement in control over their lives than those in the younger groups (MYRADA, 2002).

A national study covering 10 MFIs from different regions of the country, conducted in 2002 by EDA Rural Systems for SIDBI, brought out that microfinance had contributed to poverty reduction by supporting asset formation. The gender approach of the MFIs was found to be at best supportive and not transformative; nevertheless, there were positive impacts at individual and household levels (*www.sidbi.com*). The study was extended to 20 MFIs spread across eight states in the country. It concluded that microfinance is making a significant contribution to both the savings and borrowings of the poor in the country. Respondents reported having used 77 per cent of the loans for productive investments. It was also revealed that poorer households borrow smaller amounts and are more likely to borrow for household expenses (Sinha, 2005).

An important feature of the SHG movement is the empowerment process that it sets off amount to the poor, particularly women. Behavioural changes and self-reliance ushered in along with provision of financial services may shape the members not only as quality bank clients but also a prepared group to maximise absorption of other services. This win-win situation has been possible only through capacity building initiatives, followed with appropriate policy advocacy and promotional efforts, which has been effectively played by NABARD in enlarging the scope and outreach of the programme.

Studies have highlighted that besides pecuniary benefits, involvement in a group has significantly contributed in improving the members' self-confidence, the feeling of self-worth and communication levels as also their ability to resist social evils. Thus this movement has been an enriching experience for the banker, the government, the NGO sector and above all the rural poor.

Today the SHG-bank linkage programme encompasses active participation of over 35,000 bank branches of 560 commercial and cooperative banks and nearly 3,200 social sector initiatives in the NGO and government sector. The spread of the programme to over 11 lakh credit linked SHGs has more than validated the conceptual frame and operational feasibility of the model. About 90 per cent of over a million SHGs, which are linked to the banking system, are exclusive women groups. These one million groups have succeeded in saving with the banking system and have also accessed loans worth Rs.3,904 crore from the banking system, at market rates, without any form of subsidies associated with these loans. These groups have been formed and credit linked through the three basic approaches as given below:

Table 14.2

Three Basic Approaches

Basic Variants of SHG–Bank Linkage	*% of SHGs Financed*
SHG formed and financed by banks	20%
SHG formed by NGOs and formal agencies, but directly financed by banks	72%
SHG financed by banks using NGOs and other agencies as financial intermediaries.	8%

Mainstream banking institutions are increasingly participating in the programme because the SHG methodology leads to low transaction costs and near zero non-performing assets (NPA). These two major factors allow banks to charge interest rates of 8 per cent to 12 per cent per annum on declining basis on loans to SHGs, without sacrificing profitability concerns. This compares well with many MFIs in the world, which charge 20 per cent to 40 per cent at flat rates of interest.

The Development of Humane Action (DHAN) Foundation has evolved Kalanjiam Community Banking Programme (KCBP) of SHG federation in the past few years. Out of 50 odd federations initiated by them. Twenty have been registered as autonomous organisations and seven of these are now self-sufficient and able to meet all the costs of operations and the rest are in different stages of financial self-sufficiency ranging from 50–75 per cent. Each block is the primary unit for promoting the Kalanjiam model. The unit would have 200 groups and reach 400 families and promote 10–12 Cluster Development Associations (CDAs), finally registering as an autonomous federation.

The model focusses on cost sharing by the members from the start. Over a period of five years the proportions of costs borne by the people gradually go up and all the operational costs including professional services provided by DHAN Foundation are met by the members out of their own financial transactions. The break-even volume of business required achieving this level of financial self–sufficiency is Rs.300 lakh of worth of loan.

There has been growing excitement about SHG-bank linkage, and many believe it is destined to become the country's dominant system of mass-outreach banking for the poor. The SHG model was started in the 1980s by social development NGOs, many of whom took up group-formation (especially of women) as their main tool. Having group members learn how to pool savings into loans—mostly small, short-term consumption loans—was seen as empowering disadvantaged women, socially and politically as well as financially. By 1992 the NGOs had, heroically, persuaded government to take the idea seriously. Legal obstacles were removed and subsidies made available so that SHGs could take bulk loans from banks that could be on-lent to group members who could use them to take up or expand micro-businesses. The model evolved so that

SHG-bank linkage today involves having the group save, and then linking it to a bank (usually the rural branch of a state-owned commercial bank, but also RRBs, cooperative banks, etc. Funds saved by SHGs are placed in a group deposit account in the bank. The group then borrows from the bank (at about 12 per cent per annum), using its saving and group guarantee as the collateral. To encourage banks to lend to SHGs, NABARD has provided subsidised refinancing support to banks, although the demand for such refinancing has declined as banks begin to discover that SHG lending is quite profitable, and characterised by default rates (less than 1%) that are, in fact, much lower than the rate of default on their regular lending portfolios (11%-12%).

Banks typically provide the group a loan amounting to four times the group's savings but as the group matures, and based on the group's track record, banks are ready to lend more. Borrowed and saved funds are rotated through lending within the group using flexible repayment schedules (usually monthly repayment); SHGs thus save, borrow and repay collectively. SHG funds may be distributed either to one or more members of the group–who are personally responsible for repayment to the group, or spent collectively by the group. The group is free to decide the interest rate charged to its members, but typically, a member borrows from the group at about 24 per cent per annum. After a loan from a bank is fully repaid, the group may borrow again, often a larger amount.

Emerging Initiatives

In the midst of the apparent inadequacies of the formal financial system to cater to the needs of the rural poor despite its phenomenal physical outreach, and with the active support and patronage of some NGOs, an informal segment comprising small, indigeneous SHGs has started mobilising thrift and savings of their members and lending these resources among their members on a micro scale. The amounts involved are small, the processes followed are simple, but the operations seem to be successfully and effectively meeting at least the immediate needs of the poor. The potential of these SHGs to develop as local financial intermediaries to reach the poor has eventually gained wide recognition in India. Many NGOs have played an active role in fostering the growth of SHGs in furtherance of their basic objectives.

As the concept of informal SHGs was relatively new, the NABARD, the apex development institution with exclusive focus on integrated rural development, supported and funded in 1986-87, a MYRADA-sponsored action research project on 'Savings and Credit Management of Self-Help Groups' for assessing its efficacy to help the target groups. Thereafter, in collaboration with some of the other member institutions of Asia-Pacific Rural and Agricultural Credit Association (APRACA), NABARD undertook a survey of 43 NGOs spread over 11 states in India to study the functioning of SHGs and possibilities of collaboration between banks and SHGs in mobilisation of rural savings and improving the delivery of credit to the poor. Further, 10 other initiatives in the NGO and formal banking sector which specifically aimed at improving the access of the poor to banking were studied and analysed in great detail under the Government of Germany (The Federal Ministry for Economic Cooperation and Development, BMZ) funded research programme.

Encouraged by the results of these studies on SHGs and other initiatives, NABARD launched in 1991-92 a pilot project on linking SHGs with banks. Steady progress of the pilot project led to the mainstreaming of the SHG-bank linkage programme in 1996 as a normal lending activity of the banks with widespread acceptance.

In the wake of the successful involvement of NGOs in promoting SHGs for the benefit of the rural poor in the 1980s, particularly the women, there have been some notable initiatives under the aegis of various state governments such as Community Development Societies (CDS) in Kerala, Uttar Pradesh Land Development Corporation (UPLDC) in Uttar Pradesh, and under Development of Women and Children in Rural Areas (DWCRA) and UN Development Programme (UNDP) groups in Andhra Pradesh. These initiatives have tried to build NGO-like flexible and responsive structures within the formal systems. Some of them have also tried to develop infrastructure for the poor themselves which take on the responsibilities usually shouldered by NGOs.

Taking due note of the emergence of the NGO sector in the country and their endeavours to provide microcredit and support to micro-entrepreneurs, several other institutions, agencies, ministries and government departments of the Central and state governments have started associating NGOs for reaching out credit and other welfare services to the rural and urban poor, particularly women. Mahila Samakhya, RMK, SIDBI, HUDCO, HDFC, NHB, and Ministries of Agriculture and Human Resources Development (Department of Women and Child Development) and Rural Development Department are prominent among them.

The RMK Model

The National Credit Fund for Women or the Rashtriya Mahila Kosh (RMK) was set up in 1993 as an independent registered society by the Department of Women & Child Development in Government of India's Ministry of Human Resource Development with an initial corpus of Rs. 310,000,000—not to replace the banking sector but to fill the gap between what the banking sector offers and what the poor need. Its main objectives are:

- To provide or promote the provision of microcredit to poor women for income generation activities or for asset creation.
- To adopt a quasi-informal delivery system, which is client-friendly, uses simple and minimal procedures, disburses quickly and repeatedly, has flexibility of approach, links thrift and savings with credit and has low transaction costs both for the borrower and for the lender.
- To demonstrate and replicate participatory approaches in the organisation of women's groups for thrift and savings and effective utilisation of credit.
- To use the group concept and the provision of credit as an instrument of women's empowerment, socioeconomic change and development.
- To cooperate with and secure the cooperation of the Government of India, state governments, union territory administrations, credit institutions, industrial and commercial organisations, NGOs and others in promoting the objectives of the RMK.
- To disseminate information and experience among all these above mentioned agencies in the government and non-government sectors in the area of microfinance for poor women.

- To receive grants, donations, loans, etc., for the furtherance of the aims and objectives of the RMK.

The office of the RMK is situated in New Delhi. It does not have any branch offices. The executive director is the chief executive officer of the RMK. The executive director functions under the overall supervision, direction and control of the governing board.

The governing board comprises 16 members consisting of senior officers of the Government of India and state governments, specialists and representatives of NGOs active in the field of microfinance for women. The governing board is chaired by the minister in charge of the Department of Women & Child Development.

The general body of the RMK consists of all members of the board, institutional members and individual members.

The RMK has three main roles:

Wholesaling Role

- It acts as a wholesaling apex organisation for channelising funds from government and donors to retailing intermediate microfinance organisations (IMOs).
- The RMK has so far received only a one-time grant from government and has not needed to raise funds from any other sources.

Market Development Role

- It develops the supply side of the microfinance market by offering institution building support to new and existing-but-inexperienced IMOs by structures of incentives, transfers of technology, training of staff and other non-financial services.
- The RMK realises that it can play a value adding wholesaling role only when a sufficiently large and well established microfinance sector already exists. This depends on the number of IMOs and the sustainability of IMOs. Subsidised institution building increases the equity of any IMO as much as grants do—large and premature disbursement of funds to the IMO can reduce the effectiveness of any institution building effort.

Advocacy Role

Whereby RMK can act as an advocate or agent for influencing development and microfinance policy and creating a more enabling policy and legal environment for spread of microfinance activities in India. Being a creation and a representative of the government, RMK has a particular advantage in this area.

Its loan schemes have been designed in a sequential manner—IMOs and ultimate borrowers are expected to start with the smaller loan schemes and slowly graduate to the larger loan schemes as they gain experience and increase their own outreach.

RMK borrowers are expected to form into groups, start with their own savings, and to take the first loans from their own savings to meet their immediate consumption needs, before taking loans from RMK. Groups must learn to save before they can learn to borrow. RMK has found that it is best to think in terms of a sequence in which the very poor, by borrowing for consumption, are able to gradually reduce their income vulnerability and get into a position where they can think of riskier investments in working capital, hiring of extra-family labour, and ultimately fixed capital. Such a sequence helps the poorest to successfully overcome the barriers of self-exclusion, social exclusion and institutional exclusion that currently block their access to loans.

The common features of all loan schemes are as follows:

- Group loan mechanisms are used as a collateral substitute.
- Repeat loans are encouraged to ensure that the borrower is brought above the poverty line.
- The loans can be given to rural/urban women.
- The loans can be given for income generation activities or for acquisition of assets which will yield income.
- The loans can be given through various intermediate microfinance organisations like: NGOs, suitable state government agencies or corporations, women's cooperatives (with atleast 33 per cent women members and working in profit for atleast two years), etc.

References

Action Aid (2000). *Untouchability in Rural India* (by Ghanshyam Saha, Satish Deshpande, Sukhadeo Thorat, Harsh Mander and Amita Baviskar and Research and other Regional Staff). Delhi.

Anand, K. (2008). "I-banks lose flavour, IIM students eye Micro-finance", *The Economic Times*, New Delhi, 24 September, p.7.

Ansari, A.W. (1980). *The Changing Village India*. Delhi: Chetna Publications.

APMAS (2005). *A Study on Self Help Group (SHG)-Bank Linkage in Andhra Pradesh*. Hyderabad: APMAS. pp.76-91.

Arya, D.R. (2004). "Indian Non-Life Insurance Industry: XIV ICDC 2004", *Economic Times*, March 9, p. 4.

Attwood, Donald W. (1984). "Capital and the Transformation of Agrarian Class System: Sugar Production in India", in Meghnad Desai *et al.*, *Agrarian Power and Agricultural Productivity in South Asia*. Delhi: Oxford University Press. pp. 20-50.

Attwood, D.W. and B.S. Baviskar (1987). "Study of Co-operatives in India: Approaches and Methods", *Social Change* 17(2): 8-15.

Awasthi, D.N. (1994). "Promoting Group Entrepreneurship", in Gautam Raj Jain and Debmuni Gupta (ed.), *New Initiatives in Entrepreneurship Education and Training*. Ahmedabad: Entrepreneurship Development Institute of India.

———. (1996). "Rural Entrepreneurship Development: Relevance, Approach and Issues", *Working Paper*. Ahmedabad: Entrepreneurship Development Institute of India.

Basu, S.K. (1979). *Commercial Banks and Agriculture Credit: A Study in Regional Disparity in India*. New Delhi: Allied Publishers.

Banerjee, Biswjit and J.B. Knight (1991). "Caste Discrimination in Indian Urban Labour Market", *Journal of Developing Economics*.

Baviskar, B.S. and D.W. Attwood (1984). "Rural Co-operatives in India: A Comparative Analysis of their Economic Survival and Social Impact", *Contribution to Indian Sociology* (New Series) 18(1): 85-107, 13.

Besley, Timothy (1994): "How Do Market Failures Justify Interventions in Rural Credit Markets", *The World Bank Research Observer* 9(1).

Bhatia, Navain and Anju Bhatia (2006). "Financial Institutions as Change Agents for Rural Development: The New Paradigm", in *Rural Development and Social Change* (Vol. II). New Delhi: Discovery Publishing House.

Capoor, J. (2001). "Micro Finance Dispensation: A Policy Perspective", in K. Jindal and K.C. Sharma (eds.), *Micro Finance Institutions: Issues in Sustainability*. Lucknow: BIRD.

Census of India (2001). Government of India Press, New Delhi

Centre for Monitoring Indian Economy (2003). *Money and Banking*. December. pp. 151.

———. (2004). *National Income Statistics*. January. pp.74-75,139, 219.

Chandra, Prasanna (1998). *Financial Management, Theory & Practice*. New Delhi: Tata McGraw-Hill Publishing Company Limited, 4th edition, p.28.

Chaturvedi, H.R. and S. Mitra (1987). "Rural Co-operative: Hope or Despair? A Comparative Study of Gujarat and Orissa", *Social Change* 17(2): 16-25.

Chauhan, B.R. (1990). *Rural–Urban Articulations*. Etawah: A.C. Brothers.

Chippa, M.L. (1987). *Commercial Banking Development in India: A Study in Regional Disparity.* Jaipur: Printwell Publishers.

Christen, R.P. (1997). *Banking Services for the Poor: Managing for Financial Services.* USA: ACCION International.

Clark, A.M. (1995). "Non-Governmental Organizations and their Influence on International Society", *Journal of International Affairs* 2: 507-52.

D' Cruz, D. (2002). "Undermined: Values and Foreign Aid NGOs", *IPA Review* 54: 26-28.

Dadhich, C.L. (2001). "Microfinance: A Panacea for Poverty Alleviation: A Case of Oriental Grameen Project in India", *Indian Journal of Agricultural Economics* 56(3): 419-26.

Dasgupta, R. (2001). "An Informal Journey through Self-Help Groups", *Indian Journal of Agricultural Economics* 56(3): 370-86.

Debroy, Bibek and Shyam Babu (2004). "Remedies Against Economic Discrimination—International Experience of Reservation Policy in Private Sector", in *The Dalit Question-Reforms and Social Justice*. Delhi: Globus Books.

Desai, V. (1991). *Entrepreneurial Development: Principle, Programmes and Policies* (Vol. I). Bombay: Himalaya Publishing House.

———. (1996). *The Indian Finanacial Systems: The System that Cares*. Mumbai: Himalaya Publishing House.

Desai, B.M and N.V. Namboodiri (1994a). "Scale and Scope Economies In Rural Banking: Their Implications To Rural Credit Policies", A Keynote Paper for the National Conference on *Agricultural Credit System: The Next Stage; Paper and Proceedings*, (ed.) by Mruthyunjaya, V.C. Mathur and K. Kumar. New Delhi: Agricultural Economics Research Association, IARI.

———. (1994b). "Contributions of Institutional Credit, Self-Financing and Technological Change to Agriculture Growth in India", *Indian Journal of Agriculture Economics* 49: 3, July-September.

———. (1996) "Whither Rural Financial Institutions", *Economic and Political Weekly*, August 3.

Doh, J. and T. Guay (2003). "Globalization and Corporate Social Responsibility: How NGOs Influence Labour and Environmental Code of Conduct". Link: *www62.homepagae.villanova.edu/jonathan.doh/dohguay.mir-rev3.doc*

Economic Times, Ahmedabad edition Saturday 18th May, 1996.

Elaine, E. and L. Barton (1998). "Social Intermediation and Microfinance Programmes: A Literature Review", USA: Micro-Enterprises Best Practices. The SEEP Network.

Fernandez, A. (2000). "Putting Institutions First even in Micro-credit", Paper presented at the Workshop on *Best Practices in Group Dynamics and Micro-credit*, 15-17 February.

Fisher, T., V. Mahajan and A. Singha (1997). *The Forgotten Sector: Non-Farm Employment and Enterprises in Rural India*. New Delhi: Oxford & IBH Publishing Co. Pvt. Ltd.

Fri, R. (1992). "The Corporation as Nongovernment Organization", *The Columbia Journal of World Business* 27: 90-92.

Gain, T.S.R and P. Satish (1996). "A Micro Study on Group Dynamics and Group Functions", *Working Paper* No. 6. Lucknow: BIRD.

Ghatak, M. and T. Guinnane (1999). "The Economics of Lending with Joint Liability: Theory and Practice", *Journal of Development Economics* 60(1): 95-229.

Girija, S. (1998). *Building A Future-Group by Group: Case Studies on Self Help Groups in India*. Lucknow: BIRD.

Girija, S. and P. Satish (1999). "Transaction Cost of Lending Through SHGs: Impact on Branch Profitability", *Working Paper* No. 6. Lucknow: BIRD.

Governement of India (2004). *India 2004: A Reference Annual (Labour)*. Publications Division, Ministry of Information & Broadcasting, pp.507. As reproduced in *India 2004*, pp.15.

Haan, Arjan (1997). "Poverty and Social Exclusion: A Comparison of Debates on Deprivation", *Working Paper* No. 2, Poverty Research Unit, Sussex University, Brighton.

Harper, M. (1998). *Profit for the Poor-Cases in Microfinance*. New Delhi: Oxford and IBH Publishing Co. Ltd.

Hulme, D. and M. Paul (1996). *Finance Against Poverty*. London: Routledge.

IDBI (2000). *Report on Development Banking in India*. Mumbai.

Indian Express Group (2004). "Insurance Sector to Drive Indian CRM Market", *www.expresscomputeronline.com/20040216/indiatrends02.shtml*

Jain, L.C. (1984). "Grass Without Roots: Rural Development Under Government Auspices", *Mainstream*, October 13, New Delhi. pp. 27-32.

Kaladhar, K. (1997). "Micro Finance in India: Design, Structure and Governance", *Economic and Political Weekly*. October 18.

Karmakar, K.G. (1999). *Rural Credit and Self-help Groups: Micro-Finance Needs and Concepts in India*. New Delhi: Sage Publications. pp.168-169.

Khan, Mumtaz Ali (1995). *Human Rights and the Dalits*. Delhi: Uppal Publishers.

Korten, D. (1981). "Putting People First", in D. Korten and F.B. Alfonso (eds.), *Bureaucracy and the Poor*. Asian Institute of Management.

Kumar, Manoj (). *Development of Insurance in India. www.einsuranceprofessional.com/artgeneva.htm*

Lakshmanan, S. (2001). "Working of Self-Help Groups with Particular Reference to Mallipalayam Self-Help Group", *Indian Journal of Agricultural Economics* 56(3): 457.

Leeladhar, V. (2005). "Taking Banking Services to the Common Man: Financial Inclusion", Commemorative Lecture at the Fedbank Hormis Memorial Foundation. Ernakulam. December 2. *www.iibf.org.in/uploads/Speech_VLeeladhar_.doc + International+Experience+in+Promoting+Financial+Inclusion&hl=en&gl in&pid= bl&srcid= ADGEESI-LXp6 ujdgdFtC1F7liX8Id4B7Sh4Ucko1FG4bUHt5_o_ cBJKpWHZvVMoZD5jk4jxrL2yj0cw1ROEKVf_vN9ZAjMGCugQdn19jeCEPts24LY2oTS-ISA4rk99wzBm6hJCElZ3a&sig= AHIEtbSsjdnnRCAN-xzqA839yz2_QRtRJQ*

Light, I. (1998). "Microcredit and Informal Credit in USA: New Strategy of Economic Development", *Journal of Developmental Entrepreneurship* (Special Section) 3(1).

Mahajan, V. (2001). "Issues in Sustainability of MFIs: A Practitioner's Viewpoint", in Krishan Jindal and K.C. Sharma (eds.), *Micro Finance Institutions: Issues in Sustainability*. Lucknow: BIRD.

Martin, I., David Hulme and Stuart Rutherford (2002). *Finance for the Poor: From Microcredit to Microfinancial Services.* John Wiley & Sons Ltd.

Mathur, Kuldeep (ed.) (1996). *Development Policy and Administration*. New Delhi: Sage Publications. p.14.

Mohan, Rakesh (2003). "Economic Development of the North Eastern Region Some Reflections", *Reserve Bank of India Bulletin*. December. pp.931.

———. (2004). "Globalization: The Role of Institution Building in the Financial Sector: The Indian Case", *Reserve Bank of India Bulletin*, February. pp.121.

———. "Fiscal Issues and Central Banks in Emerging Markets: An Indian Perspective", *BIS Papers.*

Mohapatra, S.C. (2006). "Distinctive Lifestyle of Puri People", *Orissa Review*, 113-116, June.

Mustafa, K., Zulfiqar Ahmad Gill and Toseef Azid (2000). "NGOs, Micro-finance and Poverty Alleviation: Experience of the Rural Poor in Pakistan", *The Pakistan Development Review* 39: 4 (II): 771-92 (Winter). *http://www.pide.org.pk/pdf*

MYRADA (2002). *Impact of SHGs on the Social/Empowerment Status of Women Members in Southern India*. Mumbai: NABARD.

NABARD (1994). National Seminar on *Rural Credit* held on September 1, in Mumbai, Background Papers.

———. (2000). Seminar on Rural Credit held at Lucknow, Background Papers.

———. (2002). *SHG-Bank Linkage Programme for the Rural Poor-An Impact Assessment.* Mumbai.

———. (2008). *Report of the Committee on Financial Inclusion*. Mumbai.

———. (1999). *Gender Equality: Empowerment of Rural Women through NABARD Schemes.* Mumbai. p.14.

———. (1999a). *Handbook on Self-Help Groups Linkage Programme*. Ahmedabad. July.

———. (1999b). *Micro Finance and NABARD: Role and Perspectives*. Mumbai. May.

———. (1999c). *Task Force on Supportive Policy and Regulatory Framework on Micro-Finance: Summary and Recommendations*. Mumbai.

———. (1999). *Gender Equality: Empowerment of Rural Women through NABARD Schemes*. Mumbai. p.14.

NAFSCOB (2005). *Performance of Primary Agricultural Credit Societies (April 1, 2004 to March 31, 2005). http://nafscob.org/basicdata/PACS-2005.pdf*

Nair, A. (2005). "Sustainability of Microfinance Self Help Groups in India: Would Federating Help?", *Policy Research Working Paper Series* No. 3516: The World Bank.

Namboodiri, N.V. and R.L. Shiyani (2001). "Potential Role of Self-Help Groups in Rural Financial Deepening", *Indian Journal of Agricultural Economics* 56(3): 401-9.

Nayak, R.K. (ed.) (1996). "Policy and Economic Change: Emerging Situation of Scheduled Castes", in *Fourth World: Ideological Perspective and Developmental Prognoses*. New Delhi: Manohar Publication.

Netherlands Ministry of Development Co-operation (1992). *Evaluation Report-India: Cooperative Credit Pilot Training Project in Gujarat and Karnataka*. March 27, The Hague.

NSS (1983-84), (1993-94) and (1999-2000). *Employment and Unemployment situation among social groups in India.* (38th, 50th and 55th Round), Ministry of Statistics and Programme implementation, Government of India.

———. *Differences in Level of Consumption among Socio-economic Group*. Ministry of Statistics and Programme Implementation, Government of India.

NSS (1982, 1992). *Land and Livestock Holding Survey*. (37th and 48th Round), Ministry of Statistics and Programme implementation, Government of India.

Oomen, M.A. (2008). "Micro Finance and Poverty Alleviation: The Case of Kerala's Kudumbashree", *Working Paper* No. 17. Kochi: Centre for Socio-economic & Environmental Studies (CSES).

Papola, T.S. (1991). *Rural Non-Farm Employment: An Assessment of Recent Trends. Monograph*. New Delhi: Planning Commission.

Patel, A.R. (2002.) "Rural Credit Delivery System", *Journal of Kurukshetra:* 8. November. New Delhi.

Patel, I.G. (1994). "Limits of Current Consensus on Development", Proceedings of the World Bank Annual Conference on Development Economics. World Bank.

Pethiya, B.P. and S. Teki (2000a). "Role of Microfinance in Marketing NTFP and Improving the Living Standard of Rural Poor, IIFM", *Newsletter* 3(2): 8–9. June.

———. (2000b). "Financing the Environment", *Indian Journal of Forestry* 23(2): 168–173.

———. (2003a). "Micro-Finance: Small Ideas and Big Rewards", *IIFM, Bhopal News Letter* V(4) & VI(1), December, 2002 and March, 2003.

———. (2003). *Assessing the Impact of Microfinance as a Tool for Adoption of Appropriate Technology and Conserving the Environment,* (with specific reference to NWFP) sponsored Project. Bhopal: IIFM.

———. (2004). "Emerging Microfinance Practices: With Special Reference to Forest Dwelling Community in Andhra Pradesh and Madhya Pradesh States", *Journal of Paradigm* 8. August-September. Ghaziabad: MIT.

Pischke, J.D. Von (1991). *Finance at the Frontier: Debt Capacity and the Role of Credit in the Private Economy*. Washington D.C.: World Bank.

Planning Commission (2001). *Report of the Working Group on Rural Povety Alleviation Programmes for the Tenth Five Year Plan (2002-2007)*. New Delhi: Government of India. December.

Prasad, Sheela and Surayya Teki (2006). *Study on Financial Performance and Viability of State Channelising Agencies of NSFDC.*Funded by NSFDC. New Delhi.

Puhazhendi, V. (2000). *Evaluation Study of Self Help Groups in Tamil Nadu*. Mumbai: NABARD.

———. (1995). *Transaction Cost of Lending to the Rural Poor—Non-governmental Organisation and Self-help Groups of the Poor as Intermediaries for Banks in India*. Brisbane: The Foundation for Development Cooperation.

Puhazhendi, V. and K.C. Badatya (2002). *SHG-Bank Linkage Programme for Rural Poor in India: An Impact Assessment*. Mumbai: NABARD.

Puhazhendi, V. and K.J.S. Satyasai (2000). *Microfinance for Rural People: An Impact Evaluation*. Mumbai: NABARD.

———. (2001). "Econojmic and Social Empowerment of Rural Poor through Self Help Groups", *Indian Journal of Agricultural Economics* 56(3): 450.

Rajasekhar, D., N.K. Gowda and R. Manjula (2006). *Impact of Bank Interest rates on SHG Members*. New Delhi: Concept Publishing Company. p.25.

Rangarajan, C. (2001). "Financial Sector Reforms and Emerging Issues", Speech delivered at the Asian Regional Seminar on *Financial Sector Reforms and Stability: Systemic Issues*, co-sponsored by Administrative Staff College of India, Hyderabad, and the International Monetary Fund. *www.hinduonnet.com/thehindu/2001/04/19/stories/0619000f.htm*

———. (2005). "Microfinance—The Road Ahead", *Conference Papers*, 12th April, New Delhi.

Rashtriya Mahila Kosh (1998). *Features of the Main and Sub-Schemes*. New Delhi: RMK.

Ray, C.N. (1992). "Implementation of IRDP: A Comparative Study of West Bengal and Gujarat", *Journal of Rural Development* 11(1): 69-100.

Rayudu, C.S. (1992). *Agricultural Credit and Rural Development in Drought Regions: A Study of Co-operative Bank of Andhra Pradesh*. New Delhi: Concept Publishing Company.

Reddy, Y.V. (2000). "Future of Rural Banking", *Reserve Bank of India Bulletin*, January.

Reserve Bank of India Bulletin (2003), February, pp.151.

Roy Choudhury, S. (2003). "Old Classes and New Spaces: Urban Poverty, Unorganised Labour and New Unions", *Economic and Political Weekly* XXXVIII. (December 13).

Sarathi, N. Vijaya (1999). "Interdependence Structure in the Indian Financial System", *International Conference in Economics*. Economic Research Center Middle East Technical University, Ankara Turkey.

Satish, P. (2005). "Mainstreaming of Indian Microfinance", *Economic and Political Weekly* XL: 1734. (April 23).

Satyanarayana, T. (2003). "NBFCs—In the Days of Turbulence", *The Journal of Indian Management*, Strategy. New Delhi. April-June.

Seibel, Hans Dieter and Harishkumar R. Dave (2002). *Commercial Aspects of SHG Banking in India*. Mumbai: NABARD.

Sen, Amartya, (2000). "Social Exclusion: Concept, Application, and Scrutiny", *Asian Development Bank Working Paper*.

Sharad, K. (2004). *Indian Financial System and Reserve Bank of India*. Mumbai: BTC, RBI.

Simmon, P.J. (1988). "Learning to Live with NGOs", *Foreign Policy* (Fall): 82-96.

Singh, Katar and T.S. Raji Gain (1995). "Evolution and Survival of Self-help Groups: Some Theoretical Propositions and Empirical Evidences", *Working Paper* No. 4, Lucknow: BIRD.

Sinha, Frances (2005). "Access, Use and Contribution of Microfinance in India: Findings from a National Study", *Economic and Political Weekly*, 23 April.

Small Industries Development Bank of India (1999). *SIDBI Foundation for Micro Credit: A Profile*. Lucknow: SIDBI.

Solanki (ed.) (2000). "Isolation and Deprivations: Economic Situation of Tribals in India", in *Development Issue in India*, Department of Economics, Dr. Babashaheeb Marathwada University, Aurangabad, Maharashtra.

Spar, D. and L. La Mure (2003). "The Power of Activism: Assessing the Impact of NGOs on Global Business", *California Management Review* 45(3): 78-101.

Srinivasan, N. (2008). *Microfinance India, State of the Sector Report 2008*. New Delhi: Sage Publication.

Srinivasan, Girija and P. Satish (2000). *Transaction Costs of SHG Lending: Impact on Branch Viability*. Lucknow: Bankers Institute of Rural Development.

Stiglitz, Joseph E. (1994). "The Role of the State in Financial Markets", Proceedings of the World Bank Annual Conference on Development Economics. World Bank.

Sundram, K. and S.D. Tendulkar (2002). "Poverty Among Social and Economic Groups in India in the Nineties", *Working Paper* No.118. Delhi: CDE.

Teki, Surayya (2001). "Marketing of Merchant Banking, Factoring, Lease Financing, and Venture Capital as Financial Services, with Special Reference to Selected Financial Institutions in Bombay", Ph.D. thesis.

Tilekar, S.N., N.J. Naikade, B.J. Deshmukh and A.A. Patil (2001). "Women Self-Help Groups Affiliated to Chaitanya: A Study on Pune District", *Indian Journal of Agricultural Economics* 56(3): 458.

Times of India (2009). *Sunday Times*, 9th August, Times Foundation, p.10

Thorat, S. (2006). "Situation of Dalit and Adivasi: Policies and Change", in R.R. Prasad and G. Rajanikanth (eds.) *Rural Development and Social Change*, (vol. I). New Delhi: Discovery Publishing House.

———. (2004a). *Human Poverty and Socially Disadvantaged Groups in India*. New Delhi: Indian Institute of Dalit Studies.

———. (2004). "Persistence of Poverty: Why is Scheduled Castes and Scheduled Tribes stay Chronically Poor?", Paper presented in Seminar on *Chronic Poverty in India*, IIPA, Delhi and DFID, London, Centre for Studies on Chronic Poverty.

———. (2004). "Dalits After India's Independence: Where do they stand?", *International, Newsletter Waterford*, USA, October.

———. (2003a). "Caste, Exclusion/Discrimination and Deprivation: The Situation of Dalits in India", *Concept Paper for DFID*, Delhi. May.

———. (2003b). Caste, Ethnicity, and Religion: An Overview Paper on Exclusion/ Discrimination and Deprivation", *Concept Paper for DFID*, Delhi. May.

———. (2002). Oppression and Denial–Dalit Discrimination in the 1990's", *EPW* 37(6), 9th February.

———. (2001). "Strategy of Disincentive and Targeting for Population Control: Implication for Dalits and Tribals", in *Ambedkar Journal of Social Sciences and Social Justice*. MHoW.

———. (1999). "Social Security in Unorganised Sector in India: How Secure are the Scheduled Caste?", (Special Issue) *Indian Journal of Labour Economics* 42(3): 451-70. September.

Thorat, Sukhadeo and R.S. Deshpande (1999). "Caste and Labour Market Discrimination", *Indian Journal of Labour Economics*, Conference Issue, November

Tripathy, R.B. (1994). *Dalits: A Sub- Human Society*. Delhi: Ashish.

United Nations Development Programme (2001). *Human Development Report, 2001*. New York: Oxford University Press.

Van Tuijl, P. (1999). "NGOs and Human Rights: Sources of Justice and Democracy", *Journal of International Affairs* 52(2): 494-512.

Vatta, K. (2003). "Microfinance and Poverty Alleviation", *Economic and Political Weekly*. XXXVIII (February 1).

Venkateswarlu, D. (1990). *Harijan–Upper Class Conflict*. Delhi: Discovery.

Wiser, W.H. (1958). *The Hindu Jajmani System: Socio-economic Systems Interrelating Members of a Hindu Village Community in Services*. Lucknow: Lucknow Publishing House.

Willets P. (2002). *What is Non-Governmental Organisation?, http://www.staff. city.ac.uk/ p.willetts/CS-NTWKS/NGO-ART.HTM*

World Bank (2000). *World Development Report 2000/01: Attacking Poverty*. New York: Oxford University Press.

Wrenn, E. (2005). *Micro-finance Literature: A Review of Literature for Tricaire*.

XIV ICDC 2004, Economic Times, March 9, 2004.

Yunus, M. (2003). *Banker to the Poor: The Autobiography of Muhammad Yunus, Founder of Grameen Bank*. Bangladesh: Public Affairs.

Zeller, M. and M. Sharma (1998). "Rural Finance, Food Security, and Poverty Alleviation: Supporting Institutional Innovation Through Public Policy", *Food Policy Report 1998*. Washington, USA: International Food Policy Research Institute (IFPRI).

Websites:

http://www.bim.edu/pdf/lead_article/Prof-sriraman.pdf

http://www.censusindia.gov.in/Census_Data_2001/States_at_glance/State_Links/21_ori.pdf

http://www.financialexpress.com/news/poverty-reduction-rate-in-orissa-still-very-slow-eco-survey/274060

http://www.iimb.ernet.in/microfinance/Docs/mr03206b.pdf

http://www.indiadevelopmentblog.com/2009/01/governments-role-in-microfinance-how.html

http://www.newkerala.com/topstory-fullnews-12252.html

http://www.orissadiary.com/CurrentNews.asp?id=10742

http://orissagov.nic.in/portal/default.asp

http://presidentofindia.nic.in/sp250208.html

http://www.radianceweekly.com/149/3441/MICROFINANCE-A-Tool-for-Alleviating-Poverty/2009-03-08/Cover-Story/Story-Detail/MICROFINANCEA-Tool-for-Alleviating-Poverty.html

http://www.sasnet.lu.se/EASASpapers/20NareshSingh.pdf

http://en.wikipedia.org/wiki/Microcredit

http://wwwwds.worldbank.org/external/default/WDSContentServer/IW3P/IB/2005/03/06/000090341_20050306103912/Rendered/PDF/wps3516.pdf http://econ.worldbank.org/external/default/main?pagePK=64165259&theSitePK=469372&piPK=64165421&menuPK=64166093&entityID=000090341_20050306103912

www.solutionexchange-un.net.in

www.sa-dhan.net/.../Orissa%20Conclave-%20Final%20document.doc

http://www.indiatogether.org/2003/oct/pov-credscene.htm

http://www.indiatogether.org/2003/oct/pov-credscene.htm

www.arcil.co.in

www.ccilindia.com

www.crisil.com

www.censusindia.net

www.nsdl.co.in/about/index.html